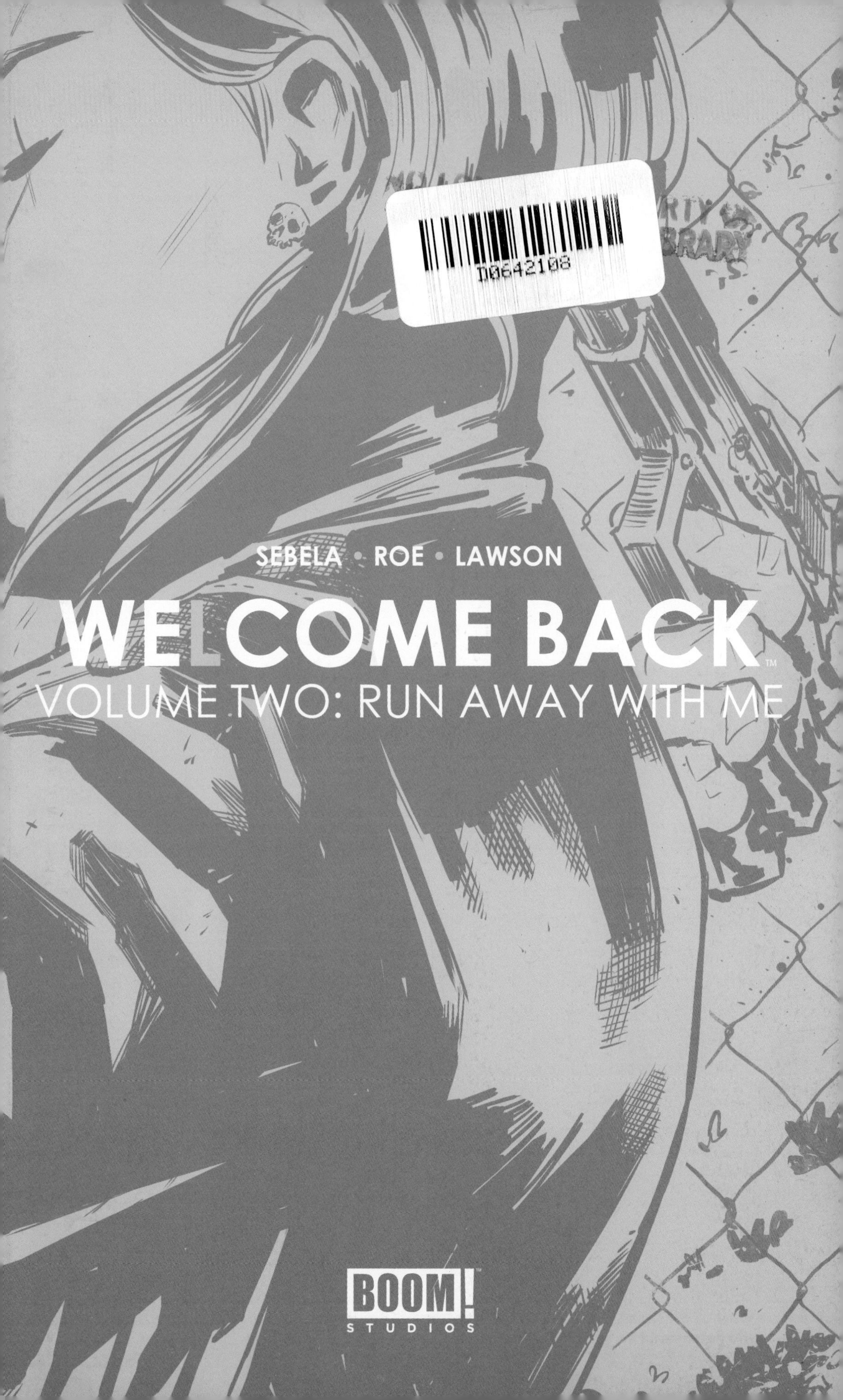

SEBELA • ROE • LAWSON

WELCOME BACK™

VOLUME TWO: RUN AWAY WITH ME

BOOM! STUDIOS

ROSS RICHIE CEO & Founder
MATT GAGNON Editor-in-Chief
FILIP SABLIK President of Publishing & Marketing
STEPHEN CHRISTY President of Development
LANCE KREITER VP of Licensing & Merchandising
PHIL BARBARO VP of Finance
BRYCE CARLSON Managing Editor
MEL CAYLO Marketing Manager
SCOTT NEWMAN Production Design Manager
KATE HENNING Operations Manager
SIERRA HAHN Senior Editor
DAFNA PLEBAN Editor, Talent Development
SHANNON WATTERS Editor
ERIC HARBURN Editor
WHITNEY LEOPARD Associate Editor
JASMINE AMIRI Associate Editor

CHRIS ROSA Associate Editor
ALEX GALER Associate Editor
CAMERON CHITTOCK Associate Editor
MATTHEW LEVINE Assistant Editor
KELSEY DIETERICH Production Designer
JILLIAN CRAB Production Designer
MICHELLE ANKLEY Production Designer
GRACE PARK Production Design Assistant
AARON FERRARA Operations Coordinator
ELIZABETH LOUGHRIDGE Accounting Coordinator
STEPHANIE HOCUTT Social Media Coordinator
JOSÉ MEZA Sales Assistant
JAMES ARRIOLA Mailroom Assistant
HOLLY AITCHISON Operations Assistant
SAM KUSEK Direct Market Representative
AMBER PARKER Administrative Assistant

WELCOME BACK Volume Two, April 2017. Published by BOOM! Studios, a division of Boom Entertainment, Inc. Welcome Back is ™ & © 2017 Christopher Sebela & Jonathan Brandon Sawyer. Originally published in single magazine form as WELCOME BACK No. 5-8. ™ & © 2016 Christopher Sebela & Jonathan Brandon Sawyer. All rights reserved. BOOM! Studios™ and the BOOM! Studios logo are trademarks of Boom Entertainment, Inc., registered in various countries and categories. All characters, events, and institutions depicted herein are fictional. Any similarity between any of the names, characters, persons, events, and/or institutions in this publication to actual names, characters, and persons, whether living or dead, events, and/or institutions is unintended and purely coincidental. BOOM! Studios does not read or accept unsolicited submissions of ideas, stories, or artwork.

A catalog record of this book is available from OCLC and from the BOOM! Studios website, www.boom-studios.com, on the Librarians page.

BOOM! Studios, 5670 Wilshire Boulevard, Suite 450, Los Angeles, CA 90036-5679. Printed in China. First Printing.

ISBN: 978-1-60886-950-3, eISBN: 978-1-61398-621-9

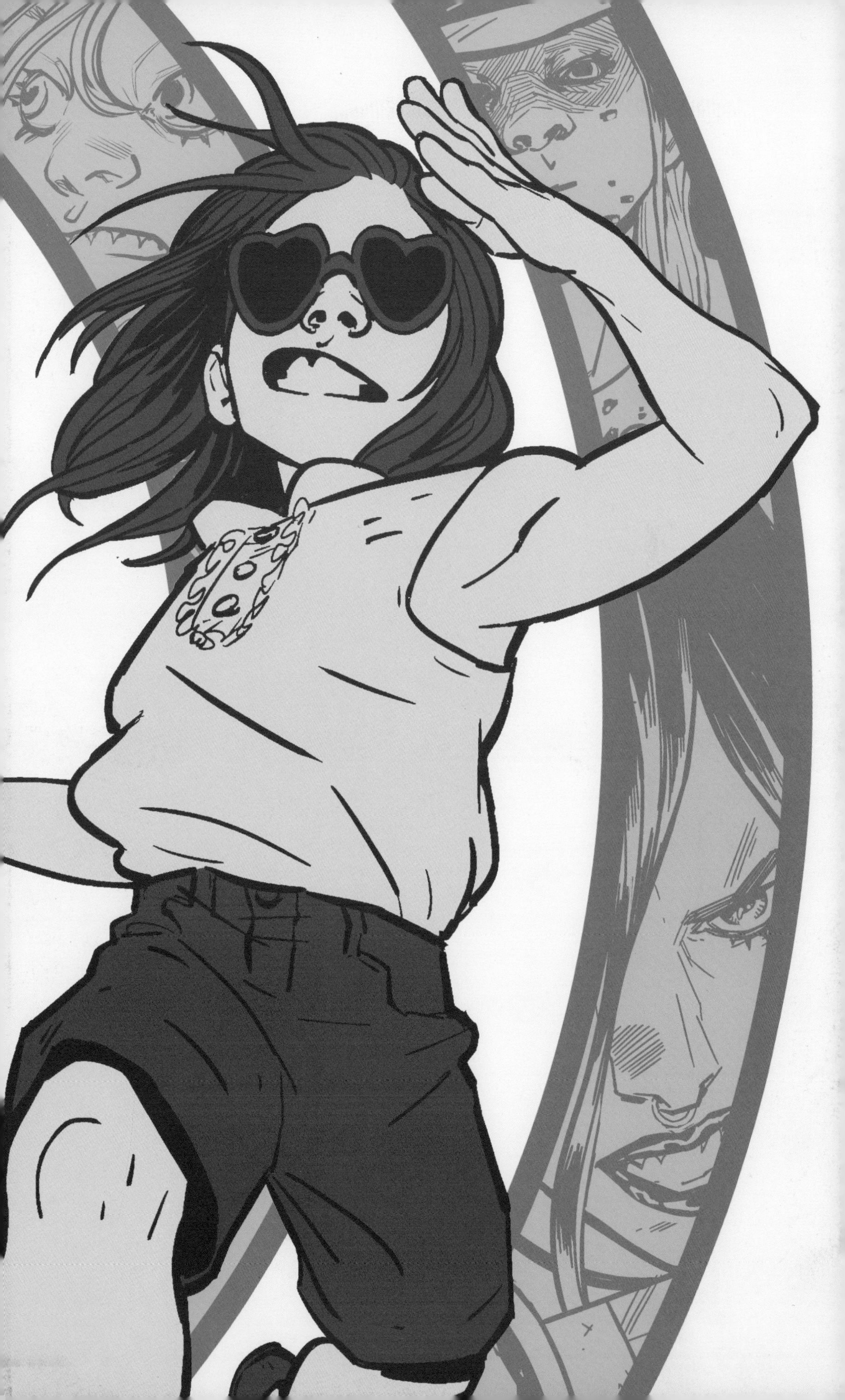

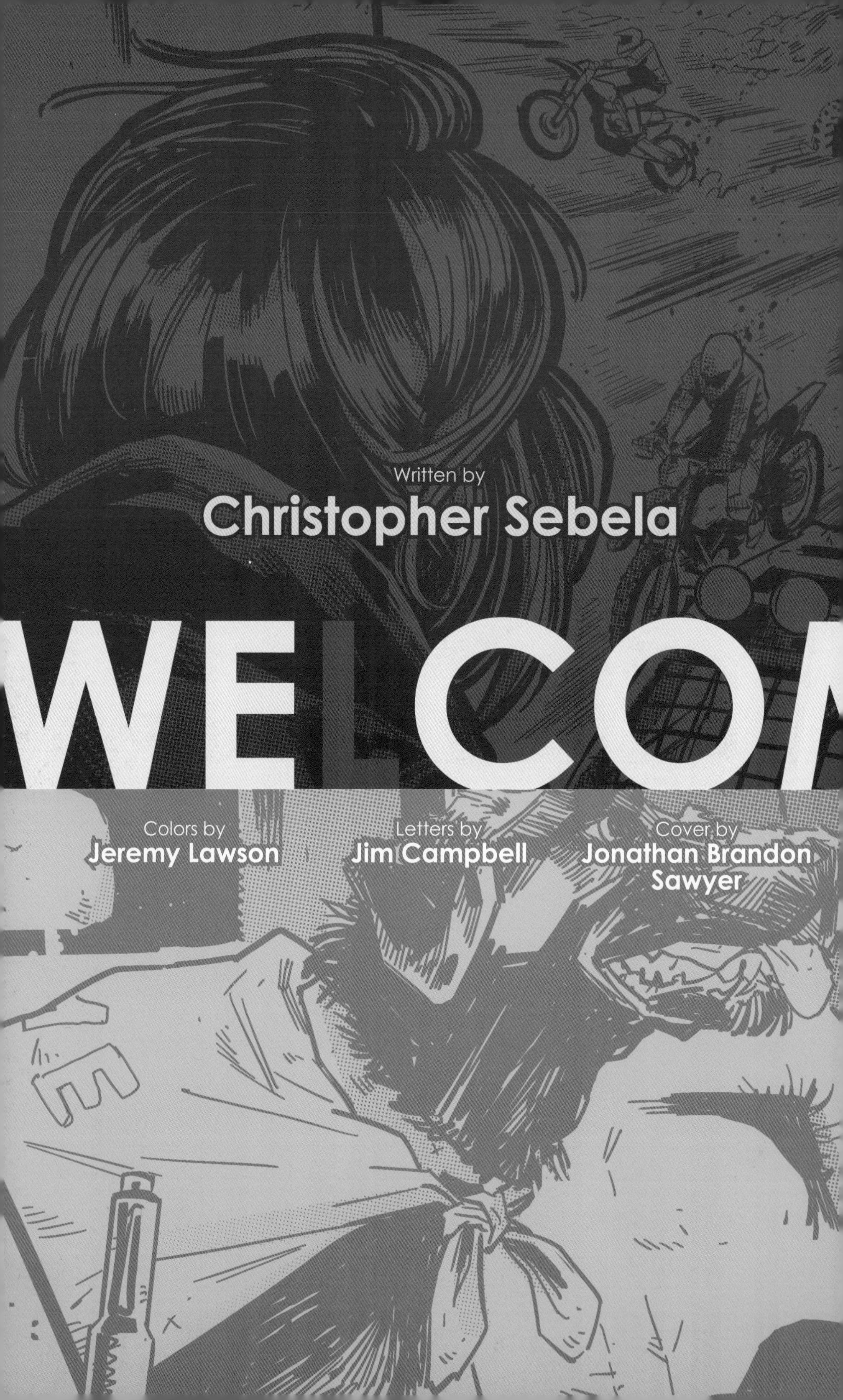

Written by
Christopher Sebela

WELCOM

Colors by
Jeremy Lawson

Letters by
Jim Campbell

Cover by
Jonathan Brandon Sawyer

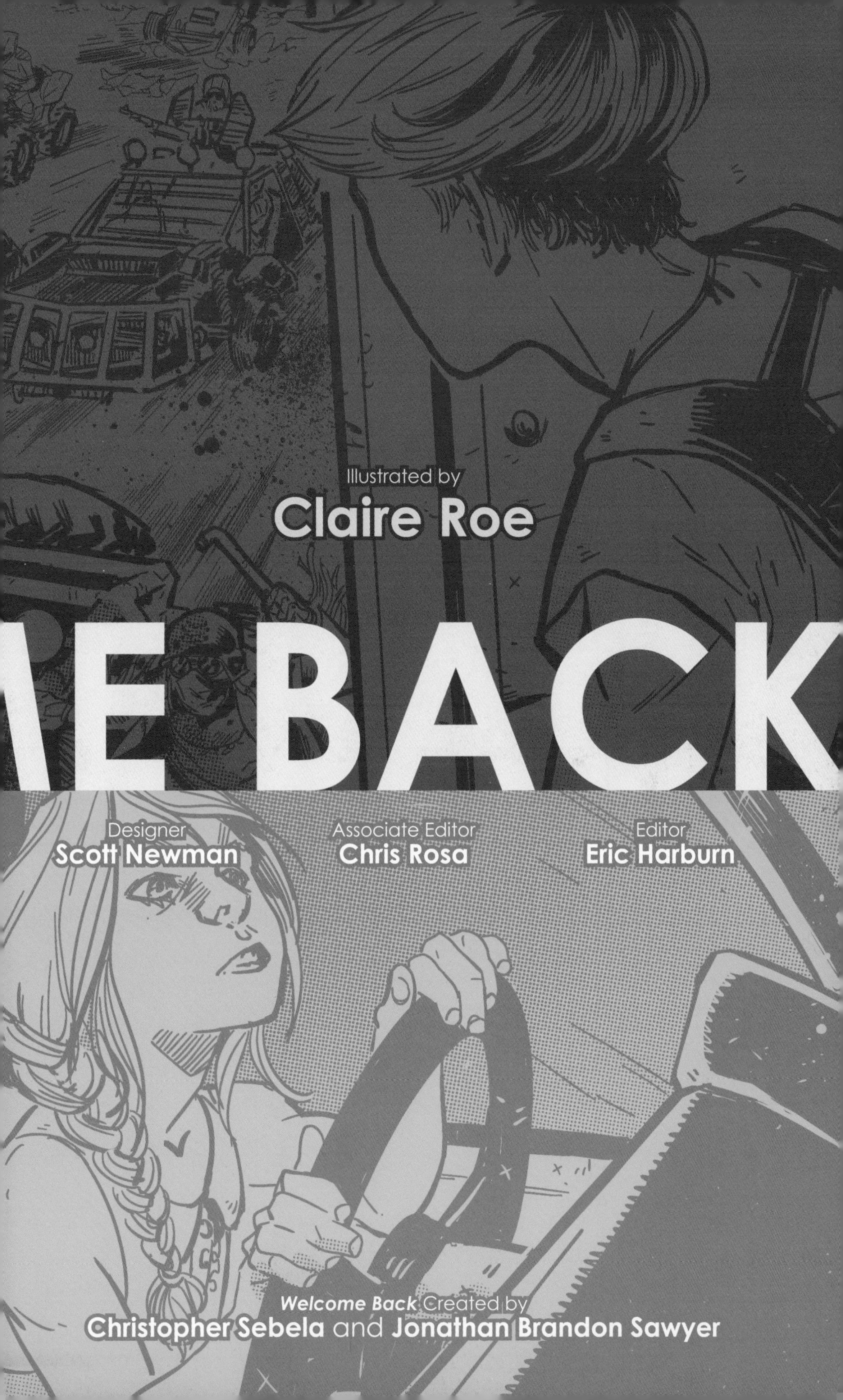

Illustrated by
Claire Roe

ME BACK

Designer
Scott Newman

Associate Editor
Chris Rosa

Editor
Eric Harburn

Welcome Back Created by
Christopher Sebela and **Jonathan Brandon Sawyer**

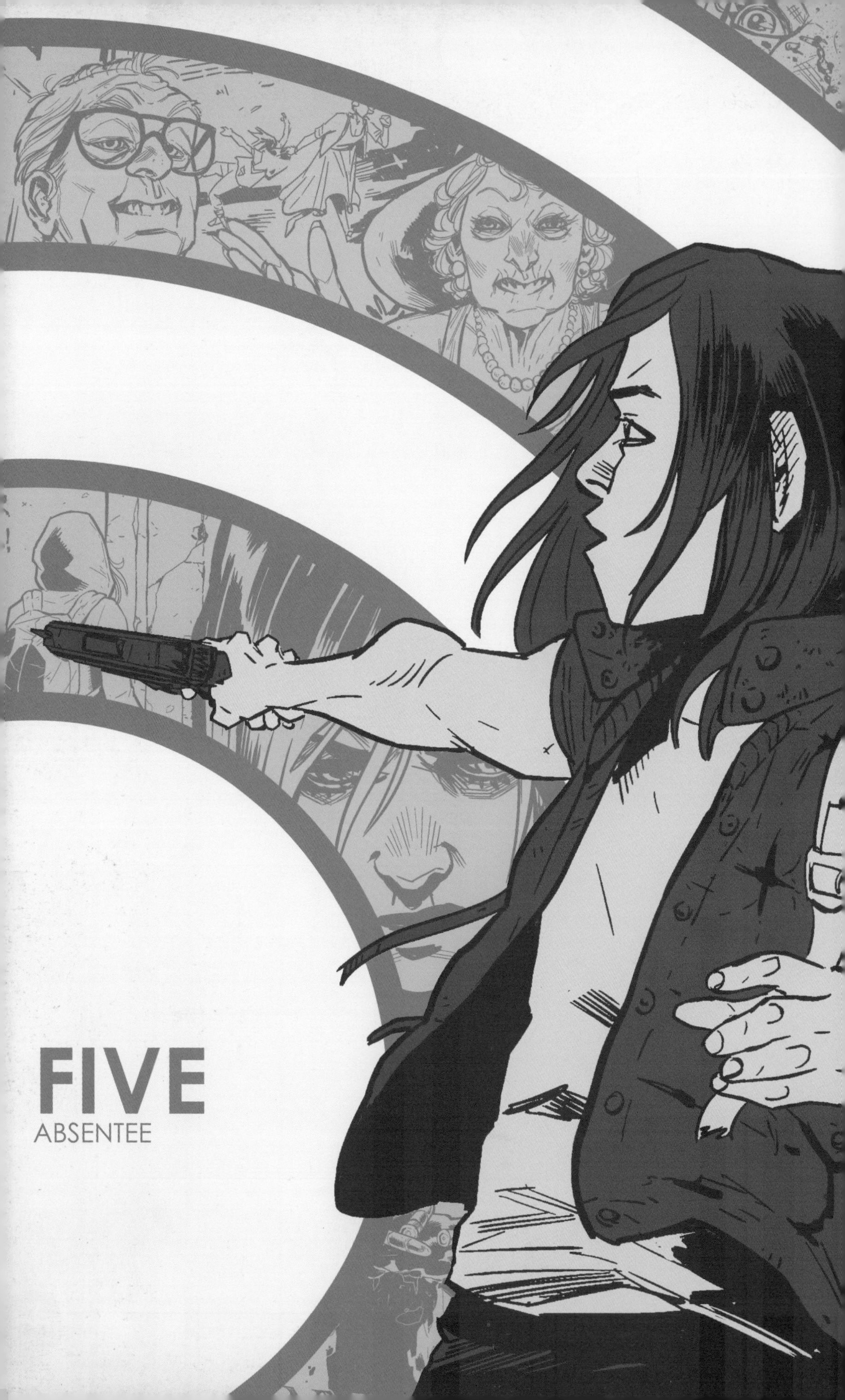

FIVE

ABSENTEE

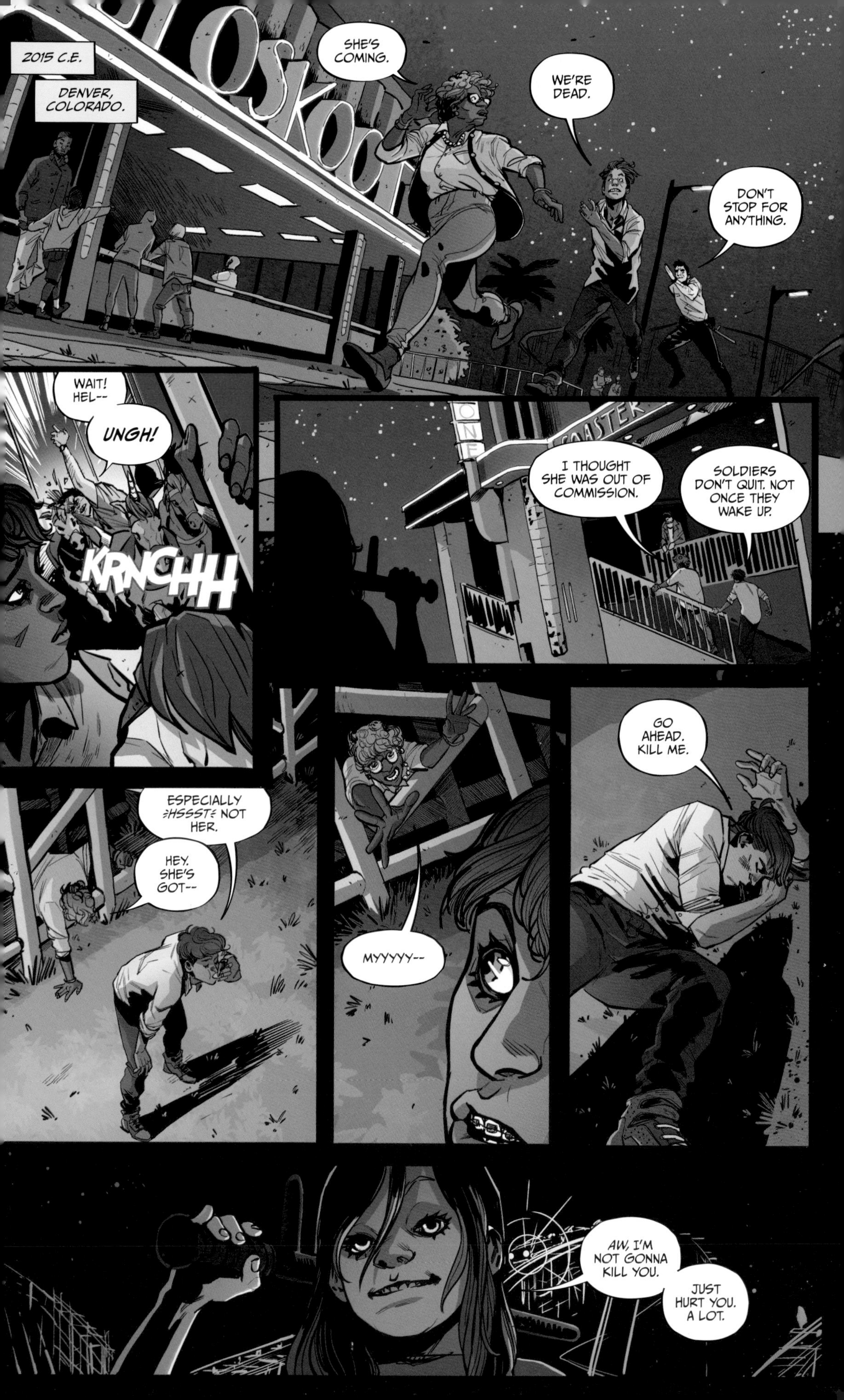
2015 C.E.
DENVER, COLORADO.
SHE'S COMING.
WE'RE DEAD.
DON'T STOP FOR ANYTHING.
WAIT! HEL--
UNGH!
KRNCHH
I THOUGHT SHE WAS OUT OF COMMISSION.
SOLDIERS DON'T QUIT. NOT ONCE THEY WAKE UP.
ESPECIALLY ≠HSSST≠ NOT HER.
HEY. SHE'S GOT--
MYYYYY--
GO AHEAD. KILL ME.
AW, I'M NOT GONNA KILL YOU.
JUST HURT YOU. A LOT.

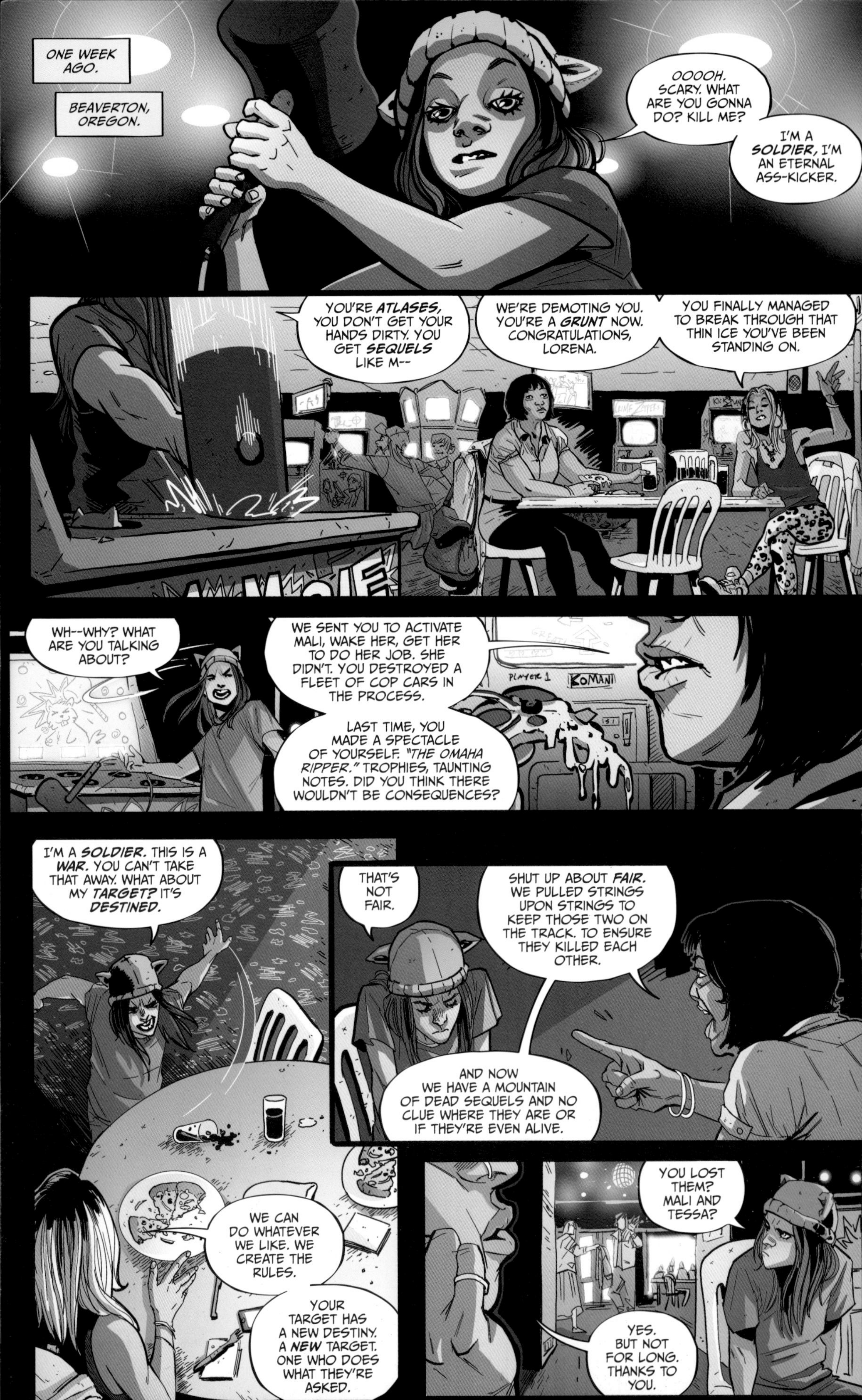

ONE WEEK AGO.
BEAVERTON, OREGON.
OOOOH. SCARY. WHAT ARE YOU GONNA DO? KILL ME?
I'M A SOLDIER, I'M AN ETERNAL ASS-KICKER.
YOU'RE ATLASES, YOU DON'T GET YOUR HANDS DIRTY. YOU GET SEQUELS LIKE M--
WE'RE DEMOTING YOU. YOU'RE A GRUNT NOW. CONGRATULATIONS, LORENA.
YOU FINALLY MANAGED TO BREAK THROUGH THAT THIN ICE YOU'VE BEEN STANDING ON.
WH--WHY? WHAT ARE YOU TALKING ABOUT?
WE SENT YOU TO ACTIVATE MALI, WAKE HER, GET HER TO DO HER JOB. SHE DIDN'T. YOU DESTROYED A FLEET OF COP CARS IN THE PROCESS.
LAST TIME, YOU MADE A SPECTACLE OF YOURSELF. "THE OMAHA RIPPER." TROPHIES, TAUNTING NOTES. DID YOU THINK THERE WOULDN'T BE CONSEQUENCES?
PLAYER 1
KOMANI
I'M A SOLDIER. THIS IS A WAR. YOU CAN'T TAKE THAT AWAY. WHAT ABOUT MY TARGET? IT'S DESTINED.
THAT'S NOT FAIR.
SHUT UP ABOUT FAIR. WE PULLED STRINGS UPON STRINGS TO KEEP THOSE TWO ON THE TRACK. TO ENSURE THEY KILLED EACH OTHER.
AND NOW WE HAVE A MOUNTAIN OF DEAD SEQUELS AND NO CLUE WHERE THEY ARE OR IF THEY'RE EVEN ALIVE.
WE CAN DO WHATEVER WE LIKE. WE CREATE THE RULES.
YOUR TARGET HAS A NEW DESTINY. A NEW TARGET. ONE WHO DOES WHAT THEY'RE ASKED.
YOU LOST THEM? MALI AND TESSA?
YES. BUT NOT FOR LONG. THANKS TO YOU.

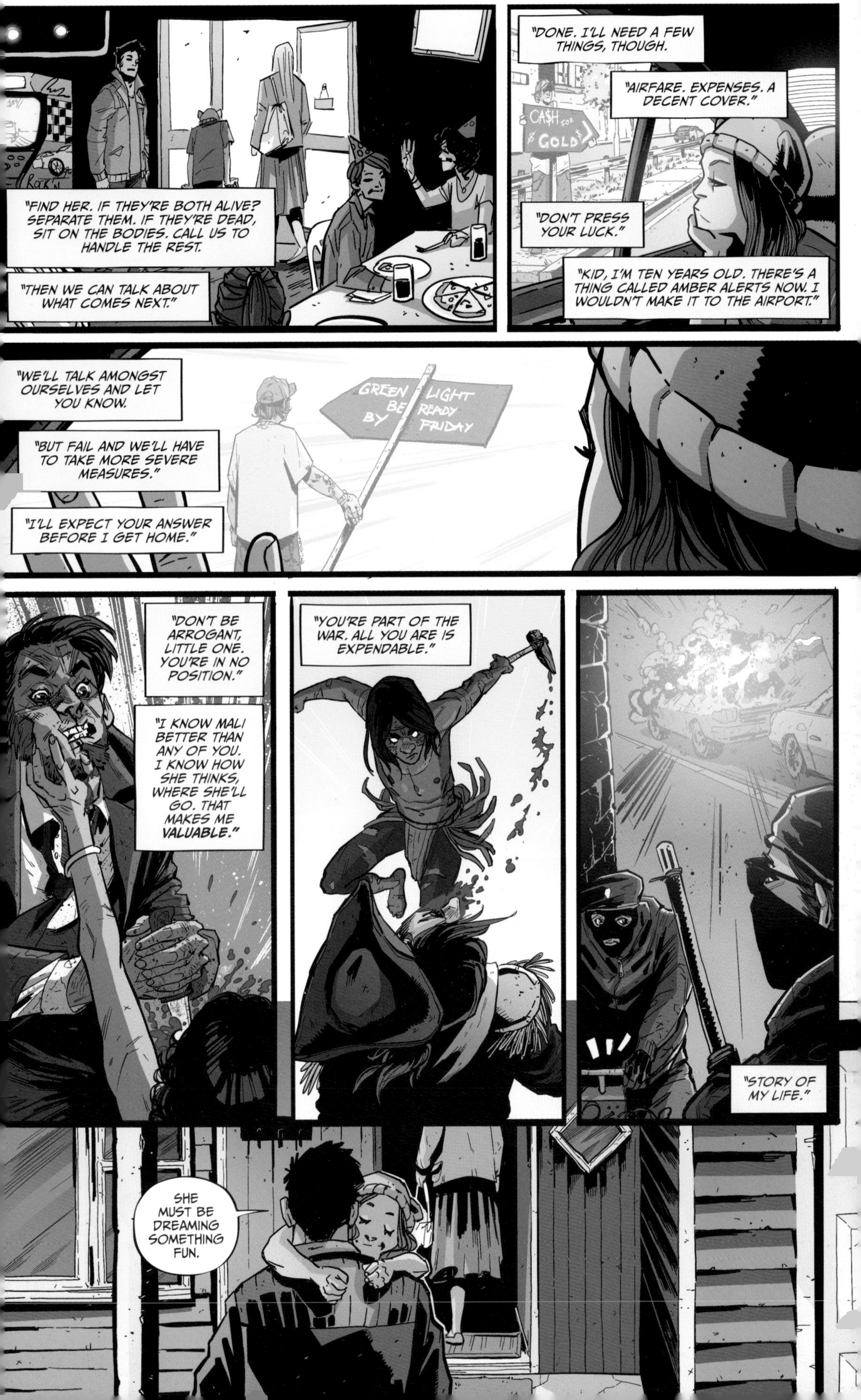
"FIND HER. IF THEY'RE BOTH ALIVE? SEPARATE THEM. IF THEY'RE DEAD, SIT ON THE BODIES. CALL US TO HANDLE THE REST.
"THEN WE CAN TALK ABOUT WHAT COMES NEXT."
"DONE. I'LL NEED A FEW THINGS, THOUGH.
"AIRFARE. EXPENSES. A DECENT COVER."
CA$H FOR GOLD
"DON'T PRESS YOUR LUCK."
"KID, I'M TEN YEARS OLD. THERE'S A THING CALLED AMBER ALERTS NOW. I WOULDN'T MAKE IT TO THE AIRPORT."
"WE'LL TALK AMONGST OURSELVES AND LET YOU KNOW.
GREEN LIGHT BE READY BY FRIDAY
"BUT FAIL AND WE'LL HAVE TO TAKE MORE SEVERE MEASURES."
"I'LL EXPECT YOUR ANSWER BEFORE I GET HOME."
"DON'T BE ARROGANT, LITTLE ONE. YOU'RE IN NO POSITION."
"I KNOW MALI BETTER THAN ANY OF YOU. I KNOW HOW SHE THINKS, WHERE SHE'LL GO. THAT MAKES ME VALUABLE."
"YOU'RE PART OF THE WAR. ALL YOU ARE IS EXPENDABLE."
"STORY OF MY LIFE."
SHE MUST BE DREAMING SOMETHING FUN.

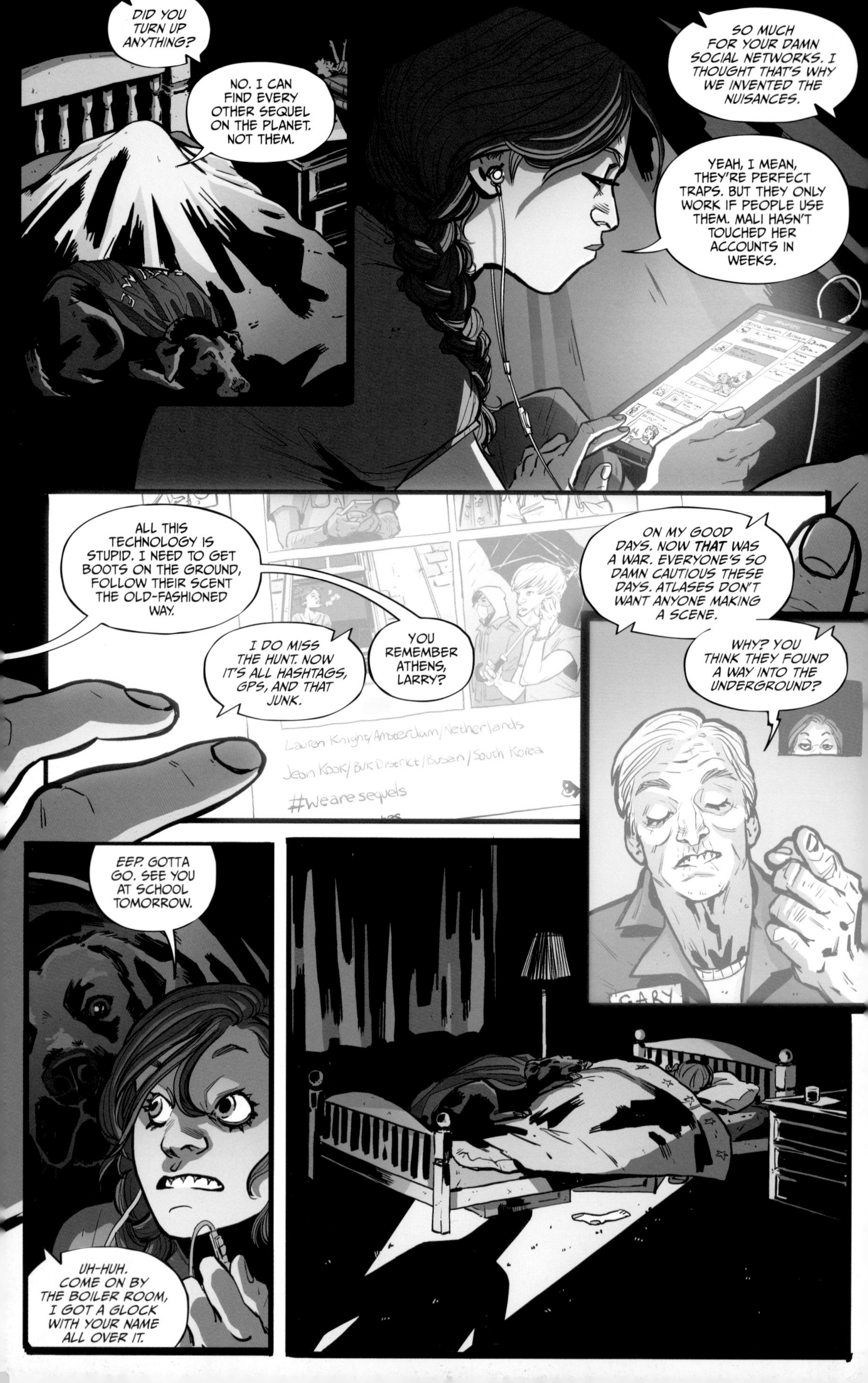
DID YOU TURN UP ANYTHING?
NO. I CAN FIND EVERY OTHER SEQUEL ON THE PLANET. NOT THEM.
SO MUCH FOR YOUR DAMN SOCIAL NETWORKS. I THOUGHT THAT'S WHY WE INVENTED THE NUISANCES.
YEAH, I MEAN, THEY'RE PERFECT TRAPS. BUT THEY ONLY WORK IF PEOPLE USE THEM. MALI HASN'T TOUCHED HER ACCOUNTS IN WEEKS.
ALL THIS TECHNOLOGY IS STUPID. I NEED TO GET BOOTS ON THE GROUND, FOLLOW THEIR SCENT THE OLD-FASHIONED WAY.
I DO MISS THE HUNT. NOW IT'S ALL HASHTAGS, GPS, AND THAT JUNK.
YOU REMEMBER ATHENS, LARRY?
Lauren Knight/Amsterdam/Netherlands
Jeon Kook/Buk District/Busan/South Korea
#wearesequels
ON MY GOOD DAYS. NOW THAT WAS A WAR. EVERYONE'S SO DAMN CAUTIOUS THESE DAYS. ATLASES DON'T WANT ANYONE MAKING A SCENE.
WHY? YOU THINK THEY FOUND A WAY INTO THE UNDERGROUND?
EEP. GOTTA GO. SEE YOU AT SCHOOL TOMORROW.
UH-HUH. COME ON BY THE BOILER ROOM, I GOT A GLOCK WITH YOUR NAME ALL OVER IT.

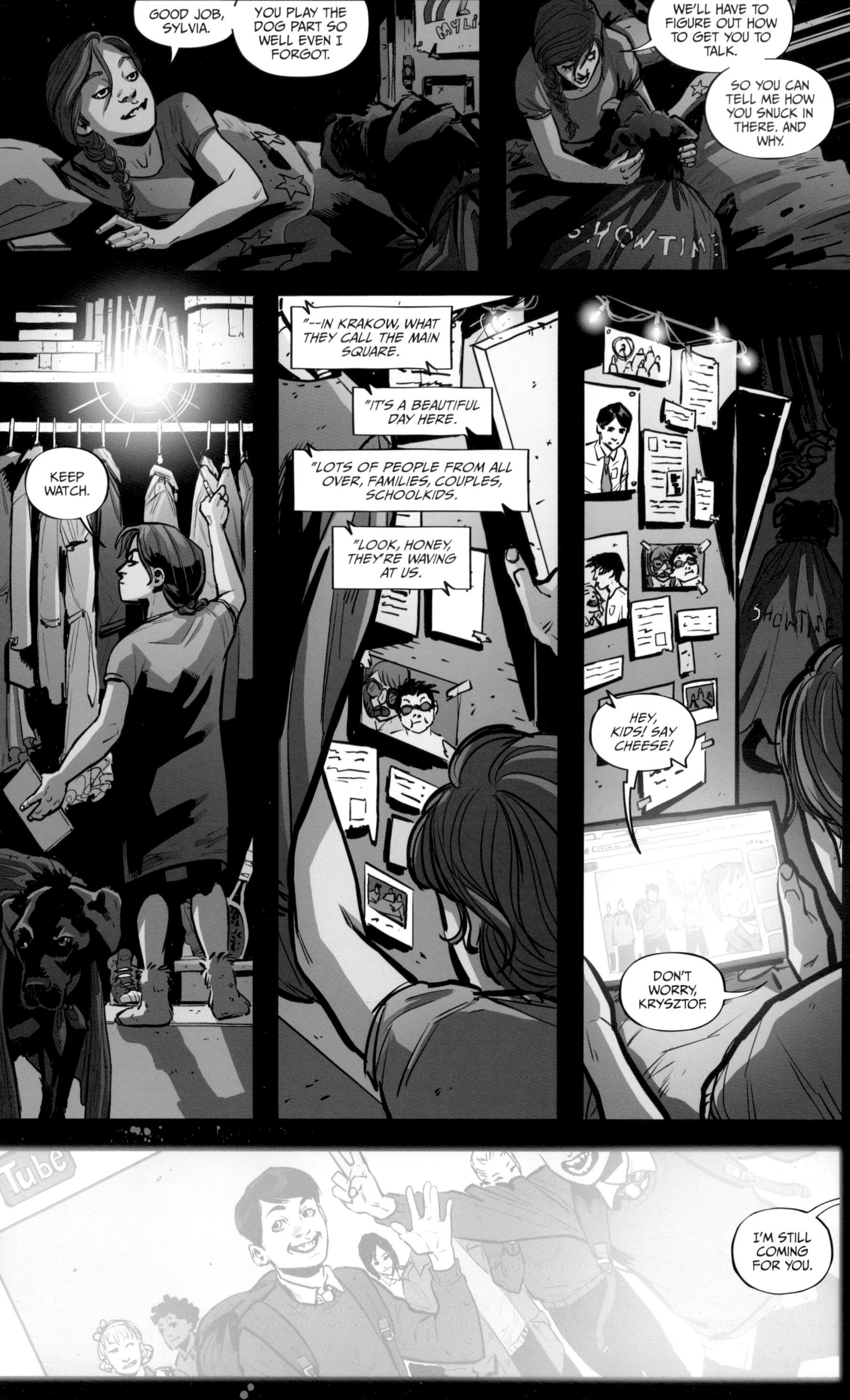
GOOD JOB, SYLVIA.
YOU PLAY THE DOG PART SO WELL EVEN I FORGOT.
WE'LL HAVE TO FIGURE OUT HOW TO GET YOU TO TALK.
SO YOU CAN TELL ME HOW YOU SNUCK IN THERE. AND WHY.
SHOWTIME
KEEP WATCH.
"--IN KRAKOW, WHAT THEY CALL THE MAIN SQUARE.
"IT'S A BEAUTIFUL DAY HERE.
"LOTS OF PEOPLE FROM ALL OVER, FAMILIES, COUPLES, SCHOOLKIDS.
"LOOK, HONEY, THEY'RE WAVING AT US.
HEY, KIDS! SAY CHEESE!
DON'T WORRY, KRYSZTOF.
Tube
I'M STILL COMING FOR YOU.

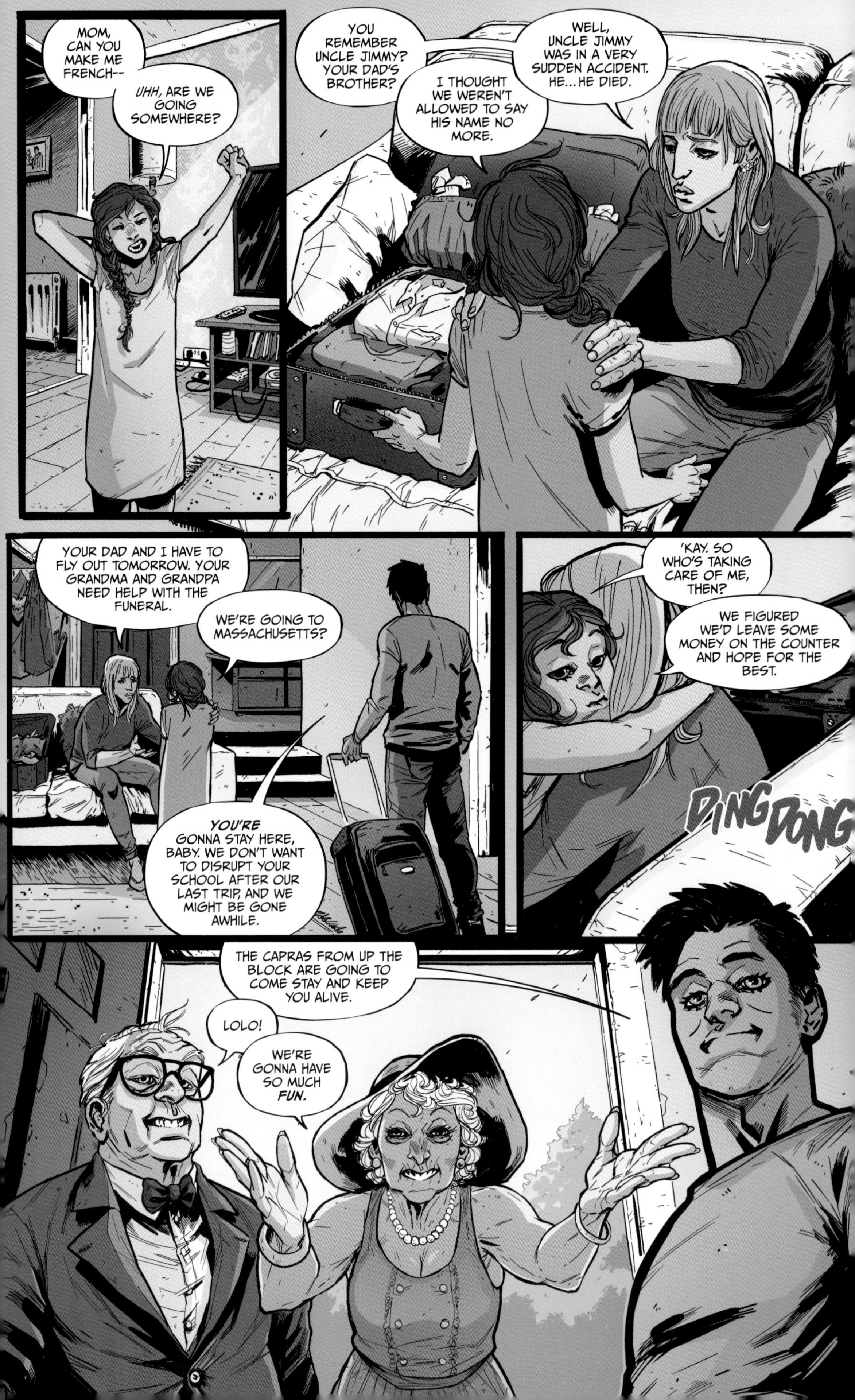
MOM, CAN YOU MAKE ME FRENCH--
UHH, ARE WE GOING SOMEWHERE?
YOU REMEMBER UNCLE JIMMY? YOUR DAD'S BROTHER?
I THOUGHT WE WEREN'T ALLOWED TO SAY HIS NAME NO MORE.
WELL, UNCLE JIMMY WAS IN A VERY SUDDEN ACCIDENT. HE... HE DIED.
YOUR DAD AND I HAVE TO FLY OUT TOMORROW. YOUR GRANDMA AND GRANDPA NEED HELP WITH THE FUNERAL.
WE'RE GOING TO MASSACHUSETTS?
YOU'RE GONNA STAY HERE, BABY. WE DON'T WANT TO DISRUPT YOUR SCHOOL AFTER OUR LAST TRIP, AND WE MIGHT BE GONE AWHILE.
'KAY. SO WHO'S TAKING CARE OF ME, THEN?
WE FIGURED WE'D LEAVE SOME MONEY ON THE COUNTER AND HOPE FOR THE BEST.
DING DONG
THE CAPRAS FROM UP THE BLOCK ARE GOING TO COME STAY AND KEEP YOU ALIVE.
LOLO!
WE'RE GONNA HAVE SO MUCH FUN.

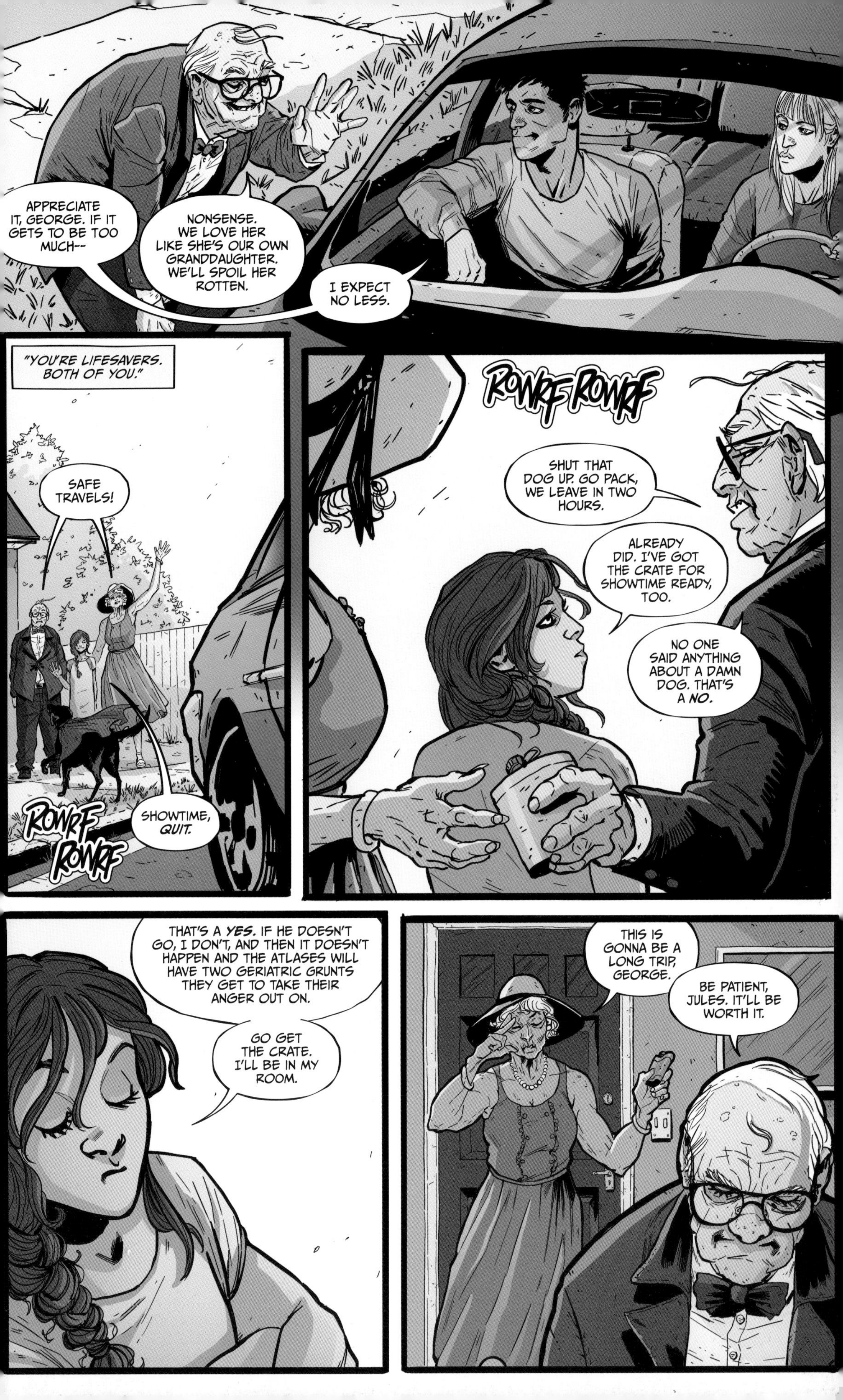

APPRECIATE IT, GEORGE. IF IT GETS TO BE TOO MUCH--
NONSENSE. WE LOVE HER LIKE SHE'S OUR OWN GRANDDAUGHTER. WE'LL SPOIL HER ROTTEN.
I EXPECT NO LESS.
"YOU'RE LIFESAVERS. BOTH OF YOU."
SAFE TRAVELS!
ROWRF ROWRF
SHOWTIME, *QUIT.*
ROWRF ROWRF
SHUT THAT DOG UP. GO PACK, WE LEAVE IN TWO HOURS.
ALREADY DID. I'VE GOT THE CRATE FOR SHOWTIME READY, TOO.
NO ONE SAID ANYTHING ABOUT A DAMN DOG. THAT'S A ***NO.***
THAT'S A ***YES.*** IF HE DOESN'T GO, I DON'T, AND THEN IT DOESN'T HAPPEN AND THE ATLASES WILL HAVE TWO GERIATRIC GRUNTS THEY GET TO TAKE THEIR ANGER OUT ON.
GO GET THE CRATE. I'LL BE IN MY ROOM.
THIS IS GONNA BE A LONG TRIP, GEORGE.
BE PATIENT, JULES. IT'LL BE WORTH IT.

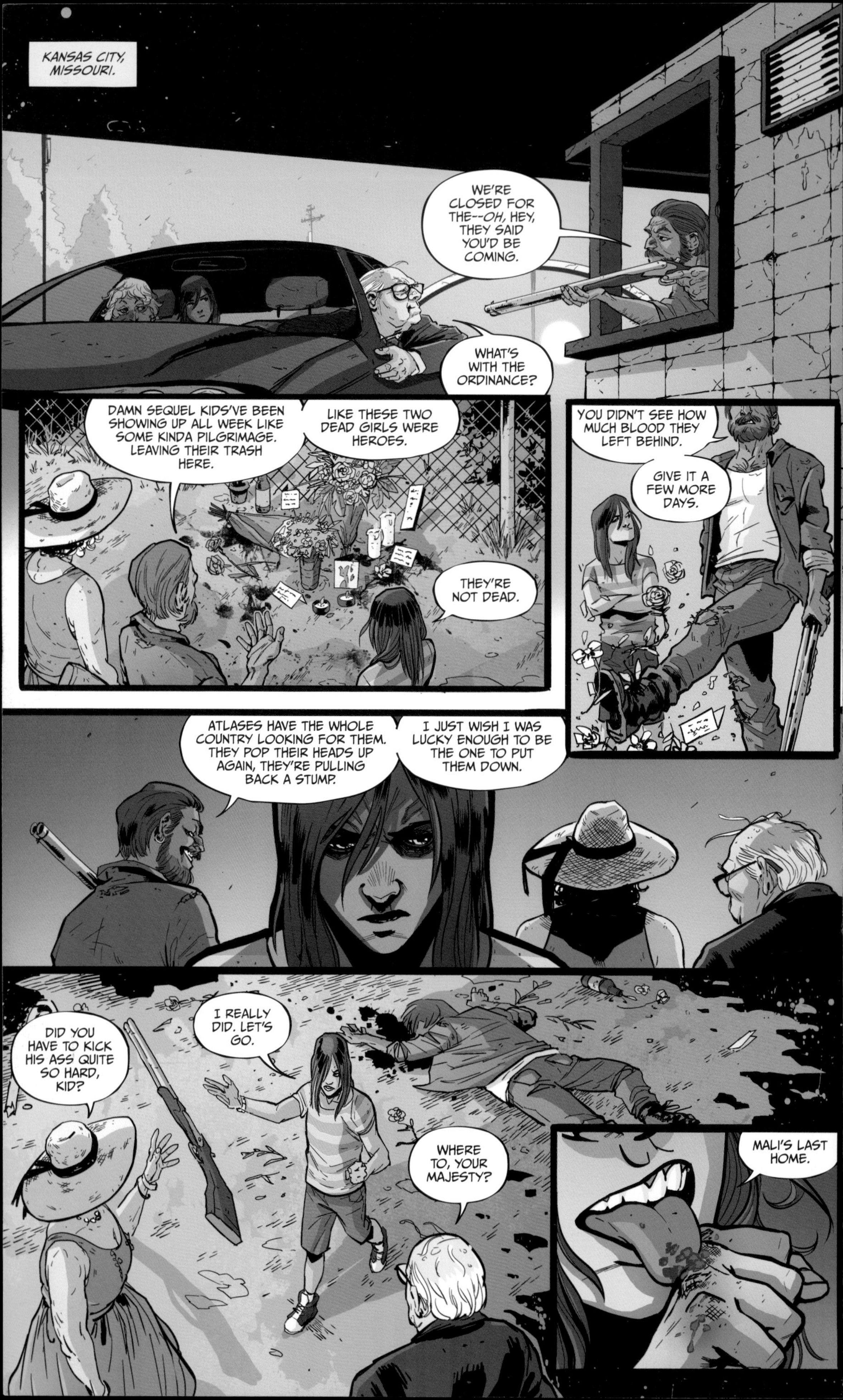
KANSAS CITY, MISSOURI.
WE'RE CLOSED FOR THE--OH, HEY, THEY SAID YOU'D BE COMING.
WHAT'S WITH THE ORDINANCE?
DAMN SEQUEL KIDS'VE BEEN SHOWING UP ALL WEEK LIKE SOME KINDA PILGRIMAGE. LEAVING THEIR TRASH HERE.
LIKE THESE TWO DEAD GIRLS WERE HEROES.
THEY'RE NOT DEAD.
YOU DIDN'T SEE HOW MUCH BLOOD THEY LEFT BEHIND.
GIVE IT A FEW MORE DAYS.
ATLASES HAVE THE WHOLE COUNTRY LOOKING FOR THEM. THEY POP THEIR HEADS UP AGAIN, THEY'RE PULLING BACK A STUMP.
I JUST WISH I WAS LUCKY ENOUGH TO BE THE ONE TO PUT THEM DOWN.
DID YOU HAVE TO KICK HIS ASS QUITE SO HARD, KID?
I REALLY DID. LET'S GO.
WHERE TO, YOUR MAJESTY?
MALI'S LAST HOME.

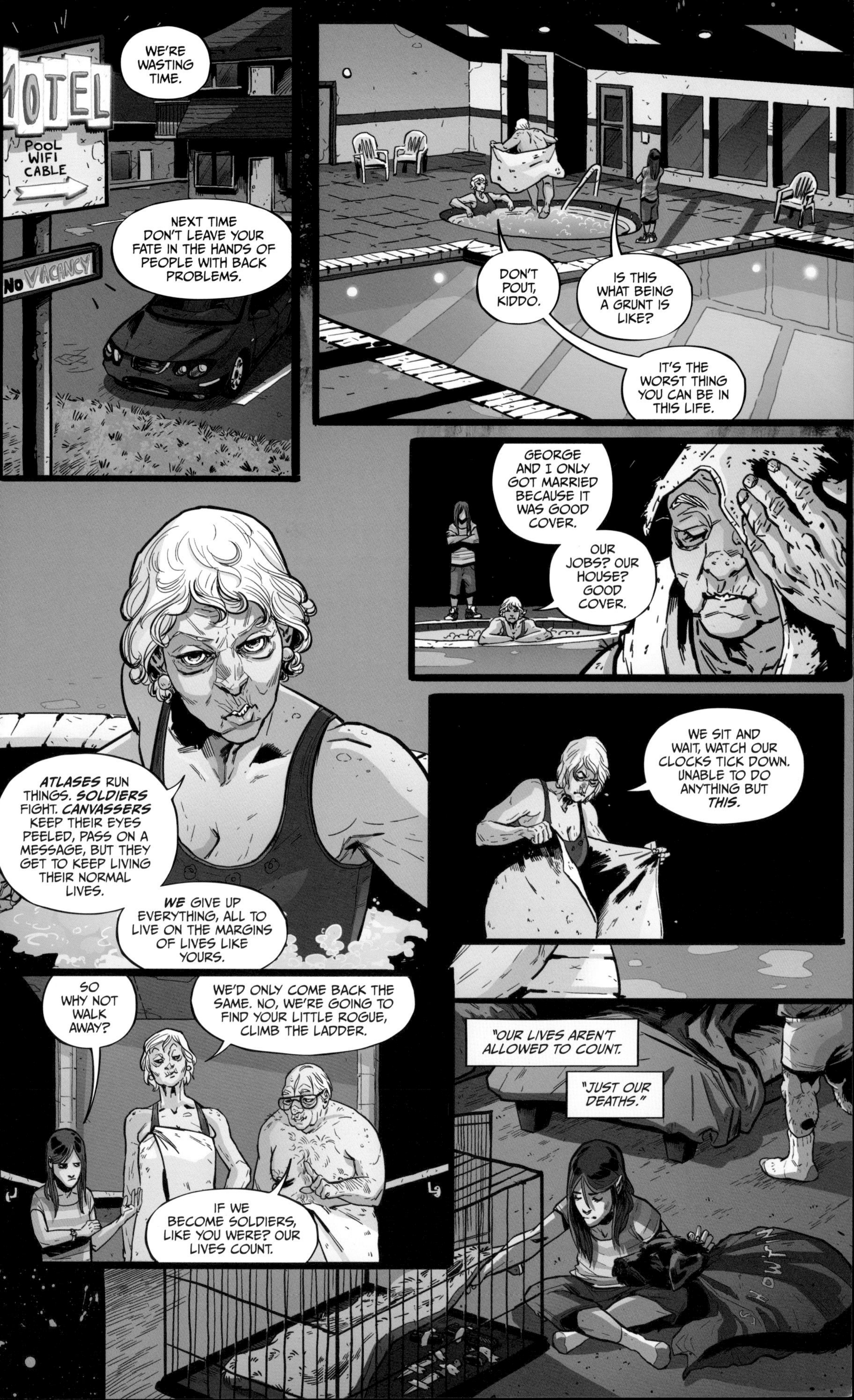
MOTEL
POOL WIFI CABLE
NO VACANCY
WE'RE WASTING TIME.
NEXT TIME DON'T LEAVE YOUR FATE IN THE HANDS OF PEOPLE WITH BACK PROBLEMS.
DON'T POUT, KIDDO.
IS THIS WHAT BEING A GRUNT IS LIKE?
IT'S THE WORST THING YOU CAN BE IN THIS LIFE.
GEORGE AND I ONLY GOT MARRIED BECAUSE IT WAS GOOD COVER.
OUR JOBS? OUR HOUSE? GOOD COVER.
ATLASES RUN THINGS. SOLDIERS FIGHT. CANVASSERS KEEP THEIR EYES PEELED, PASS ON A MESSAGE, BUT THEY GET TO KEEP LIVING THEIR NORMAL LIVES.
WE GIVE UP EVERYTHING, ALL TO LIVE ON THE MARGINS OF LIVES LIKE YOURS.
WE SIT AND WAIT, WATCH OUR CLOCKS TICK DOWN. UNABLE TO DO ANYTHING BUT THIS.
SO WHY NOT WALK AWAY?
WE'D ONLY COME BACK THE SAME. NO, WE'RE GOING TO FIND YOUR LITTLE ROGUE, CLIMB THE LADDER.
IF WE BECOME SOLDIERS, LIKE YOU WERE? OUR LIVES COUNT.
"OUR LIVES AREN'T ALLOWED TO COUNT.
"JUST OUR DEATHS."

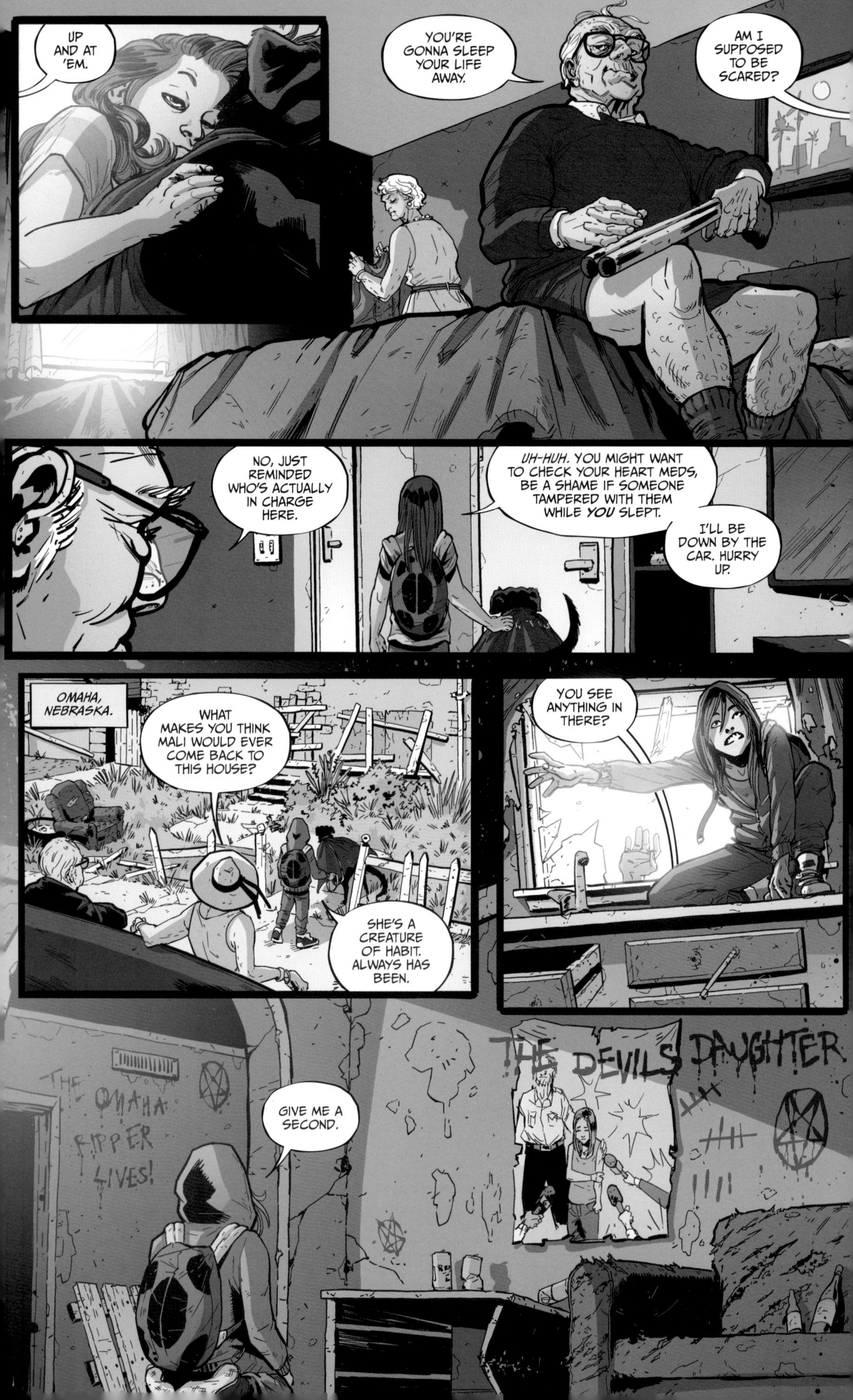
UP AND AT 'EM.
YOU'RE GONNA SLEEP YOUR LIFE AWAY.
AM I SUPPOSED TO BE SCARED?
NO, JUST REMINDED WHO'S ACTUALLY IN CHARGE HERE.
UH-HUH. YOU MIGHT WANT TO CHECK YOUR HEART MEDS, BE A SHAME IF SOMEONE TAMPERED WITH THEM WHILE YOU SLEPT.
I'LL BE DOWN BY THE CAR. HURRY UP.
OMAHA, NEBRASKA.
WHAT MAKES YOU THINK MALI WOULD EVER COME BACK TO THIS HOUSE?
SHE'S A CREATURE OF HABIT. ALWAYS HAS BEEN.
YOU SEE ANYTHING IN THERE?
THE OMAHA RIPPER LIVES!
GIVE ME A SECOND.
THE DEVILS DAUGHTER

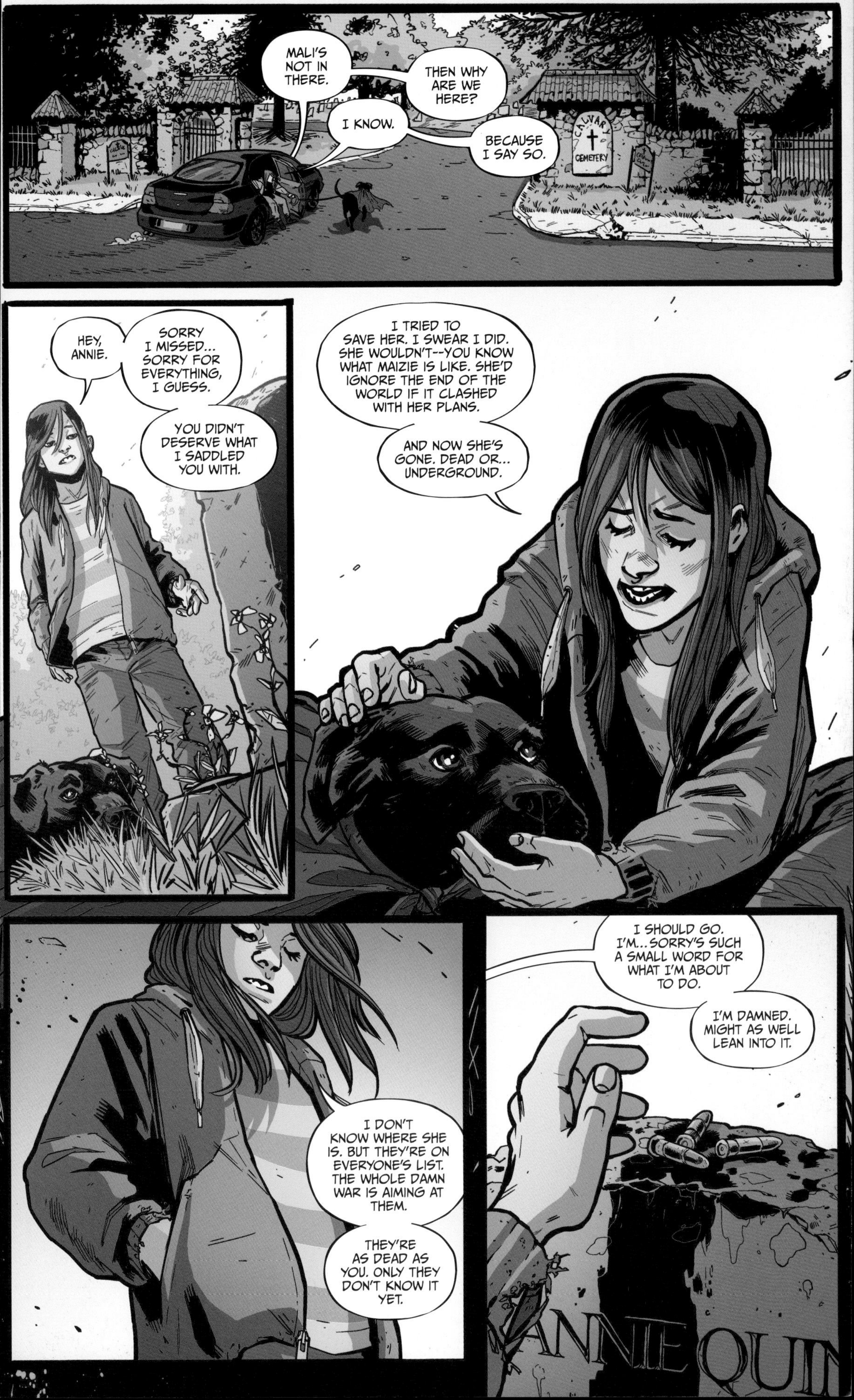
MALI'S NOT IN THERE.
THEN WHY ARE WE HERE?
I KNOW.
BECAUSE I SAY SO.
CALVARY CEMETERY
HEY, ANNIE.
SORRY I MISSED... SORRY FOR EVERYTHING, I GUESS.
YOU DIDN'T DESERVE WHAT I SADDLED YOU WITH.
I TRIED TO SAVE HER. I SWEAR I DID. SHE WOULDN'T--YOU KNOW WHAT MAIZIE IS LIKE. SHE'D IGNORE THE END OF THE WORLD IF IT CLASHED WITH HER PLANS.
AND NOW SHE'S GONE. DEAD OR... UNDERGROUND.
I DON'T KNOW WHERE SHE IS. BUT THEY'RE ON EVERYONE'S LIST. THE WHOLE DAMN WAR IS AIMING AT THEM.
THEY'RE AS DEAD AS YOU. ONLY THEY DON'T KNOW IT YET.
I SHOULD GO. I'M...SORRY'S SUCH A SMALL WORD FOR WHAT I'M ABOUT TO DO.
I'M DAMNED. MIGHT AS WELL LEAN INTO IT.
ANNIE QUIN

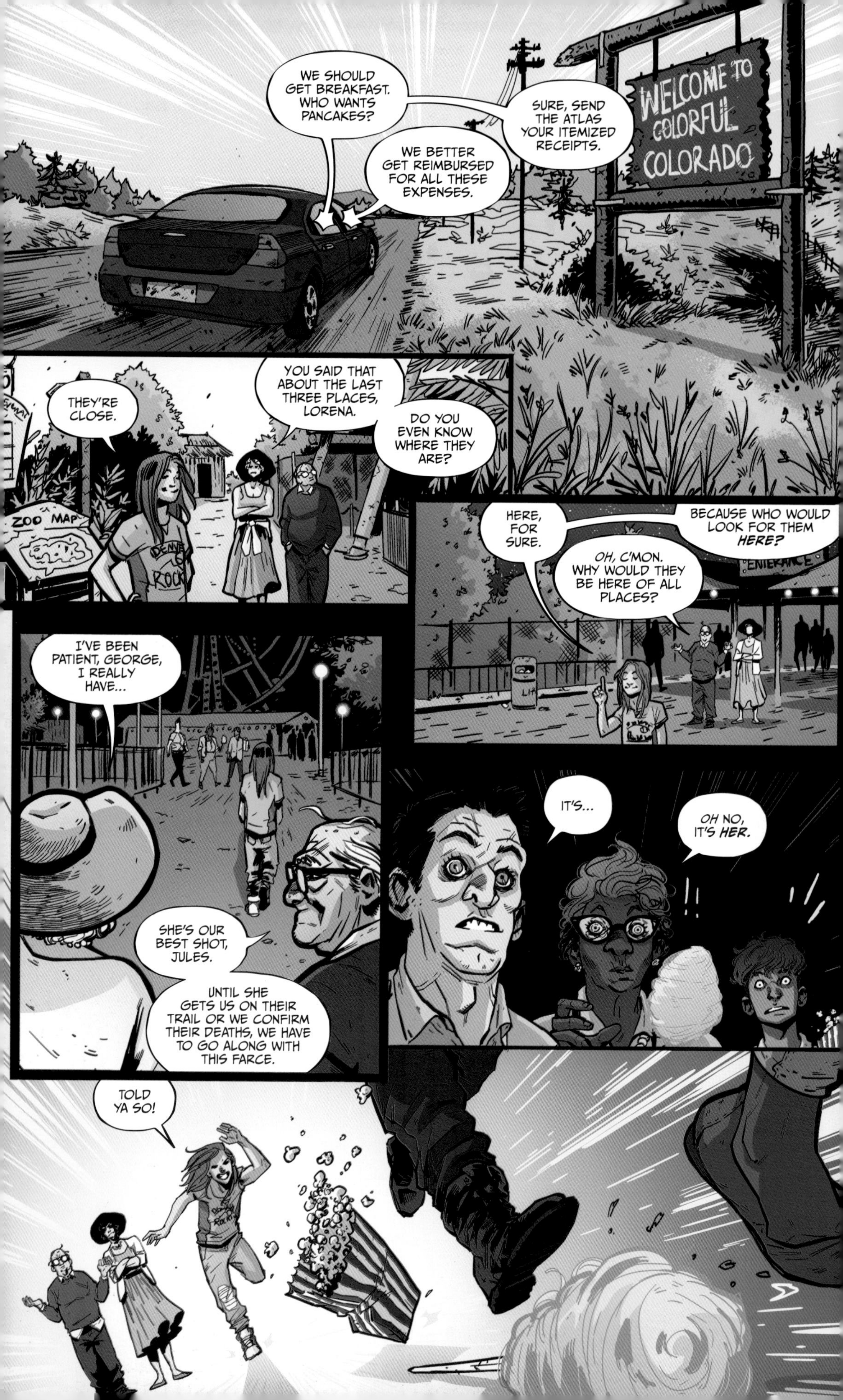
WE SHOULD GET BREAKFAST. WHO WANTS PANCAKES?
SURE, SEND THE ATLAS YOUR ITEMIZED RECEIPTS.
WE BETTER GET REIMBURSED FOR ALL THESE EXPENSES.
WELCOME TO COLORFUL COLORADO
THEY'RE CLOSE.
YOU SAID THAT ABOUT THE LAST THREE PLACES, LORENA.
DO YOU EVEN KNOW WHERE THEY ARE?
ZOO MAP
HERE, FOR SURE.
BECAUSE WHO WOULD LOOK FOR THEM *HERE?*
OH, C'MON. WHY WOULD THEY BE HERE OF ALL PLACES?
ENTRANCE
I'VE BEEN PATIENT, GEORGE, I REALLY HAVE...
SHE'S OUR BEST SHOT, JULES.
UNTIL SHE GETS US ON THEIR TRAIL OR WE CONFIRM THEIR DEATHS, WE HAVE TO GO ALONG WITH THIS FARCE.
IT'S...
OH NO, IT'S *HER.*
TOLD YA SO!

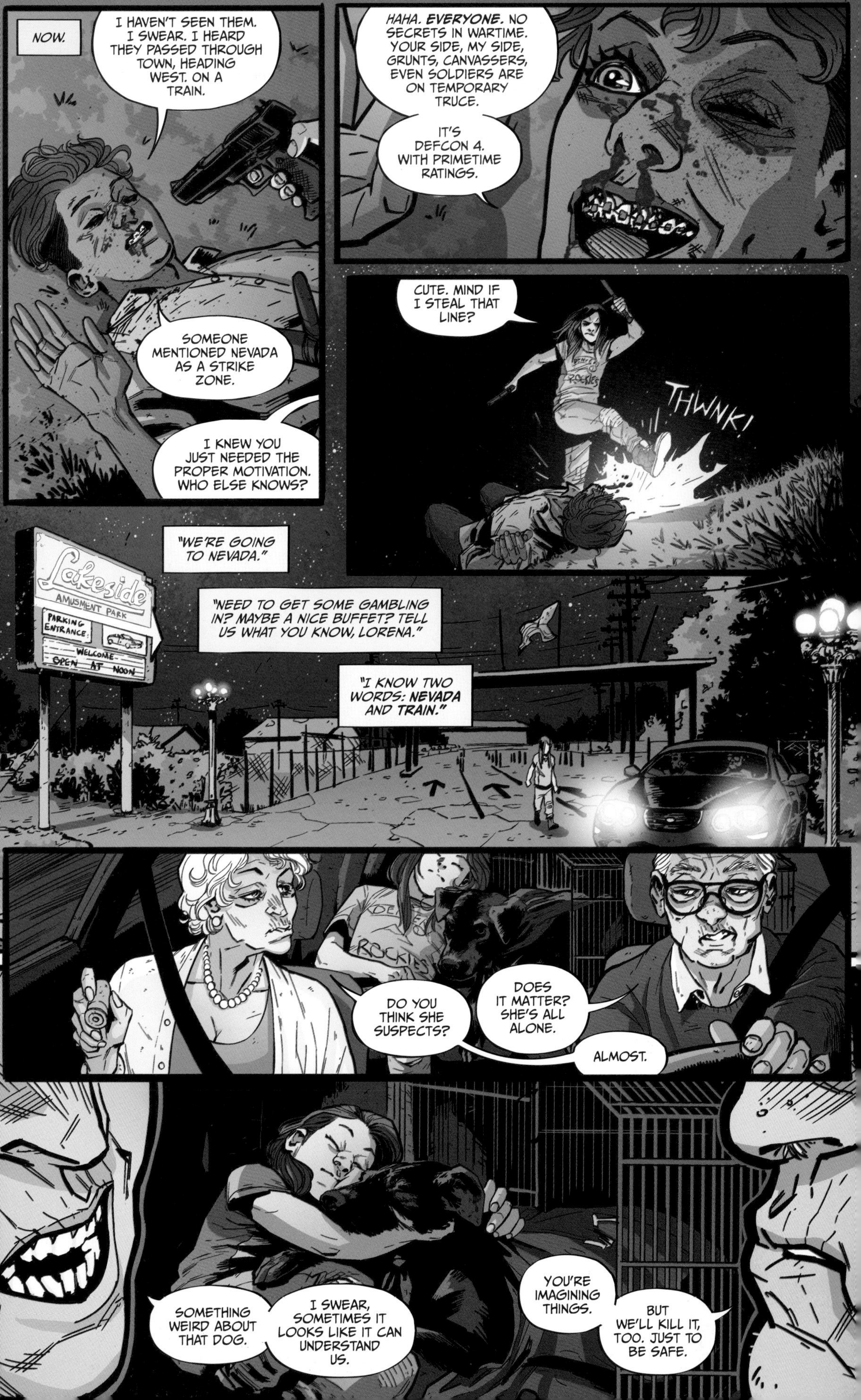
NOW.
I HAVEN'T SEEN THEM. I SWEAR. I HEARD THEY PASSED THROUGH TOWN, HEADING WEST. ON A TRAIN.
SOMEONE MENTIONED NEVADA AS A STRIKE ZONE.
I KNEW YOU JUST NEEDED THE PROPER MOTIVATION. WHO ELSE KNOWS?
HAHA. EVERYONE. NO SECRETS IN WARTIME. YOUR SIDE, MY SIDE, GRUNTS, CANVASSERS, EVEN SOLDIERS ARE ON TEMPORARY TRUCE.
IT'S DEFCON 4. WITH PRIMETIME RATINGS.
CUTE. MIND IF I STEAL THAT LINE?
THWNK!
"WE'RE GOING TO NEVADA."
Lakeside AMUSMENT PARK
PARKING ENTRANCE
WELCOME OPEN AT NOON
"NEED TO GET SOME GAMBLING IN? MAYBE A NICE BUFFET? TELL US WHAT YOU KNOW, LORENA."
"I KNOW TWO WORDS: NEVADA AND TRAIN."
DO YOU THINK SHE SUSPECTS?
DOES IT MATTER? SHE'S ALL ALONE.
ALMOST.
SOMETHING WEIRD ABOUT THAT DOG.
I SWEAR, SOMETIMES IT LOOKS LIKE IT CAN UNDERSTAND US.
YOU'RE IMAGINING THINGS.
BUT WE'LL KILL IT, TOO. JUST TO BE SAFE.

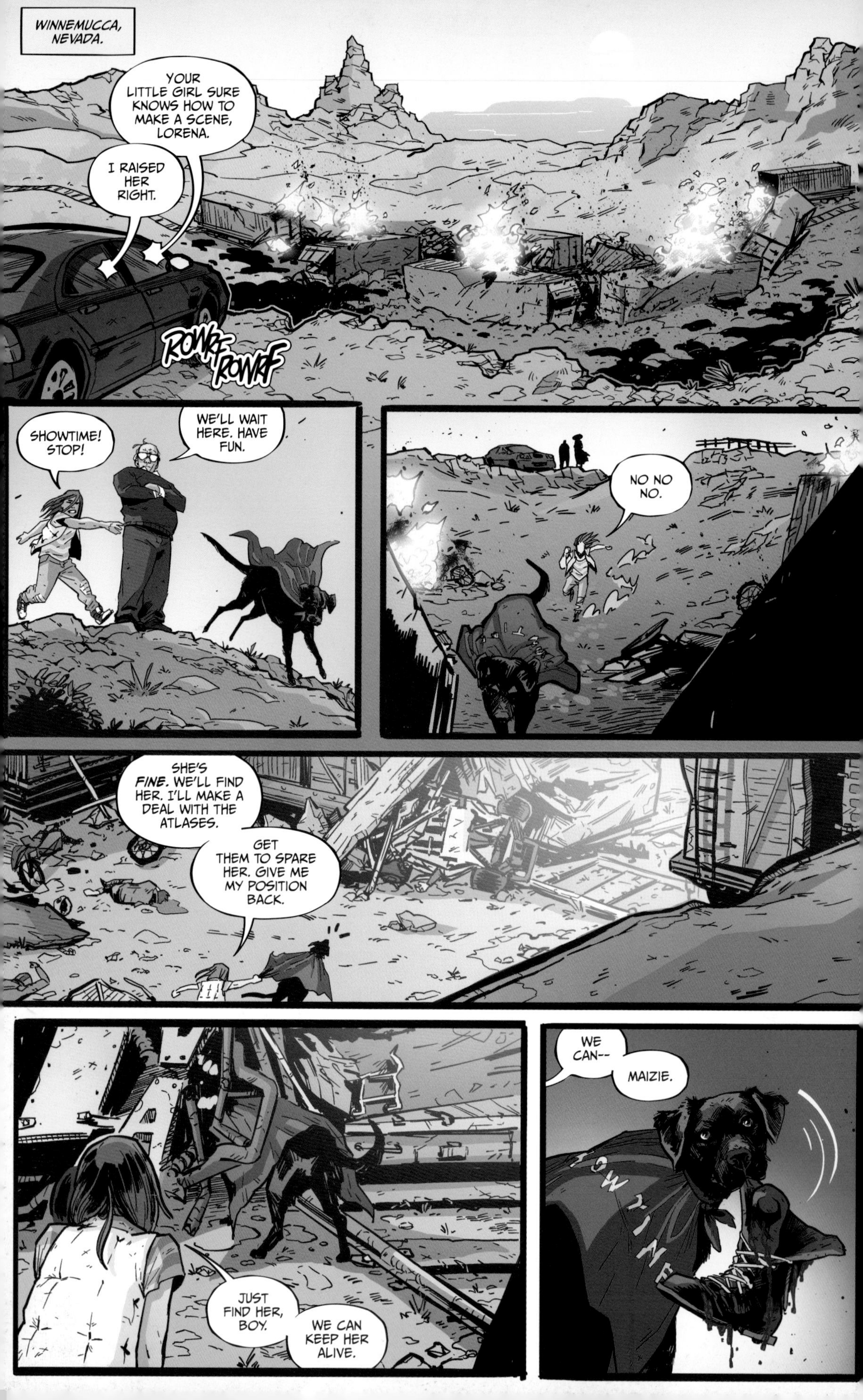
WINNEMUCCA, NEVADA.
YOUR LITTLE GIRL SURE KNOWS HOW TO MAKE A SCENE, LORENA.
I RAISED HER RIGHT.
ROWRF ROWRF
SHOWTIME! STOP!
WE'LL WAIT HERE. HAVE FUN.
NO NO NO.
SHE'S FINE. WE'LL FIND HER. I'LL MAKE A DEAL WITH THE ATLASES.
GET THEM TO SPARE HER. GIVE ME MY POSITION BACK.
JUST FIND HER, BOY.
WE CAN KEEP HER ALIVE.
WE CAN--
MAIZIE.

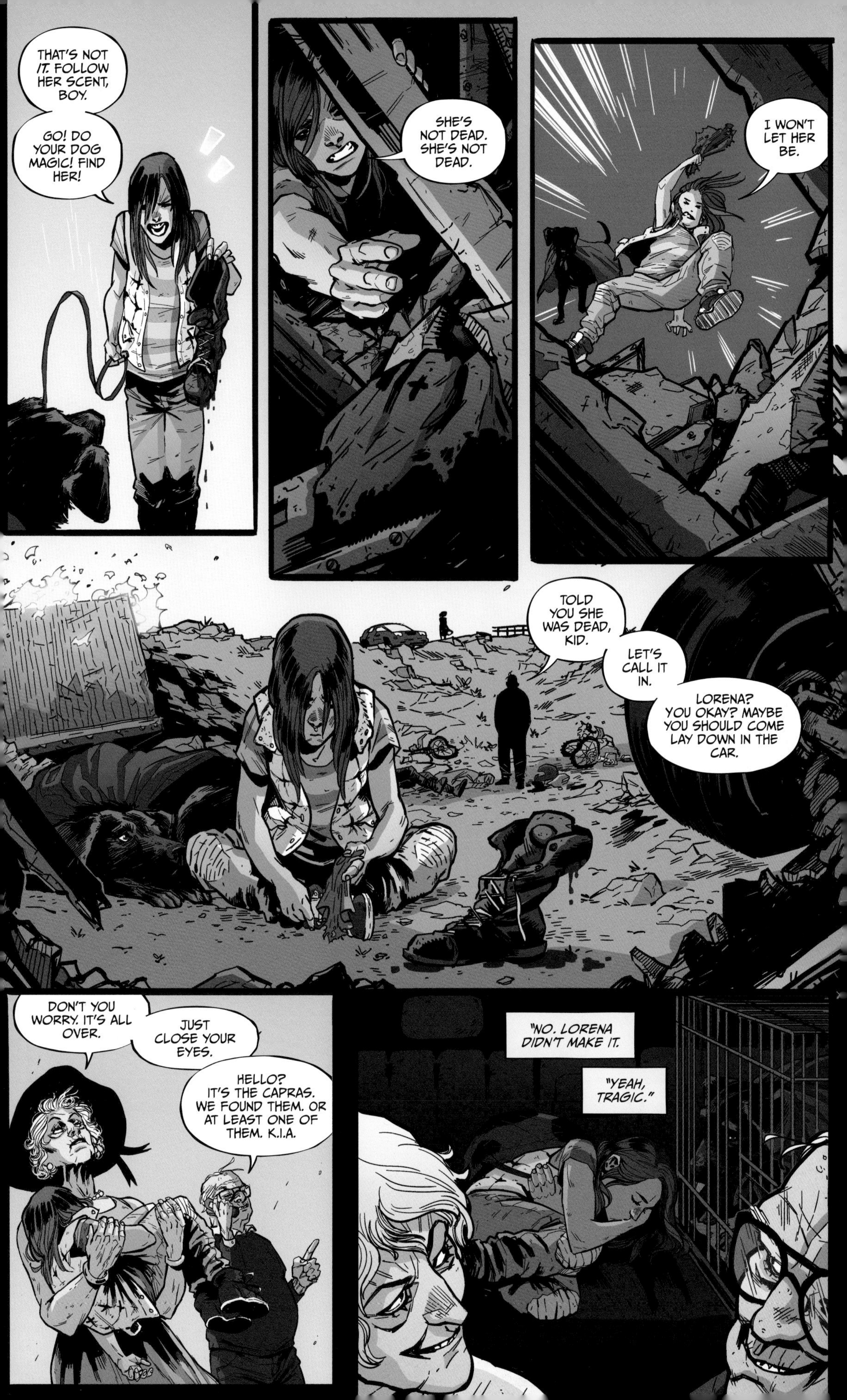
THAT'S NOT IT. FOLLOW HER SCENT, BOY.
GO! DO YOUR DOG MAGIC! FIND HER!
SHE'S NOT DEAD. SHE'S NOT DEAD.
I WON'T LET HER BE.
TOLD YOU SHE WAS DEAD, KID.
LET'S CALL IT IN.
LORENA? YOU OKAY? MAYBE YOU SHOULD COME LAY DOWN IN THE CAR.
DON'T YOU WORRY. IT'S ALL OVER.
JUST CLOSE YOUR EYES.
HELLO? IT'S THE CAPRAS. WE FOUND THEM. OR AT LEAST ONE OF THEM. K.I.A.
"NO. LORENA DIDN'T MAKE IT.
"YEAH, TRAGIC."

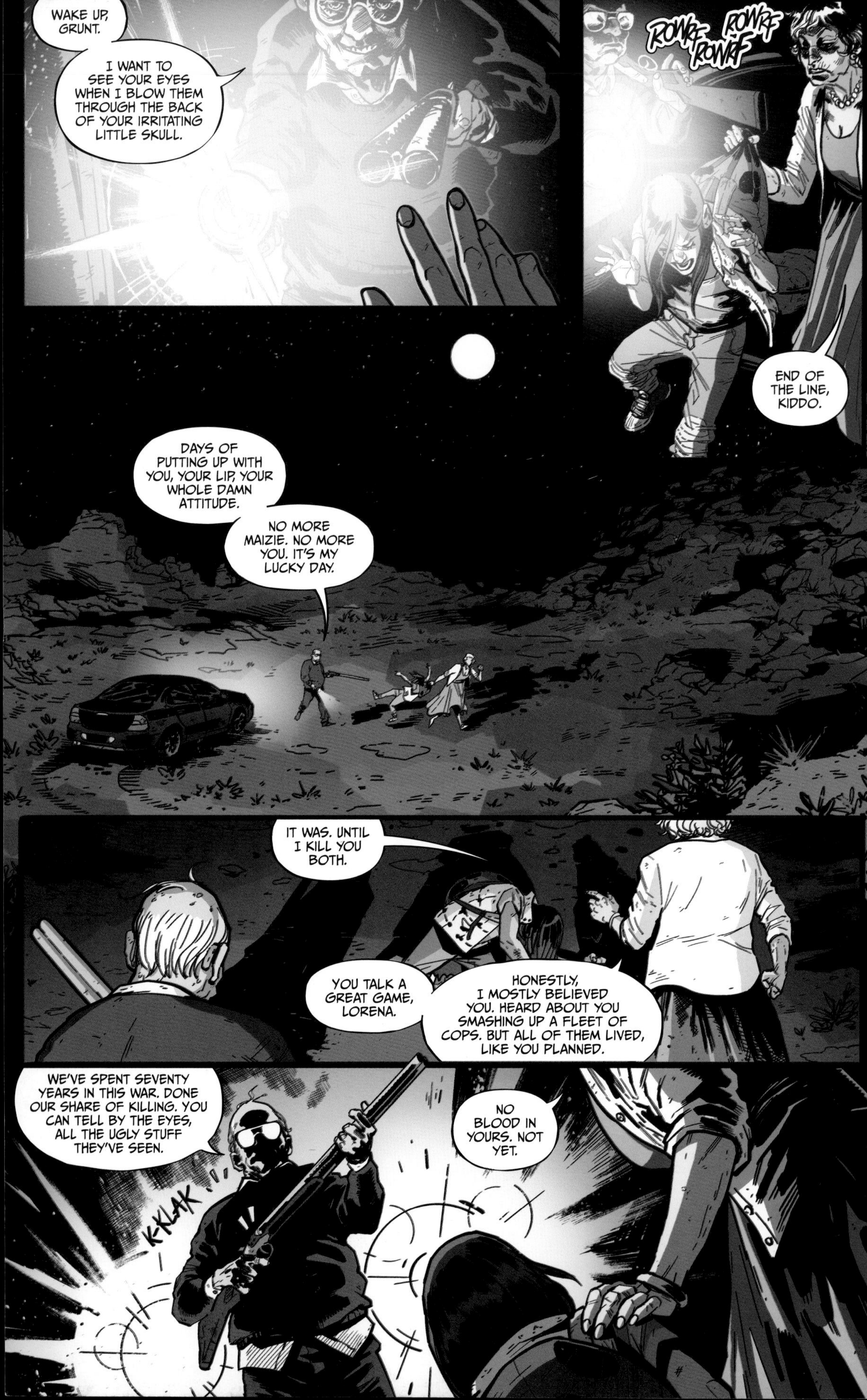
WAKE UP, GRUNT.
I WANT TO SEE YOUR EYES WHEN I BLOW THEM THROUGH THE BACK OF YOUR IRRITATING LITTLE SKULL.
ROWRF ROWRF ROWRF
END OF THE LINE, KIDDO.
DAYS OF PUTTING UP WITH YOU, YOUR LIP, YOUR WHOLE DAMN ATTITUDE.
NO MORE MAIZIE. NO MORE YOU. IT'S MY LUCKY DAY.
IT WAS. UNTIL I KILL YOU BOTH.
YOU TALK A GREAT GAME, LORENA.
HONESTLY, I MOSTLY BELIEVED YOU. HEARD ABOUT YOU SMASHING UP A FLEET OF COPS. BUT ALL OF THEM LIVED, LIKE YOU PLANNED.
WE'VE SPENT SEVENTY YEARS IN THIS WAR. DONE OUR SHARE OF KILLING. YOU CAN TELL BY THE EYES, ALL THE UGLY STUFF THEY'VE SEEN.
NO BLOOD IN YOURS. NOT YET.
K-KLAK

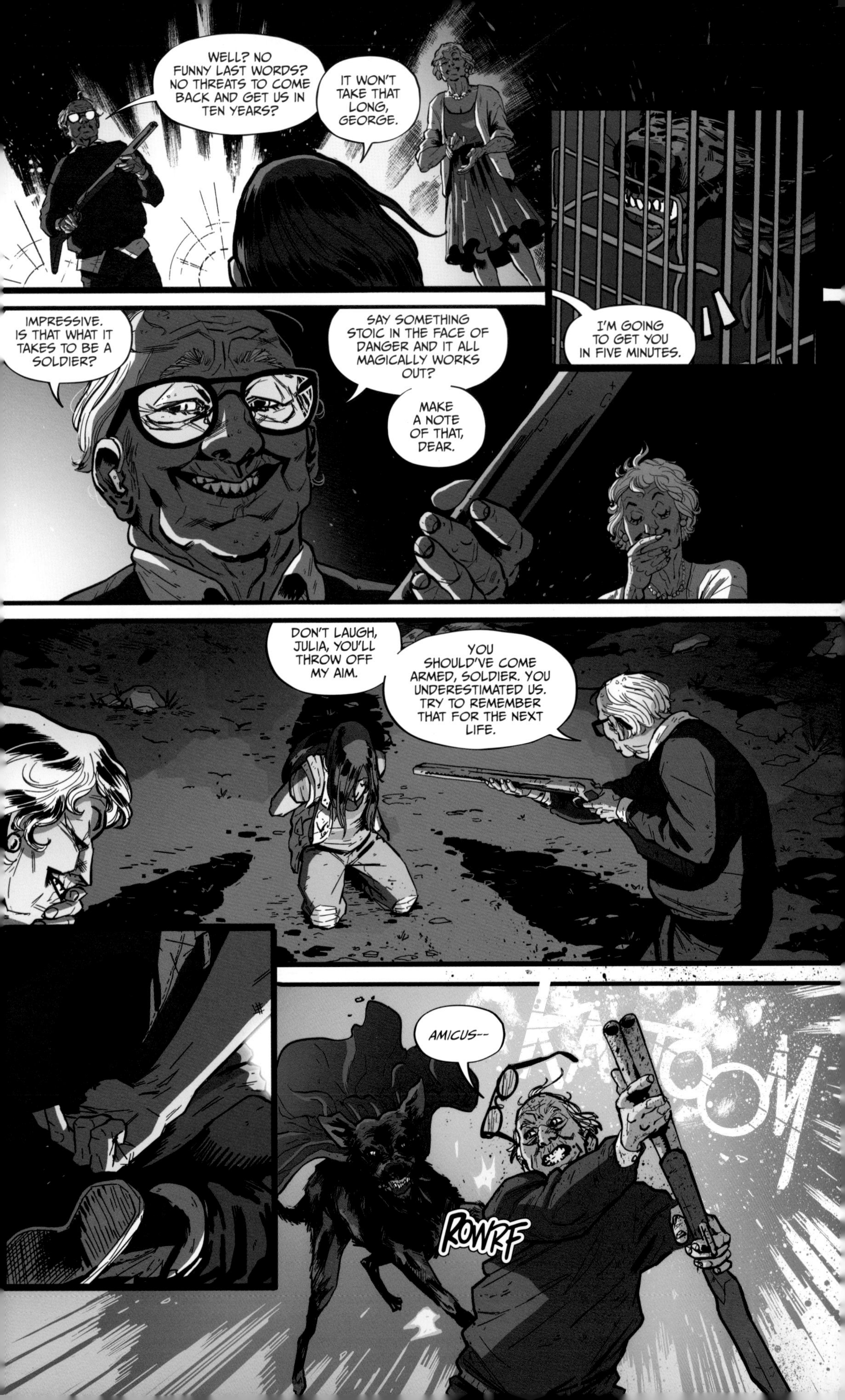
WELL? NO FUNNY LAST WORDS? NO THREATS TO COME BACK AND GET US IN TEN YEARS?
IT WON'T TAKE THAT LONG, GEORGE.
I'M GOING TO GET YOU IN FIVE MINUTES.
IMPRESSIVE. IS THAT WHAT IT TAKES TO BE A SOLDIER?
SAY SOMETHING STOIC IN THE FACE OF DANGER AND IT ALL MAGICALLY WORKS OUT?
MAKE A NOTE OF THAT, DEAR.
DON'T LAUGH, JULIA, YOU'LL THROW OFF MY AIM.
YOU SHOULD'VE COME ARMED, SOLDIER. YOU UNDERESTIMATED US. TRY TO REMEMBER THAT FOR THE NEXT LIFE.
AMICUS--
ROWRF

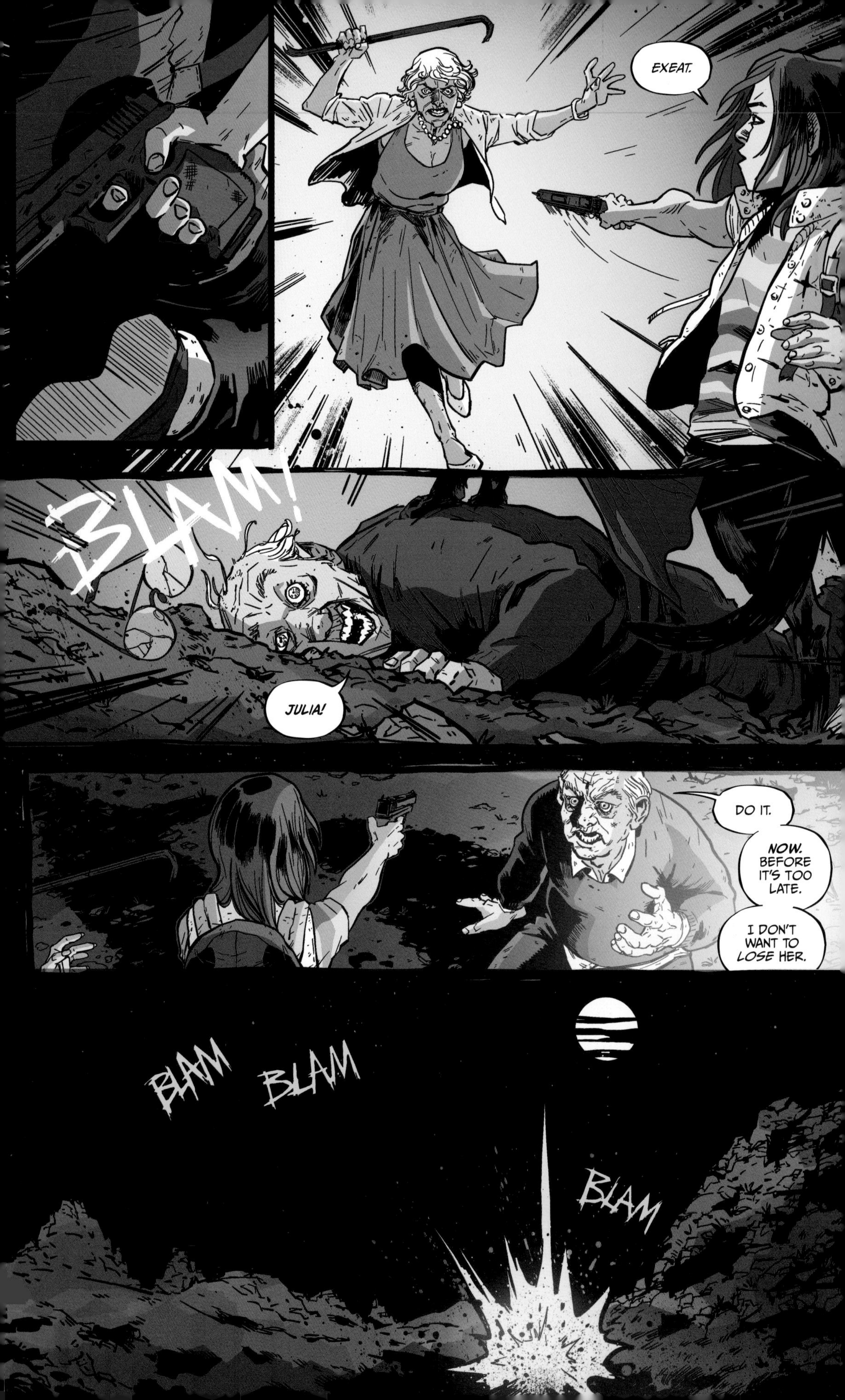
EXEAT.
BLAM!
JULIA!
DO IT.
NOW. BEFORE IT'S TOO LATE.
I DON'T WANT TO LOSE HER.
BLAM
BLAM
BLAM

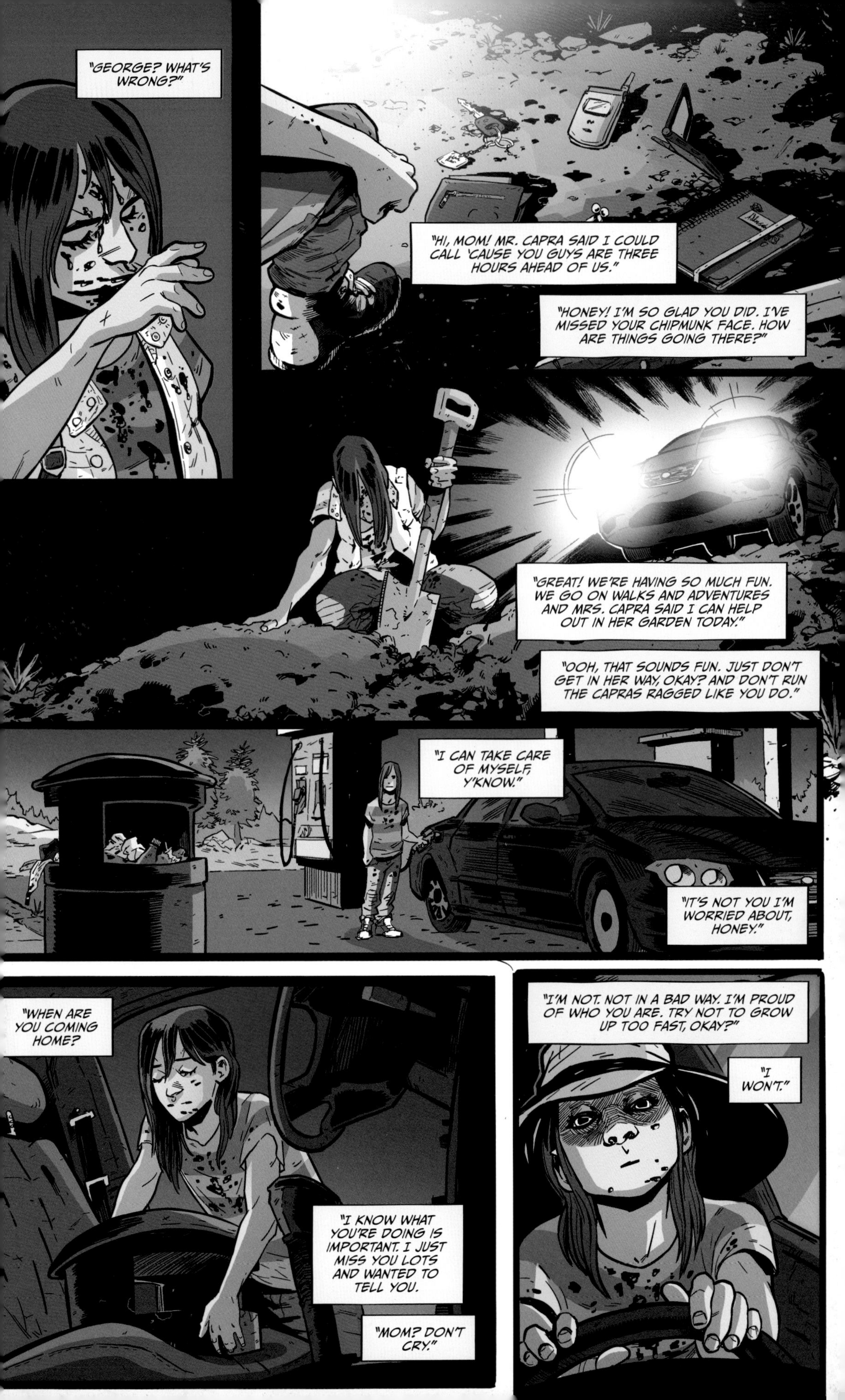
"GEORGE? WHAT'S WRONG?"
"HI, MOM! MR. CAPRA SAID I COULD CALL 'CAUSE YOU GUYS ARE THREE HOURS AHEAD OF US."
"HONEY! I'M SO GLAD YOU DID. I'VE MISSED YOUR CHIPMUNK FACE. HOW ARE THINGS GOING THERE?"
"GREAT! WE'RE HAVING SO MUCH FUN. WE GO ON WALKS AND ADVENTURES AND MRS. CAPRA SAID I CAN HELP OUT IN HER GARDEN TODAY."
"OOH, THAT SOUNDS FUN. JUST DON'T GET IN HER WAY, OKAY? AND DON'T RUN THE CAPRAS RAGGED LIKE YOU DO."
"I CAN TAKE CARE OF MYSELF, Y'KNOW."
"IT'S NOT YOU I'M WORRIED ABOUT, HONEY."
"WHEN ARE YOU COMING HOME?
"I KNOW WHAT YOU'RE DOING IS IMPORTANT. I JUST MISS YOU LOTS AND WANTED TO TELL YOU.
"MOM? DON'T CRY."
"I'M NOT. NOT IN A BAD WAY. I'M PROUD OF WHO YOU ARE. TRY NOT TO GROW UP TOO FAST, OKAY?"
"I WON'T."

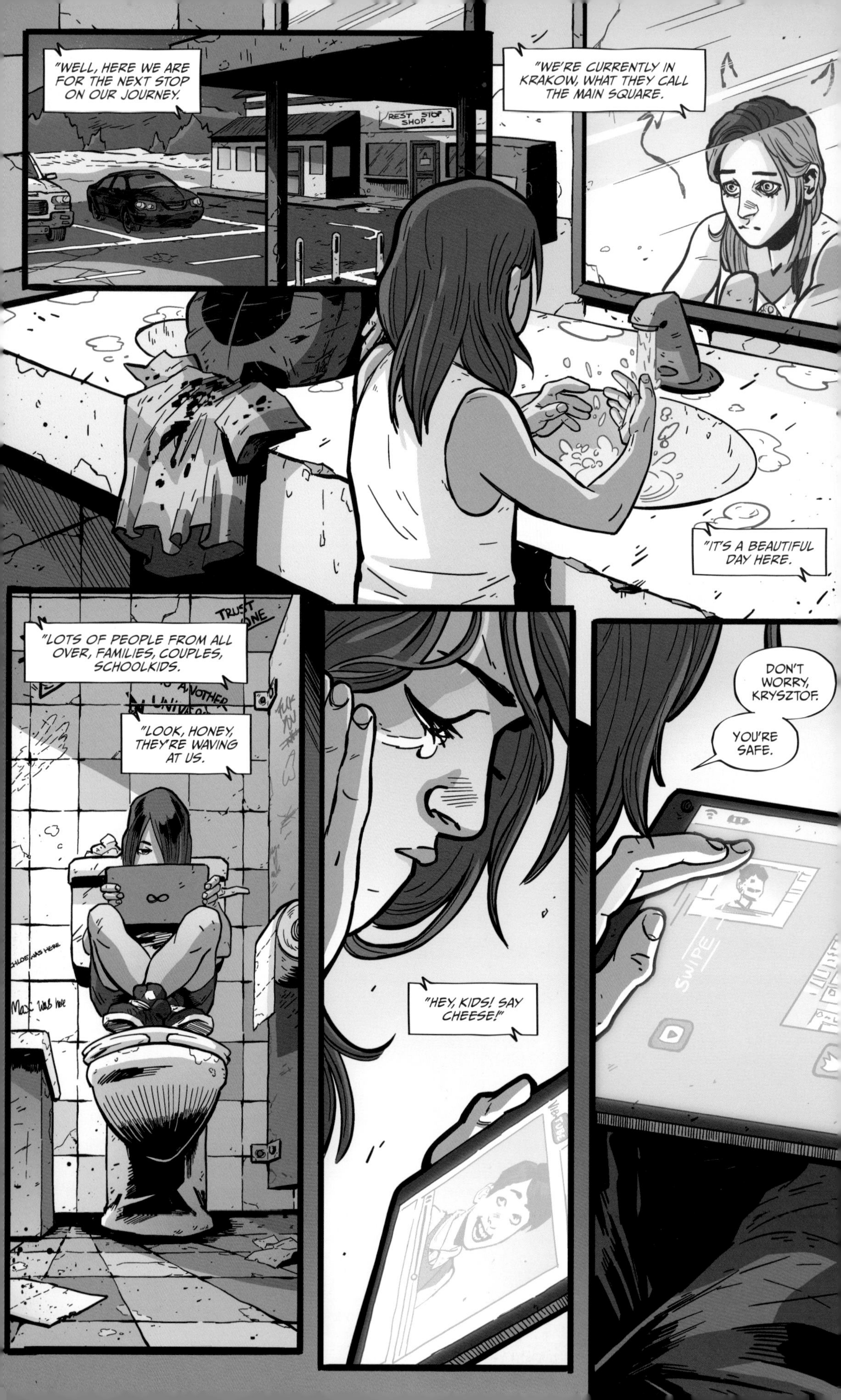
"WELL, HERE WE ARE FOR THE NEXT STOP ON OUR JOURNEY.
REST STOP SHOP
"WE'RE CURRENTLY IN KRAKOW, WHAT THEY CALL THE MAIN SQUARE.
"IT'S A BEAUTIFUL DAY HERE.
"LOTS OF PEOPLE FROM ALL OVER, FAMILIES, COUPLES, SCHOOLKIDS.
"LOOK, HONEY, THEY'RE WAVING AT US.
"HEY, KIDS! SAY CHEESE!"
DON'T WORRY, KRYSZTOF.
YOU'RE SAFE.
SWIPE

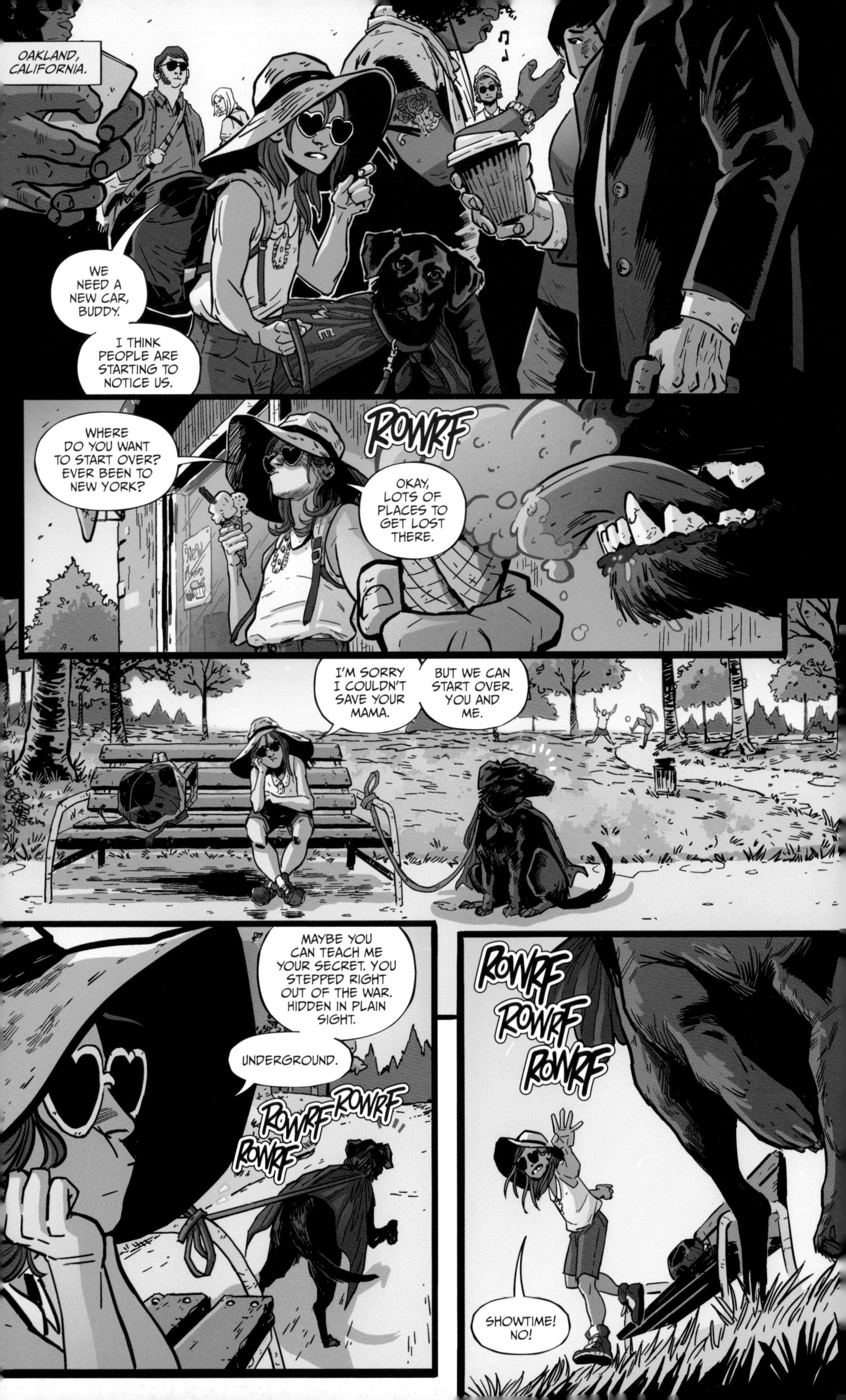
OAKLAND, CALIFORNIA.
WE NEED A NEW CAR, BUDDY.
I THINK PEOPLE ARE STARTING TO NOTICE US.
WHERE DO YOU WANT TO START OVER? EVER BEEN TO NEW YORK?
ROWRF
OKAY, LOTS OF PLACES TO GET LOST THERE.
I'M SORRY I COULDN'T SAVE YOUR MAMA.
BUT WE CAN START OVER. YOU AND ME.
MAYBE YOU CAN TEACH ME YOUR SECRET. YOU STEPPED RIGHT OUT OF THE WAR. HIDDEN IN PLAIN SIGHT.
UNDERGROUND.
ROWRF ROWRF
ROWRF
ROWRF
ROWRF
ROWRF
SHOWTIME! NO!

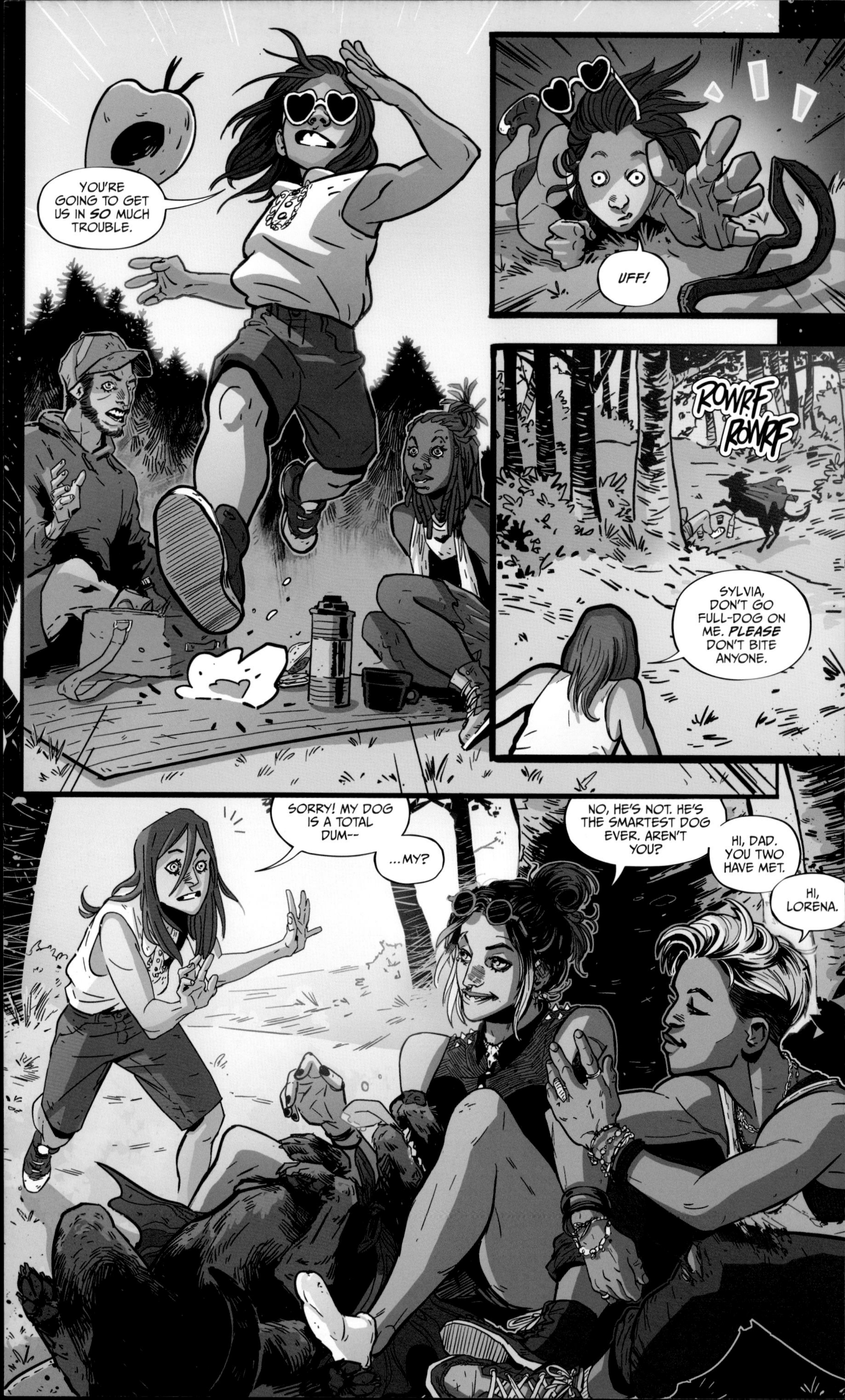
YOU'RE GOING TO GET US IN SO MUCH TROUBLE.
UFF!
ROWRF ROWRF
SYLVIA, DON'T GO FULL-DOG ON ME. PLEASE DON'T BITE ANYONE.
SORRY! MY DOG IS A TOTAL DUM--
...MY?
NO, HE'S NOT. HE'S THE SMARTEST DOG EVER. AREN'T YOU?
HI, DAD. YOU TWO HAVE MET.
HI, LORENA.

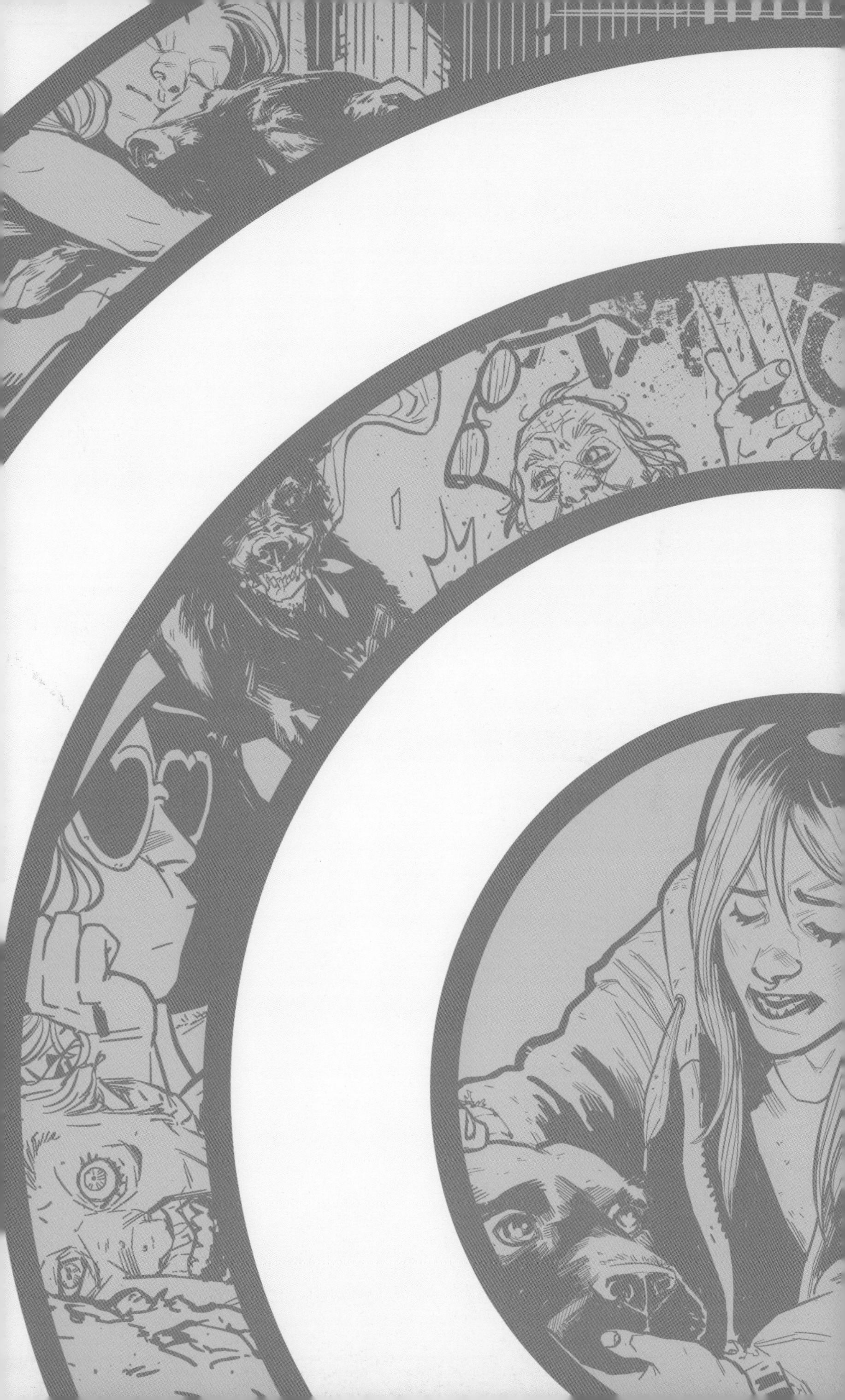

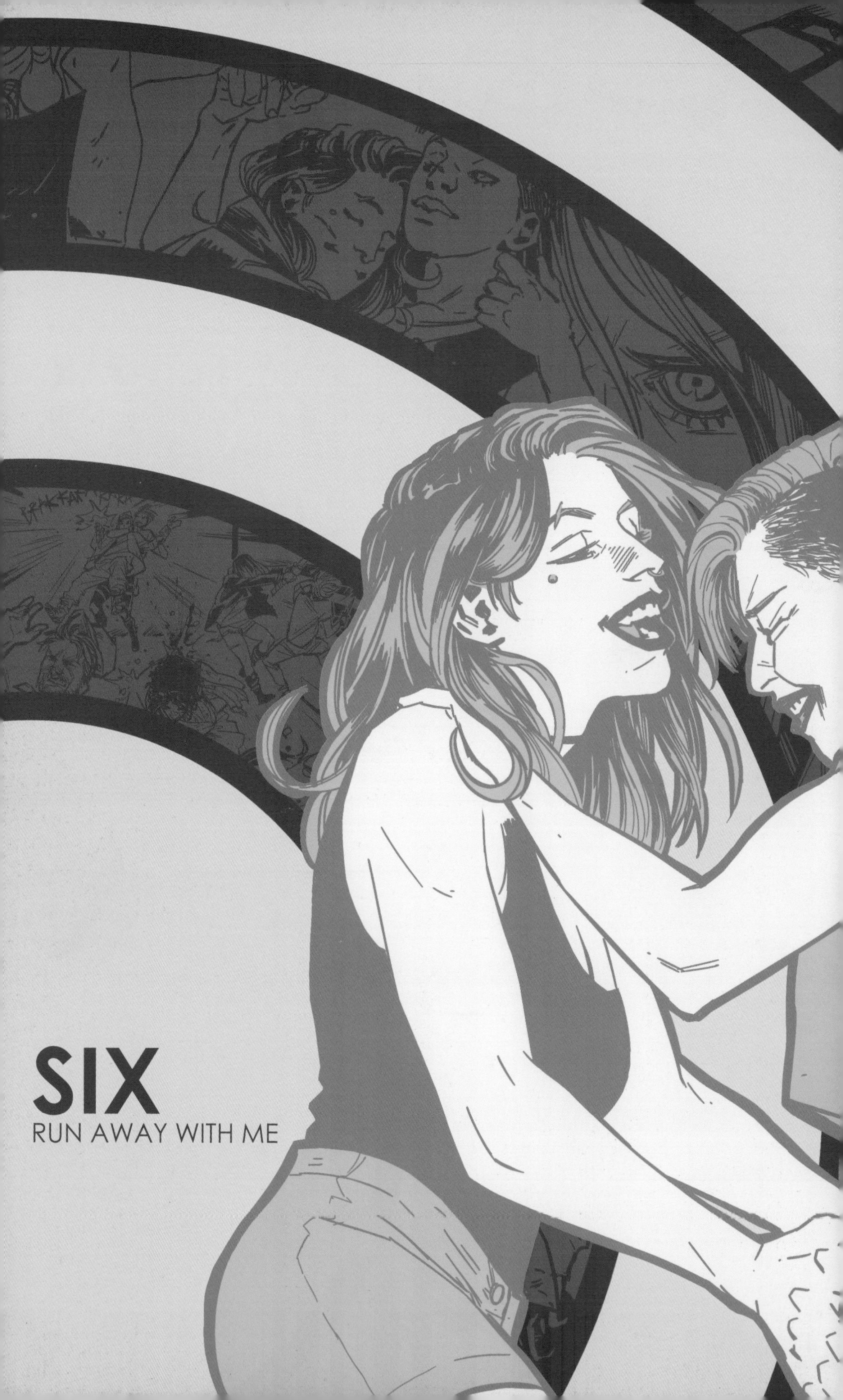

SIX
RUN AWAY WITH ME

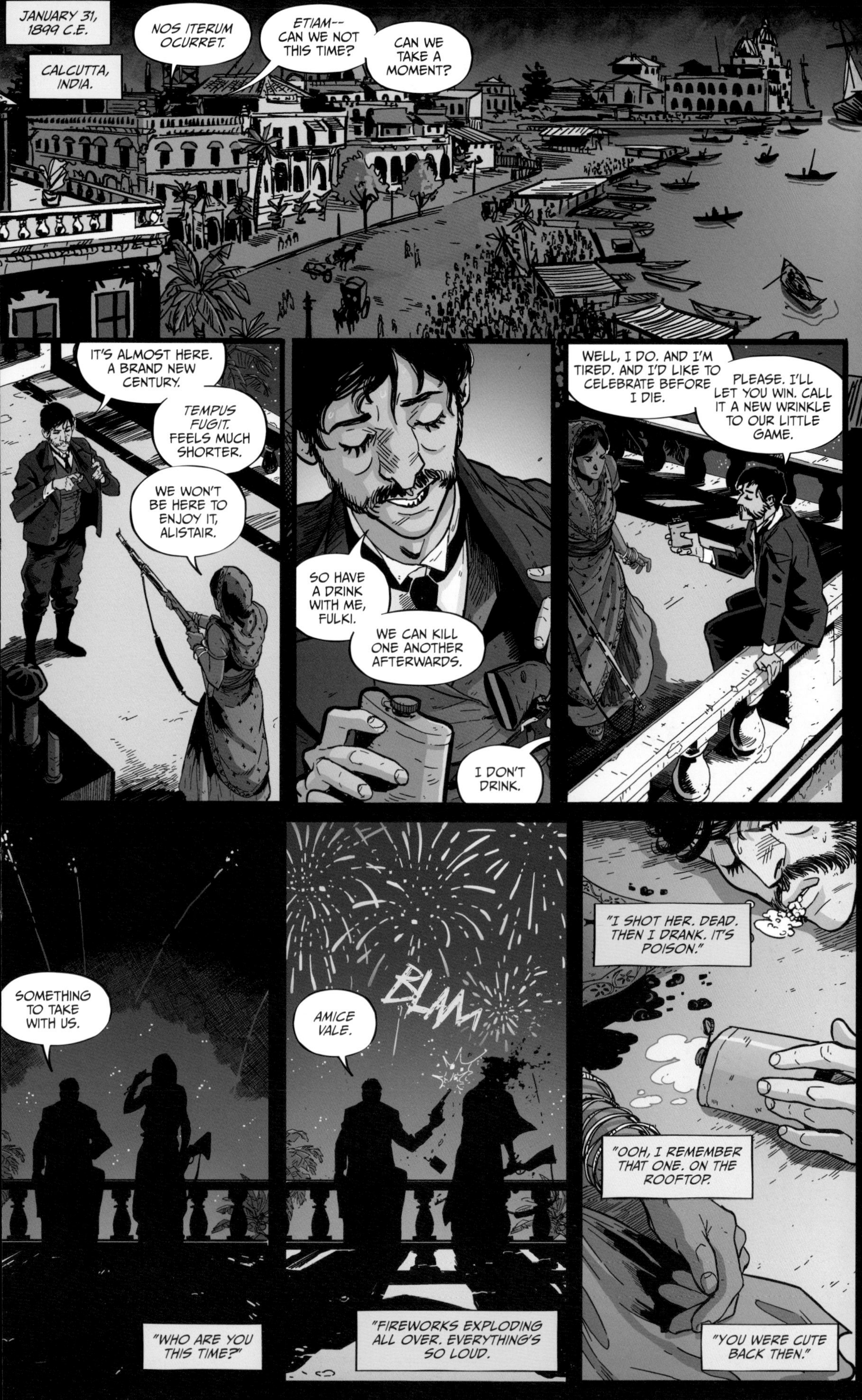
JANUARY 31, 1899 C.E.
CALCUTTA, INDIA.
NOS ITERUM OCURRET.
ETIAM-- CAN WE NOT THIS TIME?
CAN WE TAKE A MOMENT?
IT'S ALMOST HERE. A BRAND NEW CENTURY.
TEMPUS FUGIT. FEELS MUCH SHORTER.
WE WON'T BE HERE TO ENJOY IT, ALISTAIR.
SO HAVE A DRINK WITH ME, FULKI.
WE CAN KILL ONE ANOTHER AFTERWARDS.
I DON'T DRINK.
WELL, I DO. AND I'M TIRED. AND I'D LIKE TO CELEBRATE BEFORE I DIE.
PLEASE. I'LL LET YOU WIN. CALL IT A NEW WRINKLE TO OUR LITTLE GAME.
SOMETHING TO TAKE WITH US.
"WHO ARE YOU THIS TIME?"
AMICE VALE.
BLAM
"FIREWORKS EXPLODING ALL OVER. EVERYTHING'S SO LOUD.
"I SHOT HER. DEAD. THEN I DRANK. IT'S POISON."
"OOH, I REMEMBER THAT ONE. ON THE ROOFTOP.
"YOU WERE CUTE BACK THEN."

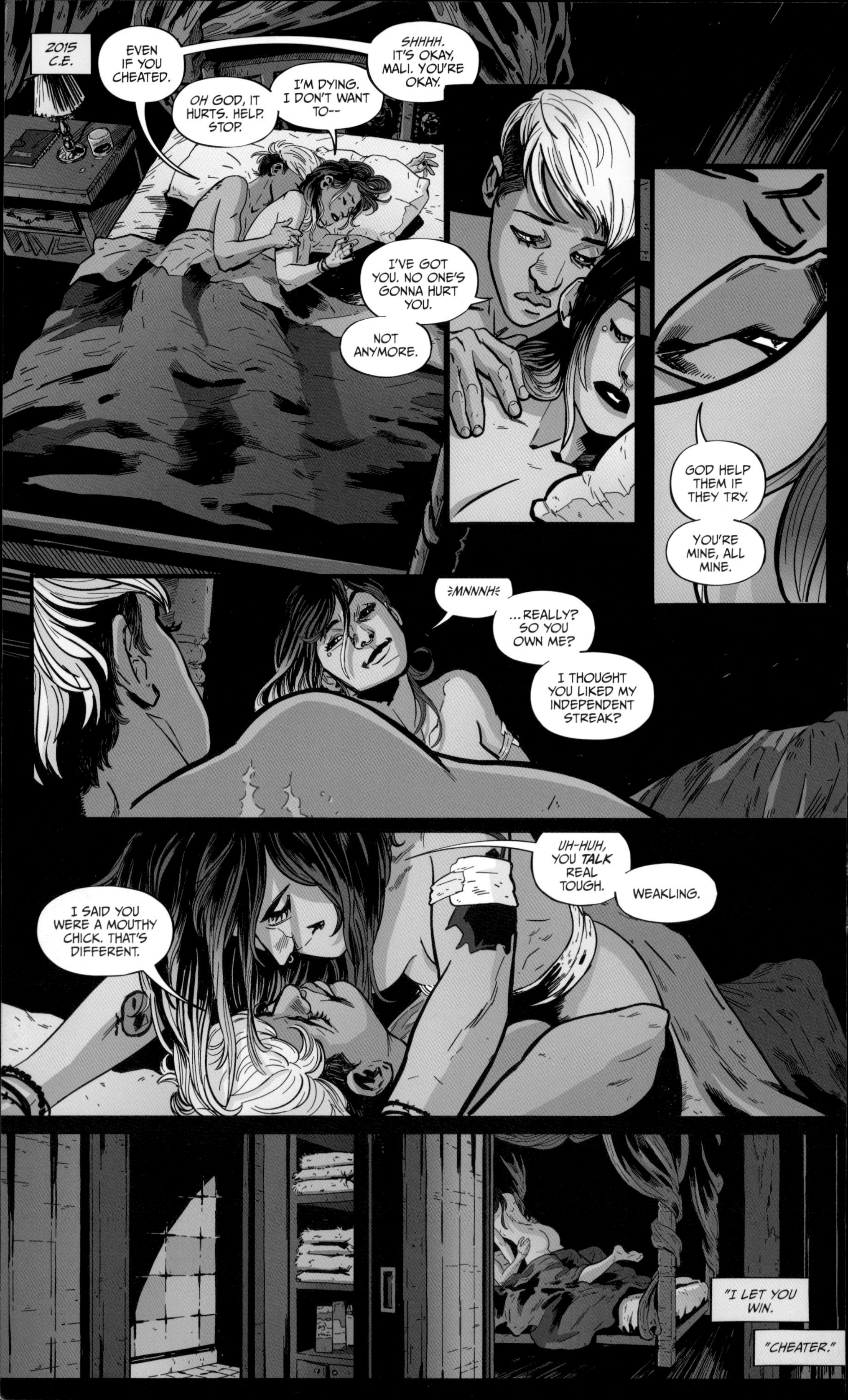
2015 C.E.
EVEN IF YOU CHEATED.
SHHHH. IT'S OKAY, MALI. YOU'RE OKAY.
OH GOD, IT HURTS. HELP. STOP.
I'M DYING. I DON'T WANT TO--
I'VE GOT YOU. NO ONE'S GONNA HURT YOU.
NOT ANYMORE.
GOD HELP THEM IF THEY TRY.
YOU'RE MINE, ALL MINE.
MNNNH
...REALLY? SO YOU OWN ME?
I THOUGHT YOU LIKED MY INDEPENDENT STREAK?
I SAID YOU WERE A MOUTHY CHICK. THAT'S DIFFERENT.
UH-HUH, YOU TALK REAL TOUGH.
WEAKLING.
"I LET YOU WIN.
"CHEATER."

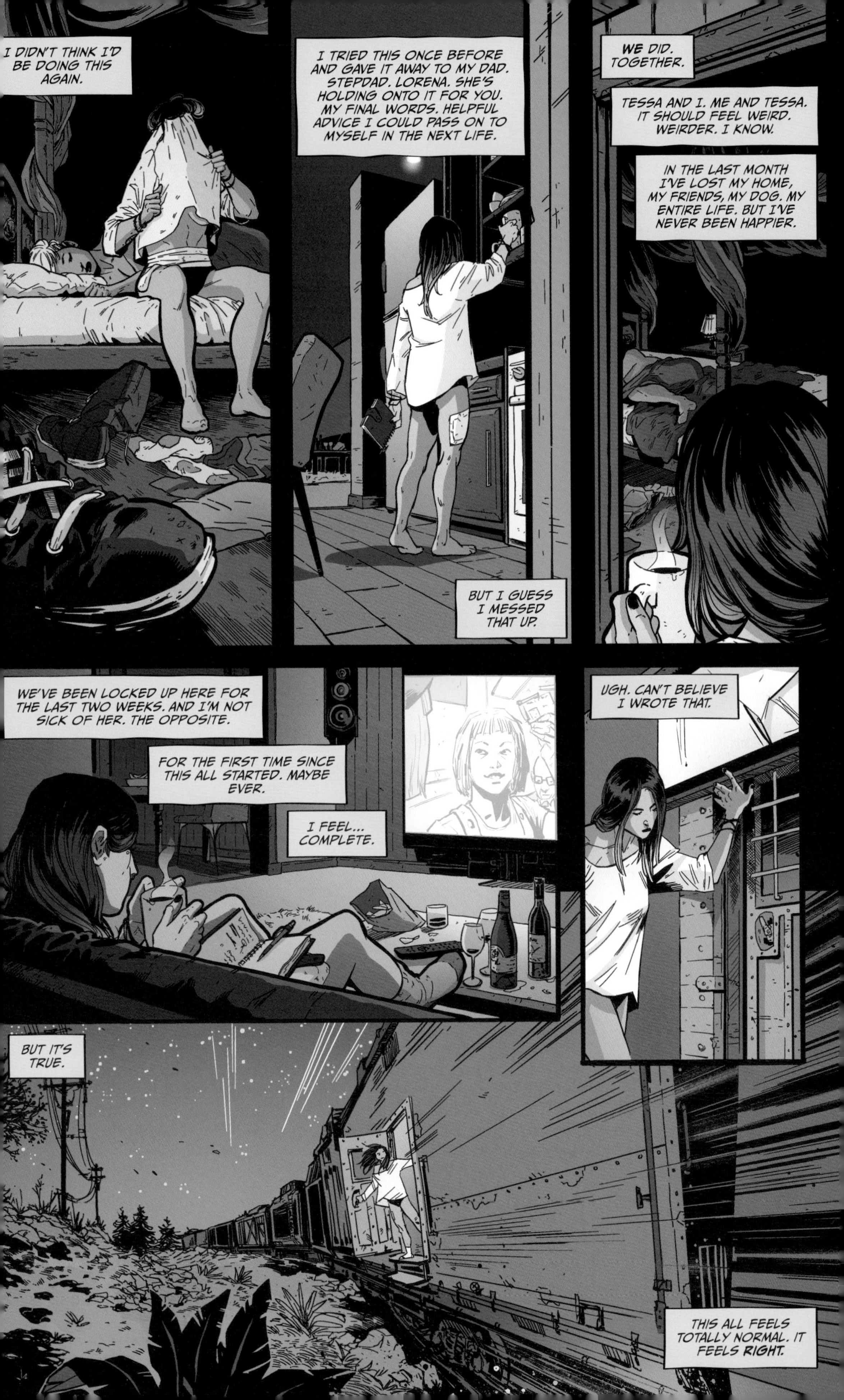
I DIDN'T THINK I'D BE DOING THIS AGAIN.
I TRIED THIS ONCE BEFORE AND GAVE IT AWAY TO MY DAD. STEPDAD. LORENA. SHE'S HOLDING ONTO IT FOR YOU. MY FINAL WORDS. HELPFUL ADVICE I COULD PASS ON TO MYSELF IN THE NEXT LIFE.
BUT I GUESS I MESSED THAT UP.
WE DID. TOGETHER.
TESSA AND I. ME AND TESSA. IT SHOULD FEEL WEIRD. WEIRDER. I KNOW.
IN THE LAST MONTH I'VE LOST MY HOME, MY FRIENDS, MY DOG. MY ENTIRE LIFE. BUT I'VE NEVER BEEN HAPPIER.
WE'VE BEEN LOCKED UP HERE FOR THE LAST TWO WEEKS. AND I'M NOT SICK OF HER. THE OPPOSITE.
FOR THE FIRST TIME SINCE THIS ALL STARTED. MAYBE EVER.
I FEEL... COMPLETE.
UGH. CAN'T BELIEVE I WROTE THAT.
BUT IT'S TRUE.
THIS ALL FEELS TOTALLY NORMAL. IT FEELS RIGHT.

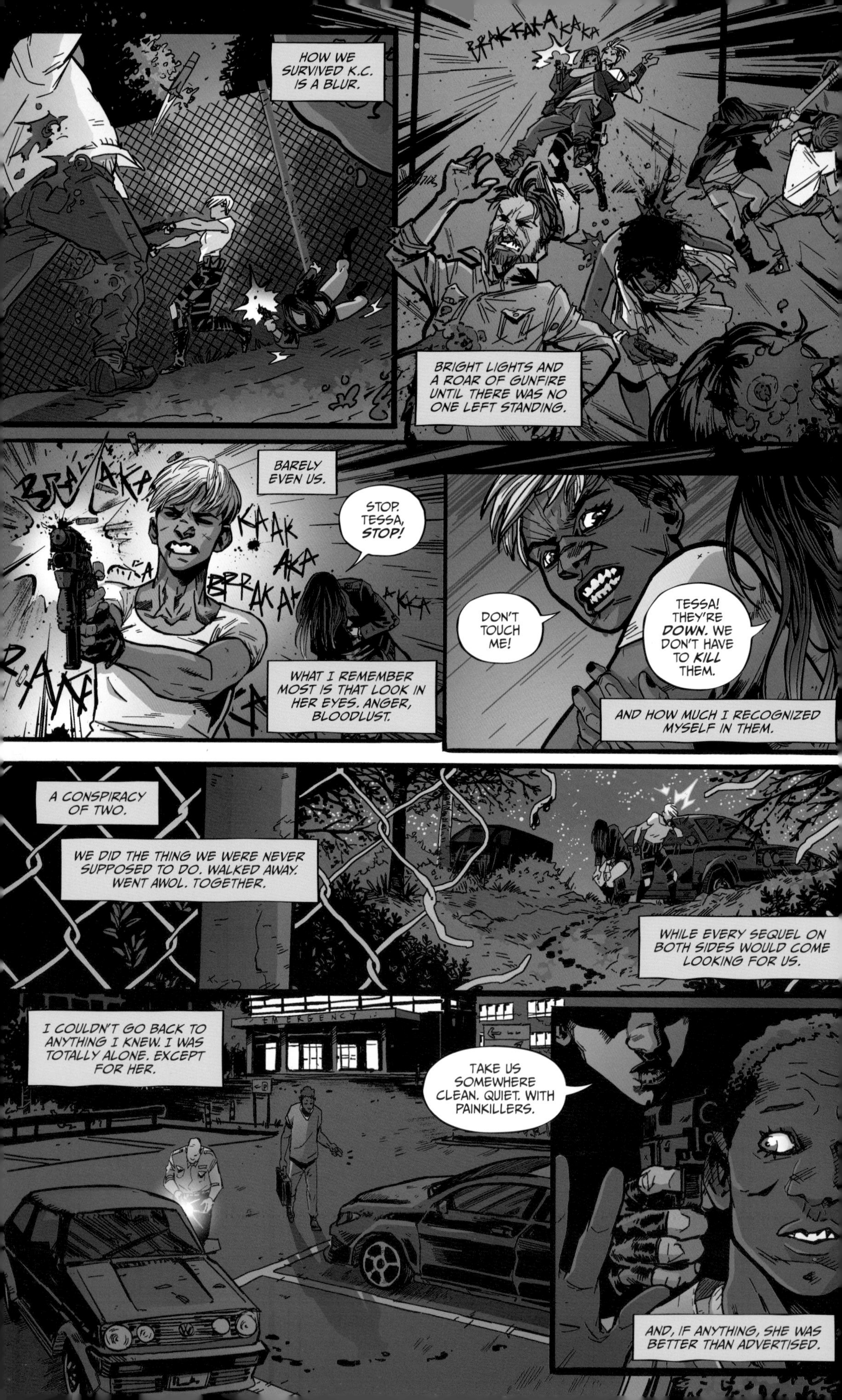
HOW WE SURVIVED K.C. IS A BLUR.
BRAKAKAKAKAKA
BRIGHT LIGHTS AND A ROAR OF GUNFIRE UNTIL THERE WAS NO ONE LEFT STANDING.
BARELY EVEN US.
STOP. TESSA, STOP!
WHAT I REMEMBER MOST IS THAT LOOK IN HER EYES. ANGER, BLOODLUST.
DON'T TOUCH ME!
TESSA! THEY'RE DOWN. WE DON'T HAVE TO KILL THEM.
AND HOW MUCH I RECOGNIZED MYSELF IN THEM.
A CONSPIRACY OF TWO.
WE DID THE THING WE WERE NEVER SUPPOSED TO DO. WALKED AWAY. WENT AWOL. TOGETHER.
WHILE EVERY SEQUEL ON BOTH SIDES WOULD COME LOOKING FOR US.
I COULDN'T GO BACK TO ANYTHING I KNEW. I WAS TOTALLY ALONE. EXCEPT FOR HER.
EMERGENCY
TAKE US SOMEWHERE CLEAN. QUIET. WITH PAINKILLERS.
AND, IF ANYTHING, SHE WAS BETTER THAN ADVERTISED.

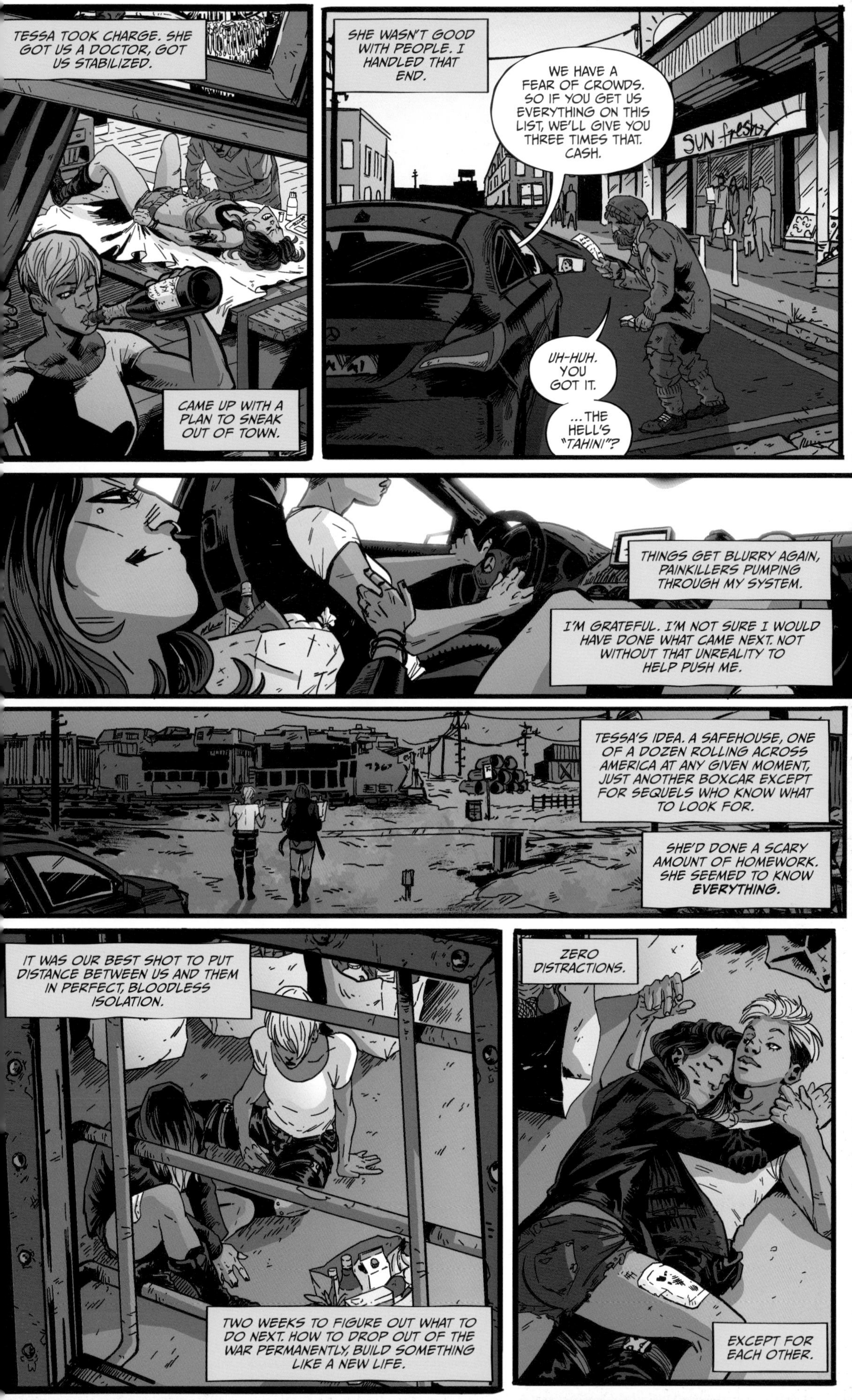

TESSA TOOK CHARGE. SHE GOT US A DOCTOR, GOT US STABILIZED.
CAME UP WITH A PLAN TO SNEAK OUT OF TOWN.
SHE WASN'T GOOD WITH PEOPLE. I HANDLED THAT END.
WE HAVE A FEAR OF CROWDS. SO IF YOU GET US EVERYTHING ON THIS LIST, WE'LL GIVE YOU THREE TIMES THAT. CASH.
SUN fresh
UH-HUH. YOU GOT IT.
...THE HELL'S "TAHINI"?
THINGS GET BLURRY AGAIN, PAINKILLERS PUMPING THROUGH MY SYSTEM.
I'M GRATEFUL. I'M NOT SURE I WOULD HAVE DONE WHAT CAME NEXT. NOT WITHOUT THAT UNREALITY TO HELP PUSH ME.
TESSA'S IDEA. A SAFEHOUSE, ONE OF A DOZEN ROLLING ACROSS AMERICA AT ANY GIVEN MOMENT, JUST ANOTHER BOXCAR EXCEPT FOR SEQUELS WHO KNOW WHAT TO LOOK FOR.
SHE'D DONE A SCARY AMOUNT OF HOMEWORK. SHE SEEMED TO KNOW **EVERYTHING.**
IT WAS OUR BEST SHOT TO PUT DISTANCE BETWEEN US AND THEM IN PERFECT, BLOODLESS ISOLATION.
TWO WEEKS TO FIGURE OUT WHAT TO DO NEXT. HOW TO DROP OUT OF THE WAR PERMANENTLY, BUILD SOMETHING LIKE A NEW LIFE.
ZERO DISTRACTIONS.
EXCEPT FOR EACH OTHER.

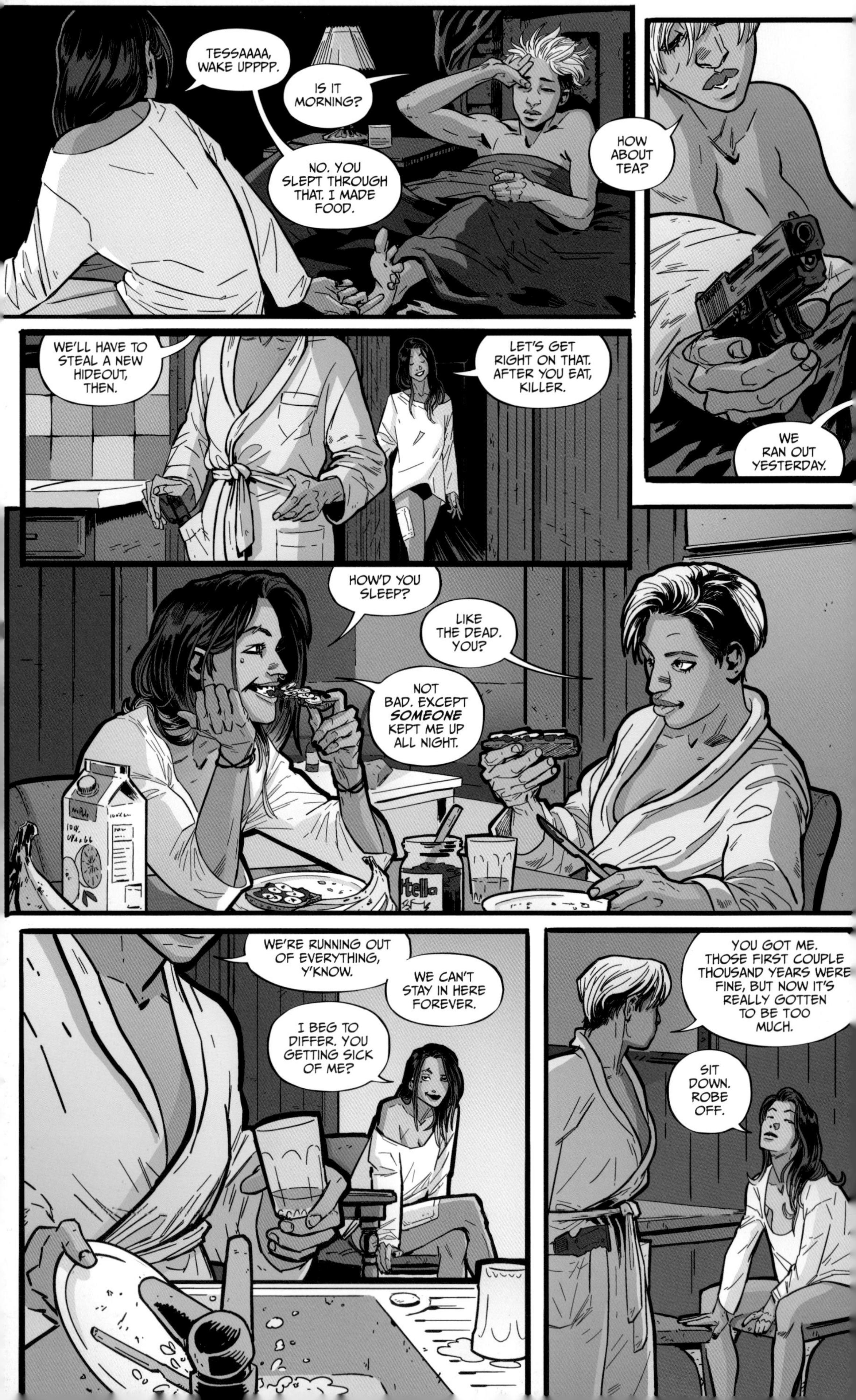
TESSAAAA, WAKE UPPPP.
IS IT MORNING?
NO. YOU SLEPT THROUGH THAT. I MADE FOOD.
HOW ABOUT TEA?
WE RAN OUT YESTERDAY.
WE'LL HAVE TO STEAL A NEW HIDEOUT, THEN.
LET'S GET RIGHT ON THAT. AFTER YOU EAT, KILLER.
HOW'D YOU SLEEP?
LIKE THE DEAD. YOU?
NOT BAD. EXCEPT SOMEONE KEPT ME UP ALL NIGHT.
WE'RE RUNNING OUT OF EVERYTHING, Y'KNOW.
WE CAN'T STAY IN HERE FOREVER.
I BEG TO DIFFER. YOU GETTING SICK OF ME?
YOU GOT ME. THOSE FIRST COUPLE THOUSAND YEARS WERE FINE, BUT NOW IT'S REALLY GOTTEN TO BE TOO MUCH.
SIT DOWN. ROBE OFF.

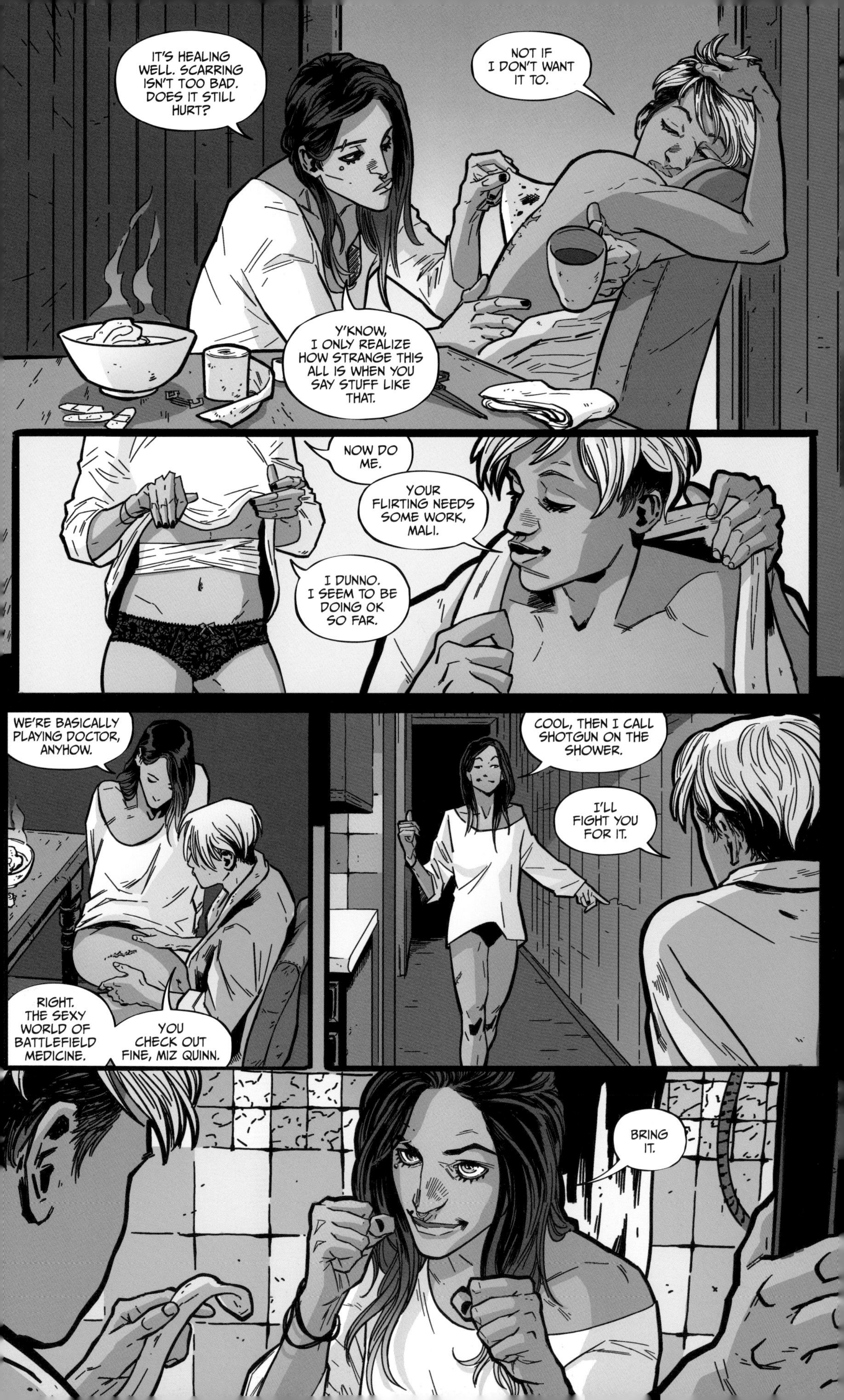
IT'S HEALING WELL. SCARRING ISN'T TOO BAD. DOES IT STILL HURT?
NOT IF I DON'T WANT IT TO.
Y'KNOW, I ONLY REALIZE HOW STRANGE THIS ALL IS WHEN YOU SAY STUFF LIKE THAT.
NOW DO ME.
YOUR FLIRTING NEEDS SOME WORK, MALI.
I DUNNO. I SEEM TO BE DOING OK SO FAR.
WE'RE BASICALLY PLAYING DOCTOR, ANYHOW.
RIGHT. THE SEXY WORLD OF BATTLEFIELD MEDICINE.
YOU CHECK OUT FINE, MIZ QUINN.
COOL, THEN I CALL SHOTGUN ON THE SHOWER.
I'LL FIGHT YOU FOR IT.
BRING IT.

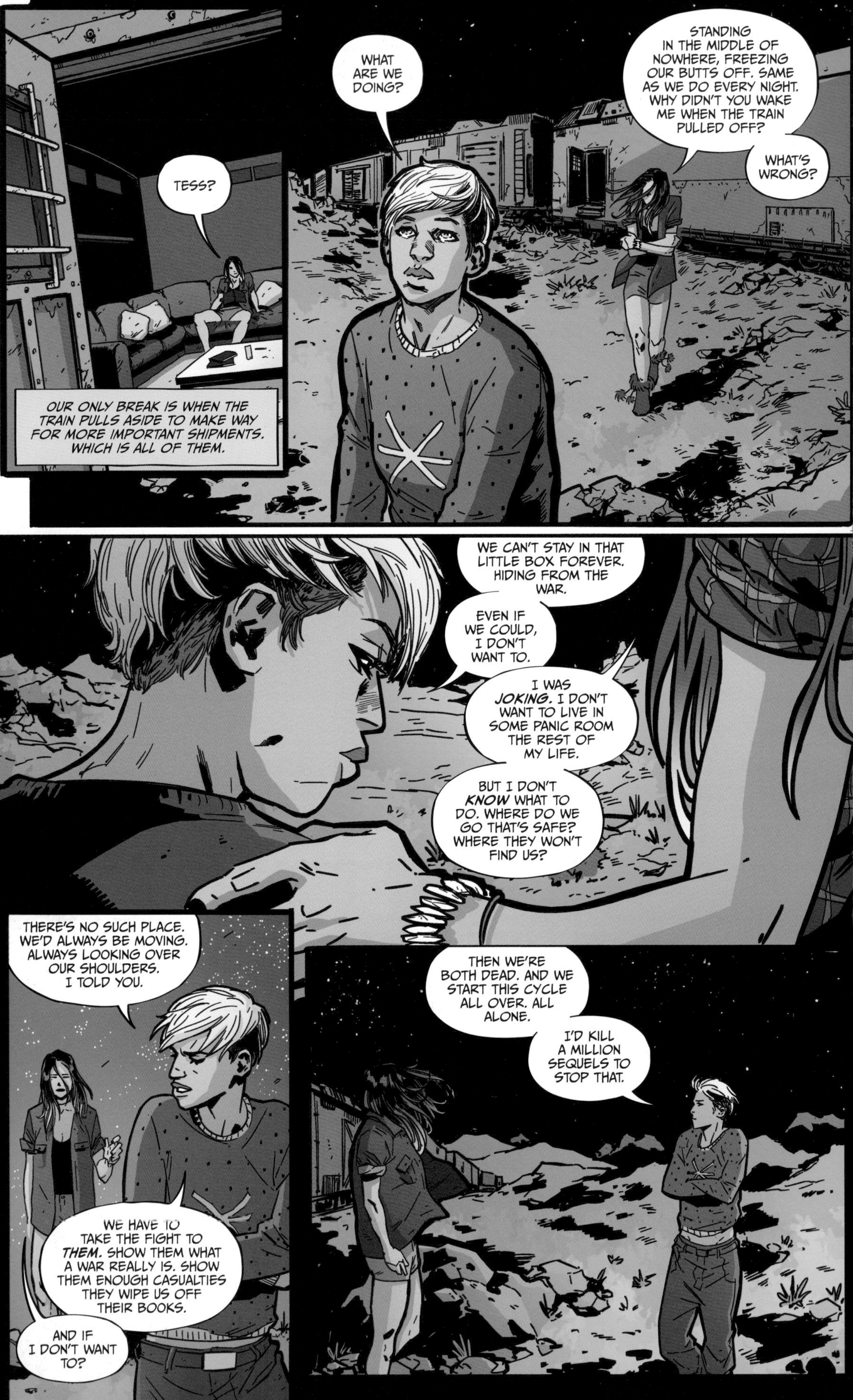
TESS?
OUR ONLY BREAK IS WHEN THE TRAIN PULLS ASIDE TO MAKE WAY FOR MORE IMPORTANT SHIPMENTS. WHICH IS ALL OF THEM.
WHAT ARE WE DOING?
STANDING IN THE MIDDLE OF NOWHERE, FREEZING OUR BUTTS OFF. SAME AS WE DO EVERY NIGHT. WHY DIDN'T YOU WAKE ME WHEN THE TRAIN PULLED OFF?
WHAT'S WRONG?
WE CAN'T STAY IN THAT LITTLE BOX FOREVER. HIDING FROM THE WAR.
EVEN IF WE COULD, I DON'T WANT TO.
I WAS JOKING. I DON'T WANT TO LIVE IN SOME PANIC ROOM THE REST OF MY LIFE.
BUT I DON'T KNOW WHAT TO DO. WHERE DO WE GO THAT'S SAFE? WHERE THEY WON'T FIND US?
THERE'S NO SUCH PLACE. WE'D ALWAYS BE MOVING. ALWAYS LOOKING OVER OUR SHOULDERS. I TOLD YOU.
WE HAVE TO TAKE THE FIGHT TO THEM. SHOW THEM WHAT A WAR REALLY IS. SHOW THEM ENOUGH CASUALTIES THEY WIPE US OFF THEIR BOOKS.
AND IF I DON'T WANT TO?
THEN WE'RE BOTH DEAD. AND WE START THIS CYCLE ALL OVER. ALL ALONE.
I'D KILL A MILLION SEQUELS TO STOP THAT.

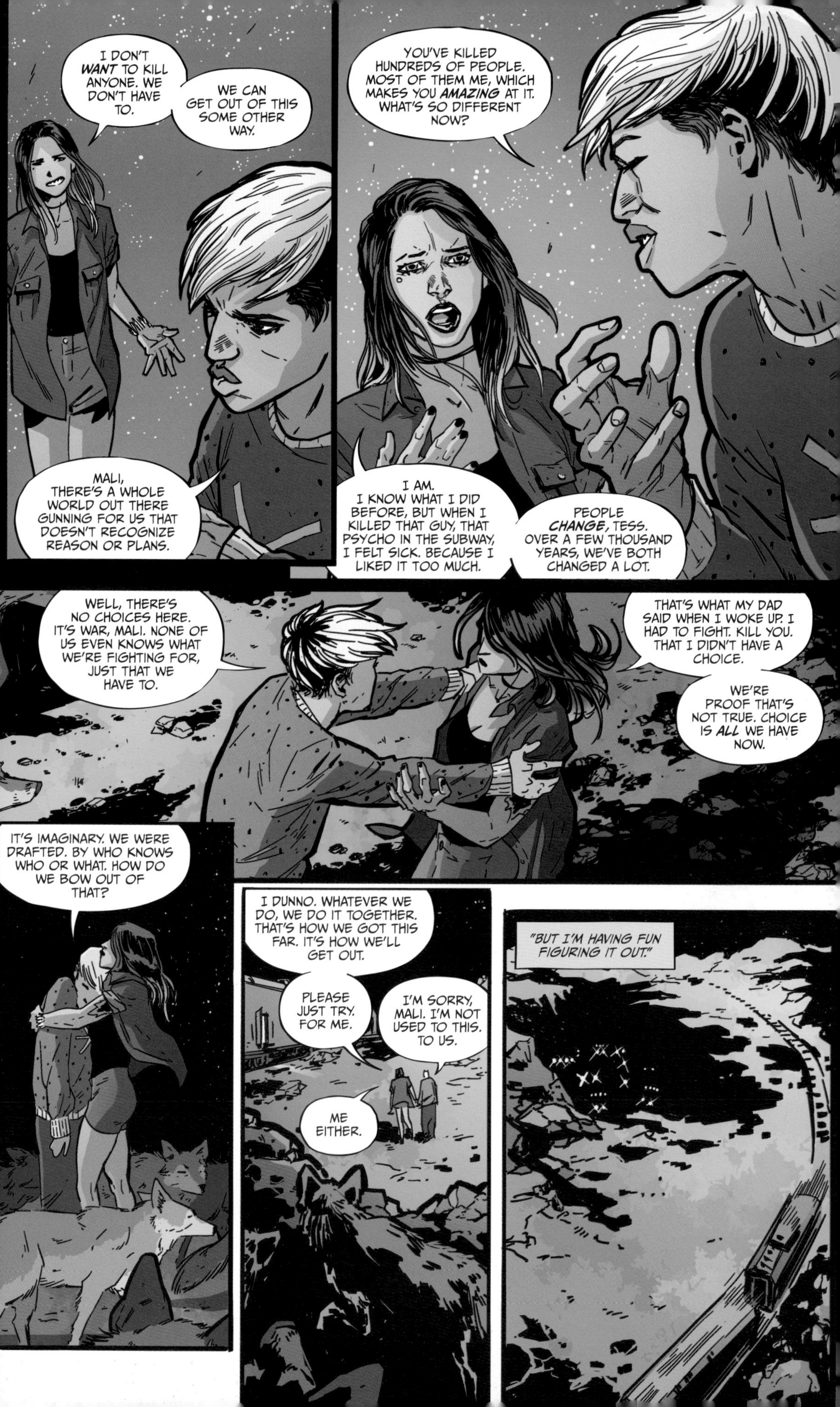

I DON'T *WANT* TO KILL ANYONE. WE DON'T HAVE TO.
WE CAN GET OUT OF THIS SOME OTHER WAY.
MALI, THERE'S A WHOLE WORLD OUT THERE GUNNING FOR US THAT DOESN'T RECOGNIZE REASON OR PLANS.
YOU'VE KILLED HUNDREDS OF PEOPLE. MOST OF THEM ME, WHICH MAKES YOU *AMAZING* AT IT. WHAT'S SO DIFFERENT NOW?
I AM. I KNOW WHAT I DID BEFORE, BUT WHEN I KILLED THAT GUY, THAT PSYCHO IN THE SUBWAY, I FELT SICK. BECAUSE I LIKED IT TOO MUCH.
PEOPLE *CHANGE,* TESS. OVER A FEW THOUSAND YEARS, WE'VE BOTH CHANGED A LOT.
WELL, THERE'S NO CHOICES HERE. IT'S WAR, MALI. NONE OF US EVEN KNOWS WHAT WE'RE FIGHTING FOR, JUST THAT WE HAVE TO.
THAT'S WHAT MY DAD SAID WHEN I WOKE UP. I HAD TO FIGHT. KILL YOU. THAT I DIDN'T HAVE A CHOICE.
WE'RE PROOF THAT'S NOT TRUE. CHOICE IS *ALL* WE HAVE NOW.
IT'S IMAGINARY. WE WERE DRAFTED. BY WHO KNOWS WHO OR WHAT. HOW DO WE BOW OUT OF THAT?
I DUNNO. WHATEVER WE DO, WE DO IT TOGETHER. THAT'S HOW WE GOT THIS FAR. IT'S HOW WE'LL GET OUT.
PLEASE JUST TRY. FOR ME.
I'M SORRY, MALI. I'M NOT USED TO THIS. TO US.
ME EITHER.
"BUT I'M HAVING FUN FIGURING IT OUT."

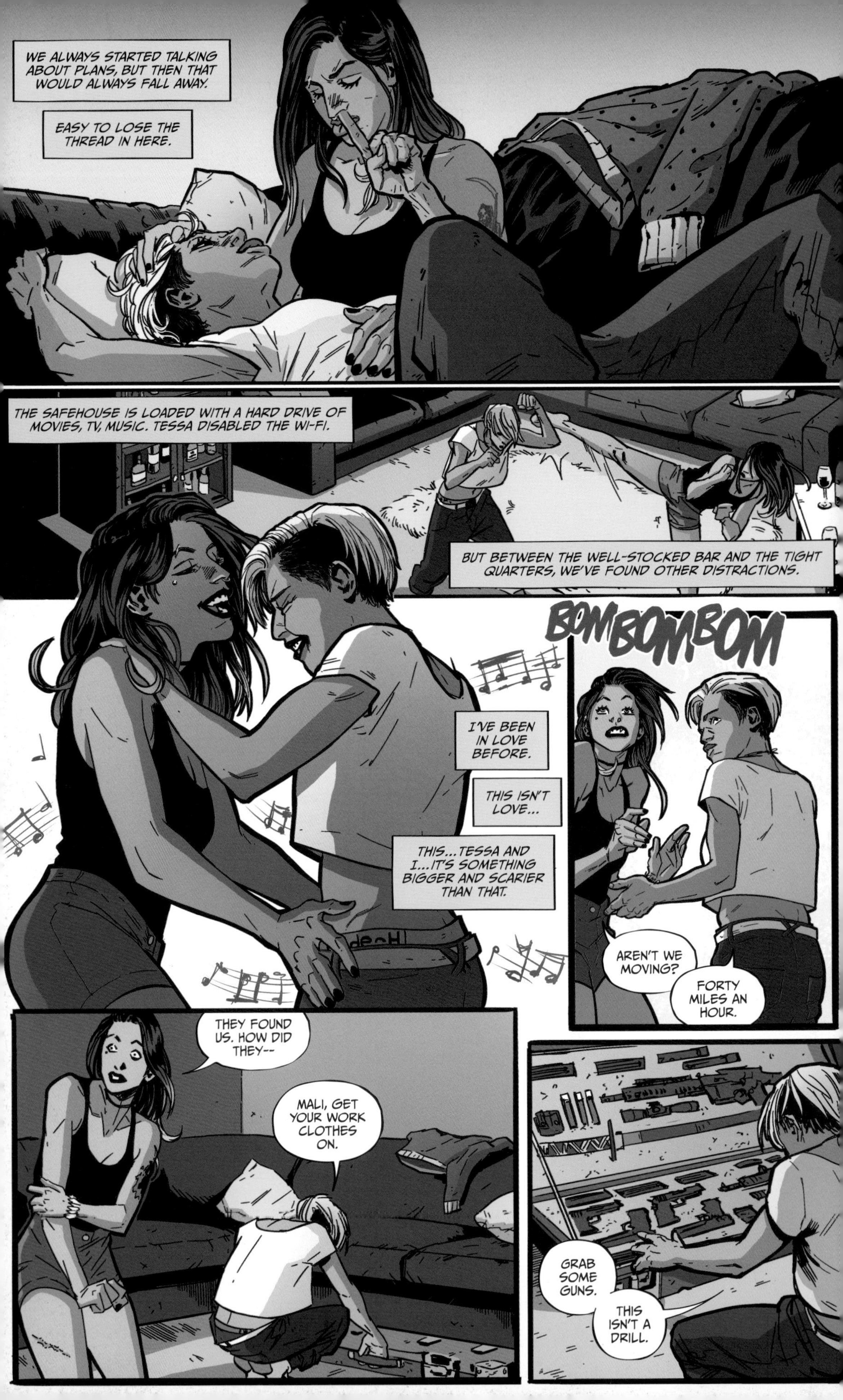
WE ALWAYS STARTED TALKING ABOUT PLANS, BUT THEN THAT WOULD ALWAYS FALL AWAY.
EASY TO LOSE THE THREAD IN HERE.
THE SAFEHOUSE IS LOADED WITH A HARD DRIVE OF MOVIES, TV, MUSIC. TESSA DISABLED THE WI-FI.
BUT BETWEEN THE WELL-STOCKED BAR AND THE TIGHT QUARTERS, WE'VE FOUND OTHER DISTRACTIONS.
I'VE BEEN IN LOVE BEFORE.
THIS ISN'T LOVE...
THIS...TESSA AND I...IT'S SOMETHING BIGGER AND SCARIER THAN THAT.
BOM BOM BOM
AREN'T WE MOVING?
FORTY MILES AN HOUR.
THEY FOUND US. HOW DID THEY--
MALI, GET YOUR WORK CLOTHES ON.
GRAB SOME GUNS.
THIS ISN'T A DRILL.

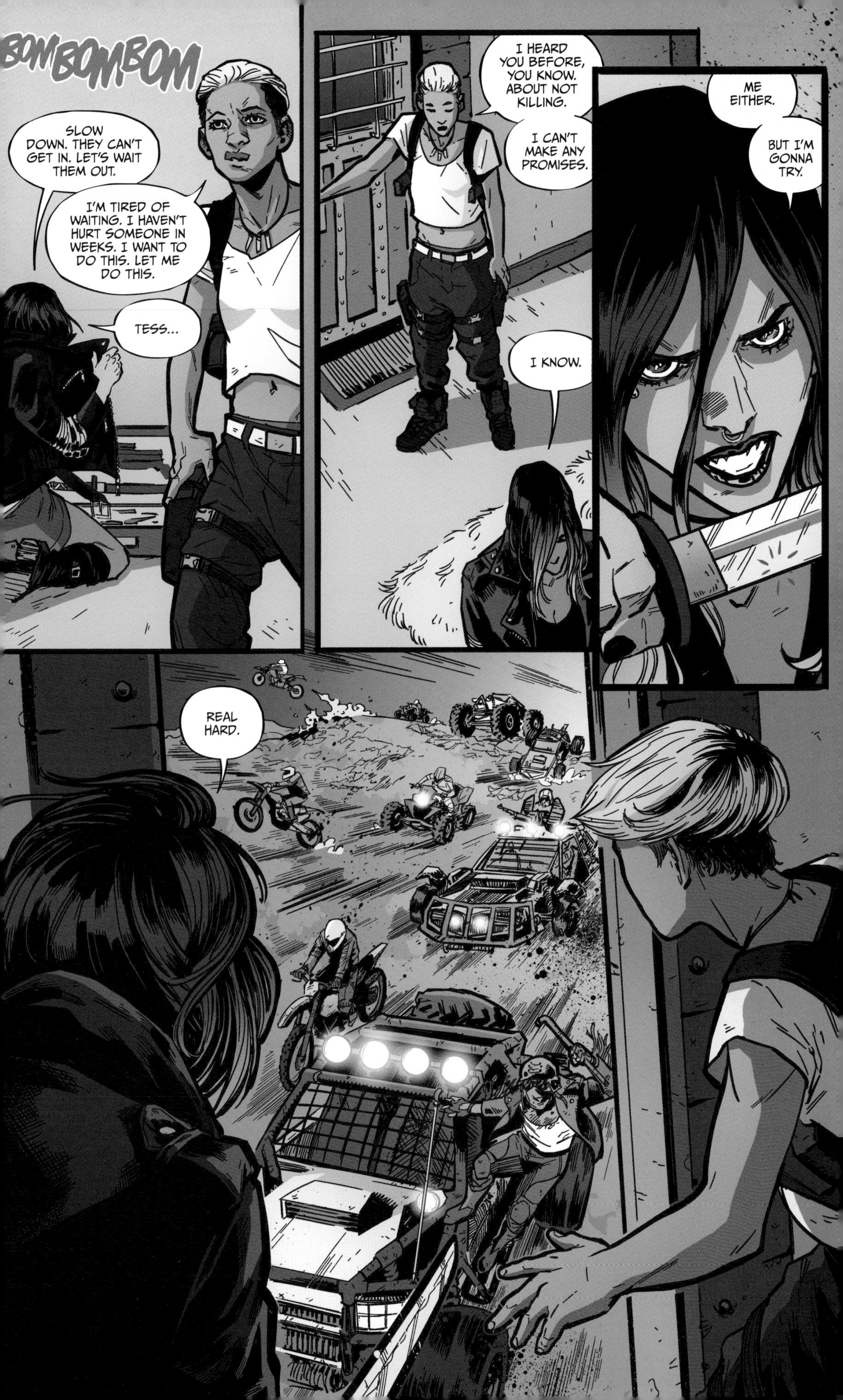
BOMBOMBOM
SLOW DOWN. THEY CAN'T GET IN. LET'S WAIT THEM OUT.
I'M TIRED OF WAITING. I HAVEN'T HURT SOMEONE IN WEEKS. I WANT TO DO THIS. LET ME DO THIS.
TESS...
I HEARD YOU BEFORE, YOU KNOW. ABOUT NOT KILLING.
I CAN'T MAKE ANY PROMISES.
I KNOW.
ME EITHER.
BUT I'M GONNA TRY.
REAL HARD.

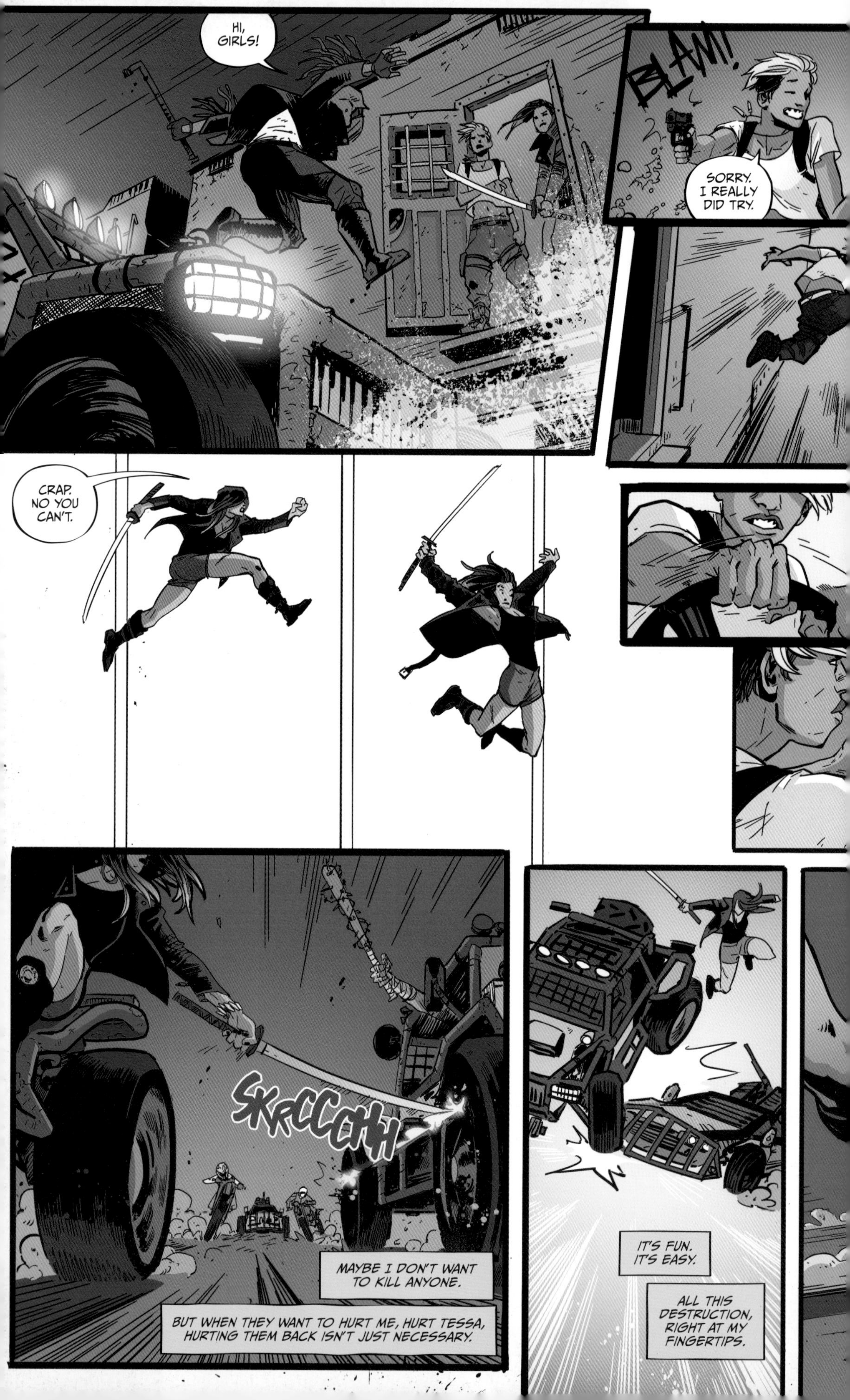
HI, GIRLS!
BLAM!
SORRY. I REALLY DID TRY.
CRAP. NO YOU CAN'T.
SKRCCCHH
MAYBE I DON'T WANT TO KILL ANYONE.
BUT WHEN THEY WANT TO HURT ME, HURT TESSA, HURTING THEM BACK ISN'T JUST NECESSARY.
IT'S FUN. IT'S EASY.
ALL THIS DESTRUCTION, RIGHT AT MY FINGERTIPS.

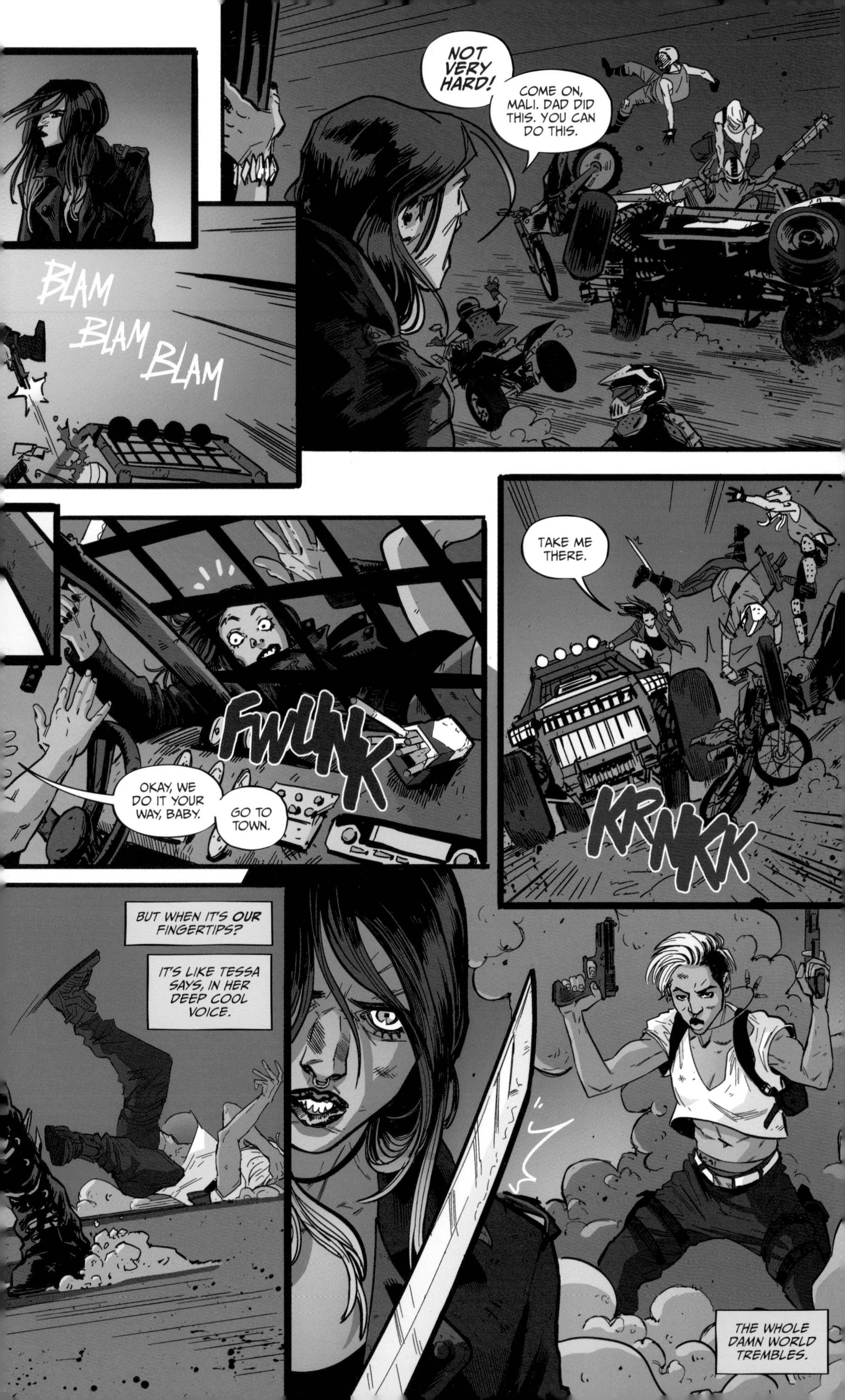
BLAM
BLAM
BLAM
NOT VERY HARD!
COME ON, MALI. DAD DID THIS. YOU CAN DO THIS.
FWUNK
OKAY, WE DO IT YOUR WAY, BABY.
GO TO TOWN.
TAKE ME THERE.
KRNKK
BUT WHEN IT'S OUR FINGERTIPS?
IT'S LIKE TESSA SAYS, IN HER DEEP COOL VOICE.
THE WHOLE DAMN WORLD TREMBLES.

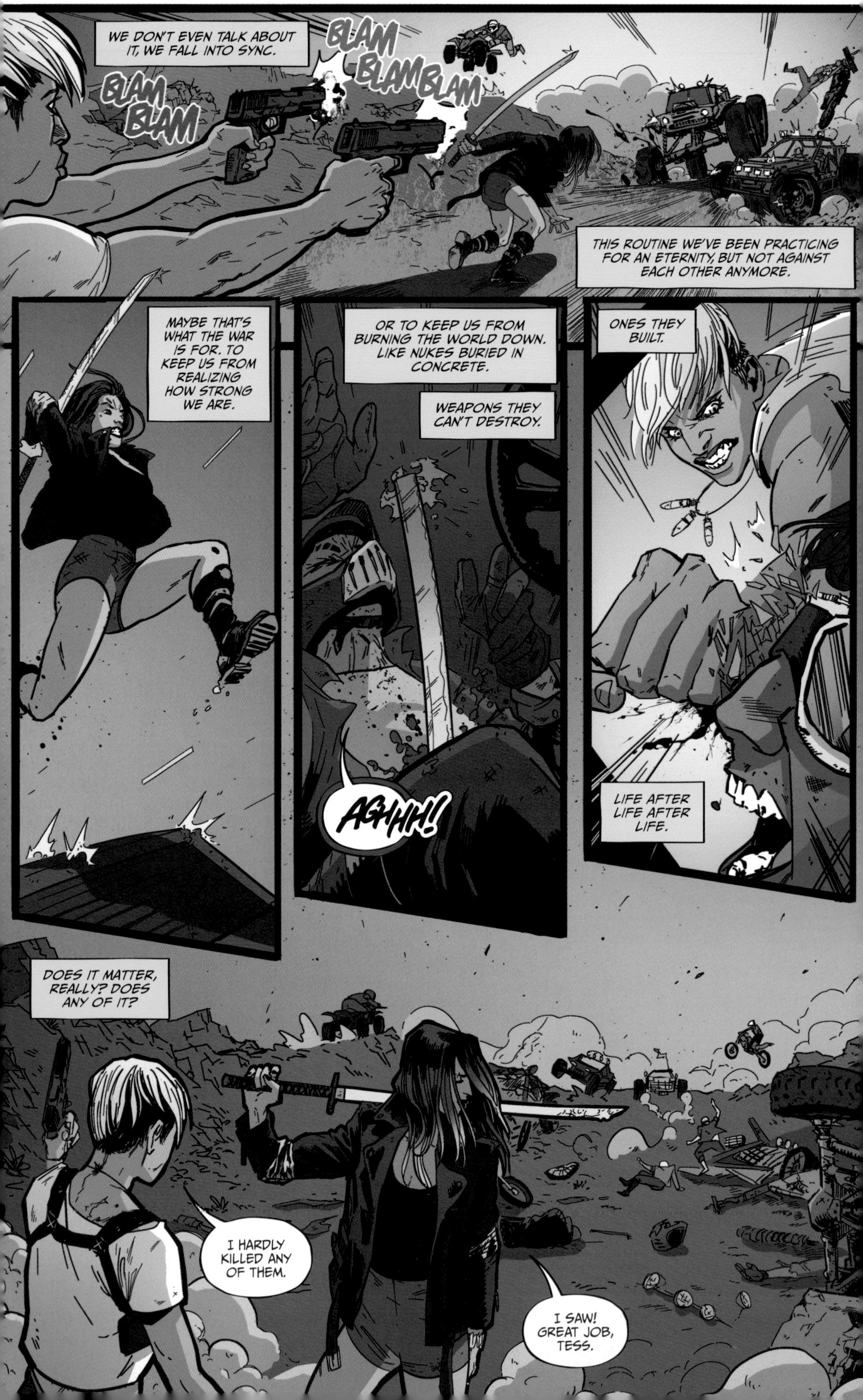
WE DON'T EVEN TALK ABOUT IT, WE FALL INTO SYNC.
BLAM BLAM
BLAM BLAM BLAM
THIS ROUTINE WE'VE BEEN PRACTICING FOR AN ETERNITY, BUT NOT AGAINST EACH OTHER ANYMORE.
MAYBE THAT'S WHAT THE WAR IS FOR. TO KEEP US FROM REALIZING HOW STRONG WE ARE.
OR TO KEEP US FROM BURNING THE WORLD DOWN. LIKE NUKES BURIED IN CONCRETE.
WEAPONS THEY CAN'T DESTROY.
AGHHH!
ONES THEY BUILT.
LIFE AFTER LIFE AFTER LIFE.
DOES IT MATTER, REALLY? DOES ANY OF IT?
I HARDLY KILLED ANY OF THEM.
I SAW! GREAT JOB, TESS.

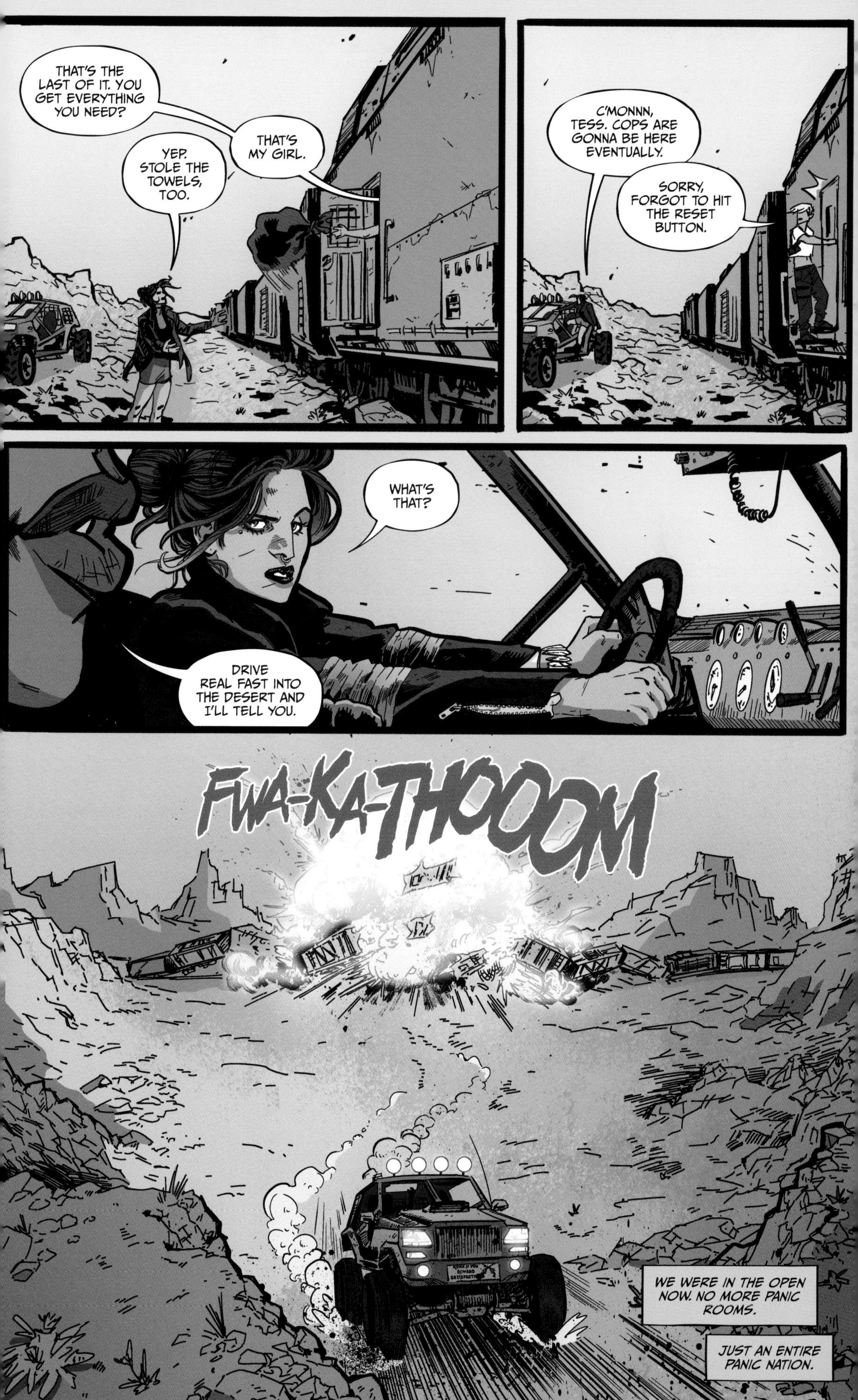
THAT'S THE LAST OF IT. YOU GET EVERYTHING YOU NEED?
YEP. STOLE THE TOWELS, TOO.
THAT'S MY GIRL.
C'MONNN, TESS. COPS ARE GONNA BE HERE EVENTUALLY.
SORRY, FORGOT TO HIT THE RESET BUTTON.
WHAT'S THAT?
DRIVE REAL FAST INTO THE DESERT AND I'LL TELL YOU.
FWA-KA-THOOOM
WE WERE IN THE OPEN NOW. NO MORE PANIC ROOMS.
JUST AN ENTIRE PANIC NATION.

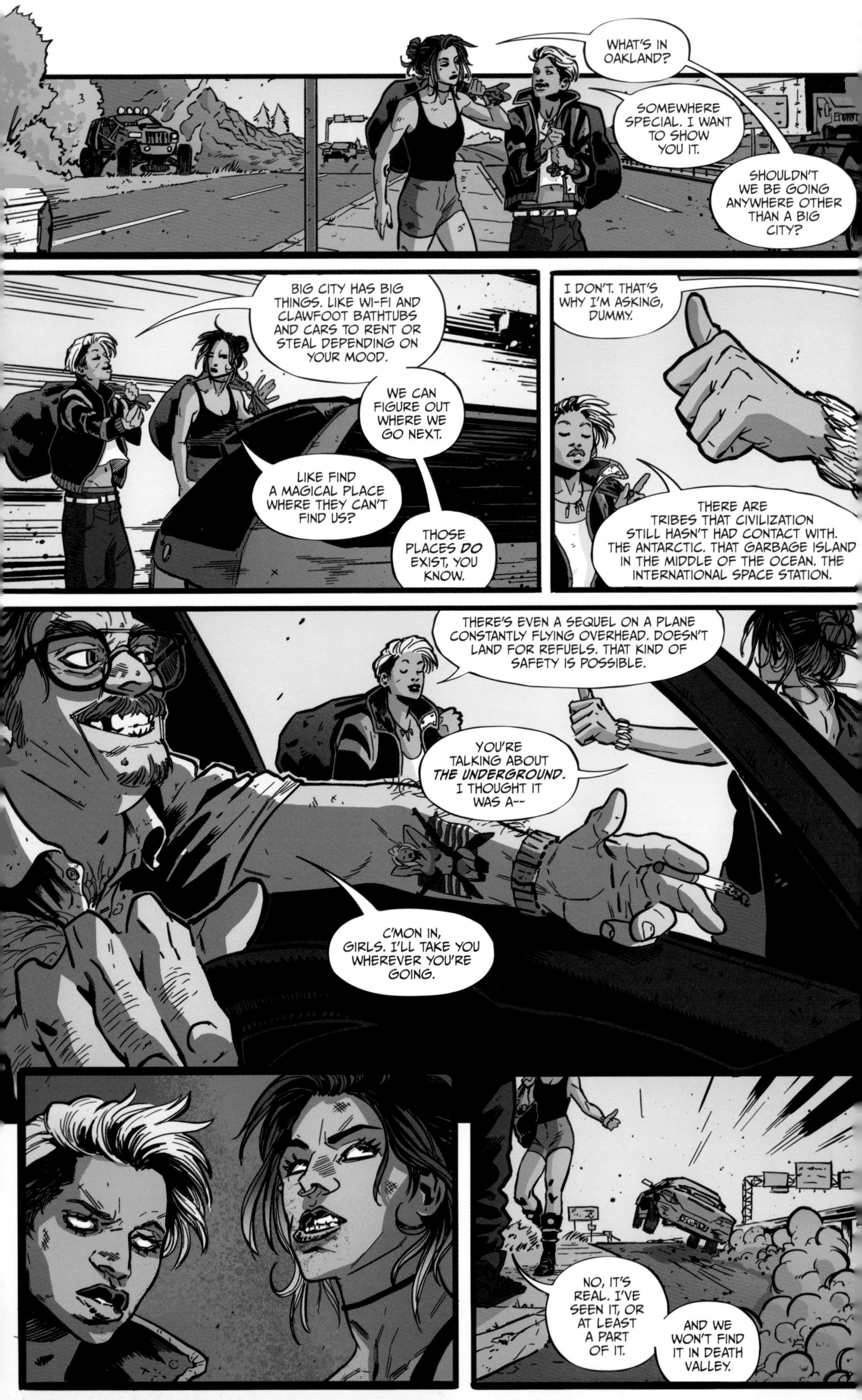
WHAT'S IN OAKLAND?
SOMEWHERE SPECIAL. I WANT TO SHOW YOU IT.
SHOULDN'T WE BE GOING ANYWHERE OTHER THAN A BIG CITY?
BIG CITY HAS BIG THINGS. LIKE WI-FI AND CLAWFOOT BATHTUBS AND CARS TO RENT OR STEAL DEPENDING ON YOUR MOOD.
WE CAN FIGURE OUT WHERE WE GO NEXT.
LIKE FIND A MAGICAL PLACE WHERE THEY CAN'T FIND US?
THOSE PLACES DO EXIST, YOU KNOW.
I DON'T. THAT'S WHY I'M ASKING, DUMMY.
THERE ARE TRIBES THAT CIVILIZATION STILL HASN'T HAD CONTACT WITH. THE ANTARCTIC. THAT GARBAGE ISLAND IN THE MIDDLE OF THE OCEAN. THE INTERNATIONAL SPACE STATION.
THERE'S EVEN A SEQUEL ON A PLANE CONSTANTLY FLYING OVERHEAD. DOESN'T LAND FOR REFUELS. THAT KIND OF SAFETY IS POSSIBLE.
YOU'RE TALKING ABOUT THE UNDERGROUND. I THOUGHT IT WAS A--
C'MON IN, GIRLS. I'LL TAKE YOU WHEREVER YOU'RE GOING.
NO, IT'S REAL. I'VE SEEN IT, OR AT LEAST A PART OF IT.
AND WE WON'T FIND IT IN DEATH VALLEY.

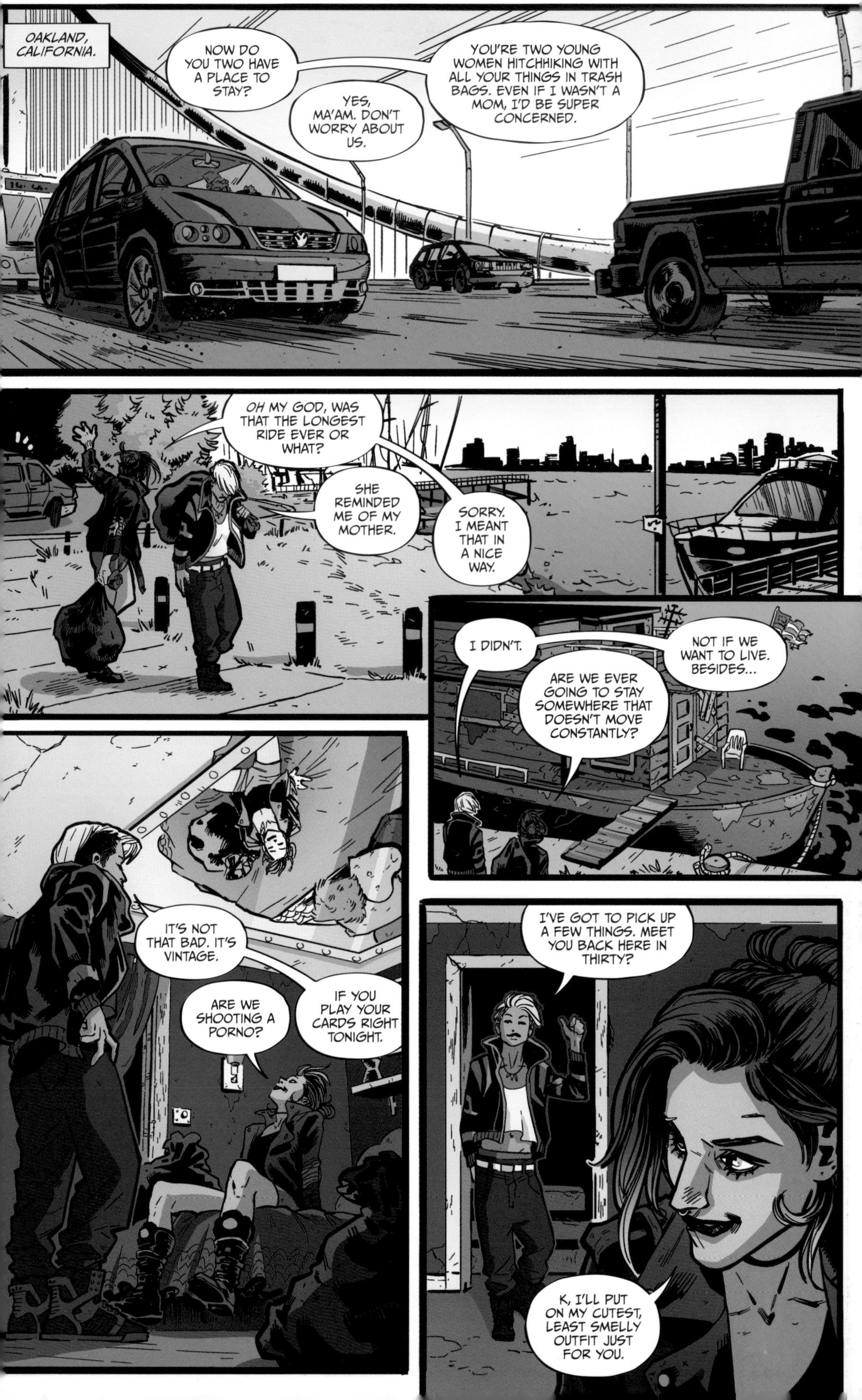

OAKLAND, CALIFORNIA.
NOW DO YOU TWO HAVE A PLACE TO STAY?
YES, MA'AM. DON'T WORRY ABOUT US.
YOU'RE TWO YOUNG WOMEN HITCHHIKING WITH ALL YOUR THINGS IN TRASH BAGS. EVEN IF I WASN'T A MOM, I'D BE SUPER CONCERNED.
OH MY GOD, WAS THAT THE LONGEST RIDE EVER OR WHAT?
SHE REMINDED ME OF MY MOTHER.
SORRY. I MEANT THAT IN A NICE WAY.
I DIDN'T.
ARE WE EVER GOING TO STAY SOMEWHERE THAT DOESN'T MOVE CONSTANTLY?
NOT IF WE WANT TO LIVE. BESIDES...
IT'S NOT THAT BAD. IT'S VINTAGE.
ARE WE SHOOTING A PORNO?
IF YOU PLAY YOUR CARDS RIGHT TONIGHT.
I'VE GOT TO PICK UP A FEW THINGS. MEET YOU BACK HERE IN THIRTY?
K, I'LL PUT ON MY CUTEST, LEAST SMELLY OUTFIT JUST FOR YOU.

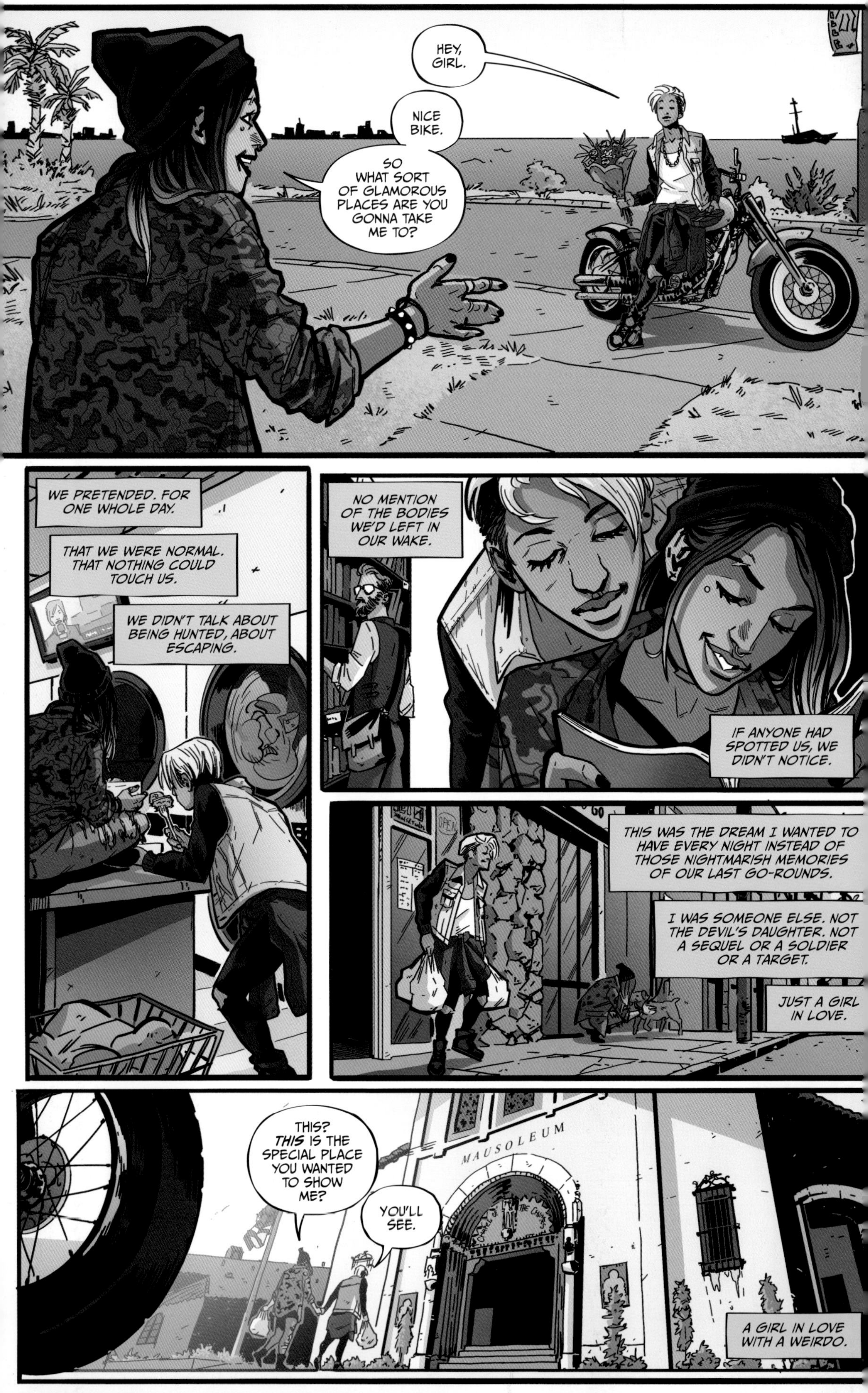
HEY, GIRL.
NICE BIKE.
SO WHAT SORT OF GLAMOROUS PLACES ARE YOU GONNA TAKE ME TO?
WE PRETENDED. FOR ONE WHOLE DAY.
THAT WE WERE NORMAL. THAT NOTHING COULD TOUCH US.
WE DIDN'T TALK ABOUT BEING HUNTED, ABOUT ESCAPING.
NO MENTION OF THE BODIES WE'D LEFT IN OUR WAKE.
IF ANYONE HAD SPOTTED US, WE DIDN'T NOTICE.
THIS WAS THE DREAM I WANTED TO HAVE EVERY NIGHT INSTEAD OF THOSE NIGHTMARISH MEMORIES OF OUR LAST GO-ROUNDS.
I WAS SOMEONE ELSE. NOT THE DEVIL'S DAUGHTER. NOT A SEQUEL OR A SOLDIER OR A TARGET.
JUST A GIRL IN LOVE.
MAUSOLEUM
THIS? *THIS* IS THE SPECIAL PLACE YOU WANTED TO SHOW ME?
YOU'LL SEE.
A GIRL IN LOVE WITH A WEIRDO.

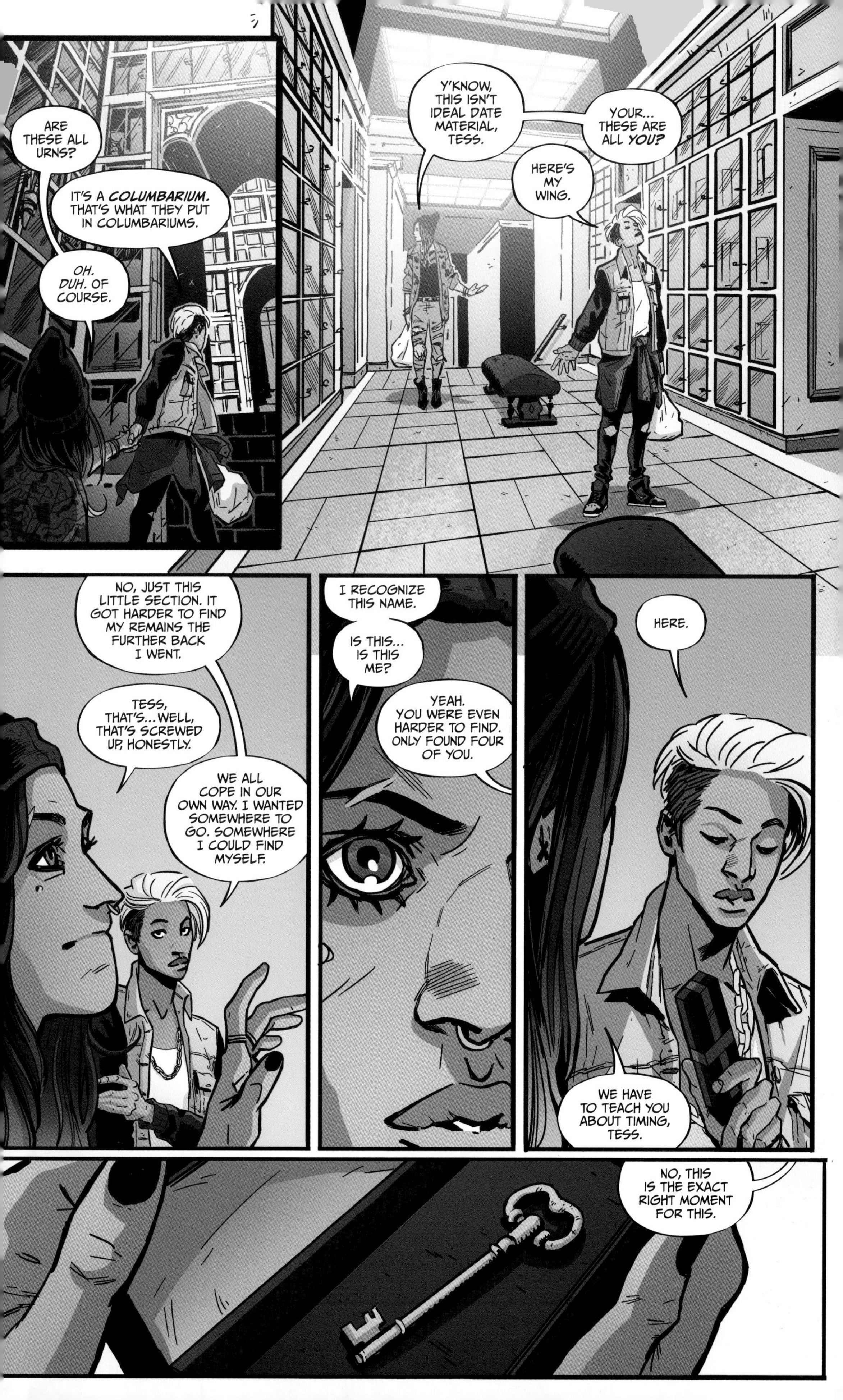
ARE THESE ALL URNS?
IT'S A COLUMBARIUM. THAT'S WHAT THEY PUT IN COLUMBARIUMS.
OH. DUH. OF COURSE.
Y'KNOW, THIS ISN'T IDEAL DATE MATERIAL, TESS.
YOUR... THESE ARE ALL YOU?
HERE'S MY WING.
NO, JUST THIS LITTLE SECTION. IT GOT HARDER TO FIND MY REMAINS THE FURTHER BACK I WENT.
TESS, THAT'S...WELL, THAT'S SCREWED UP, HONESTLY.
WE ALL COPE IN OUR OWN WAY. I WANTED SOMEWHERE TO GO. SOMEWHERE I COULD FIND MYSELF.
I RECOGNIZE THIS NAME.
IS THIS... IS THIS ME?
YEAH. YOU WERE EVEN HARDER TO FIND. ONLY FOUND FOUR OF YOU.
HERE.
WE HAVE TO TEACH YOU ABOUT TIMING, TESS.
NO, THIS IS THE EXACT RIGHT MOMENT FOR THIS.

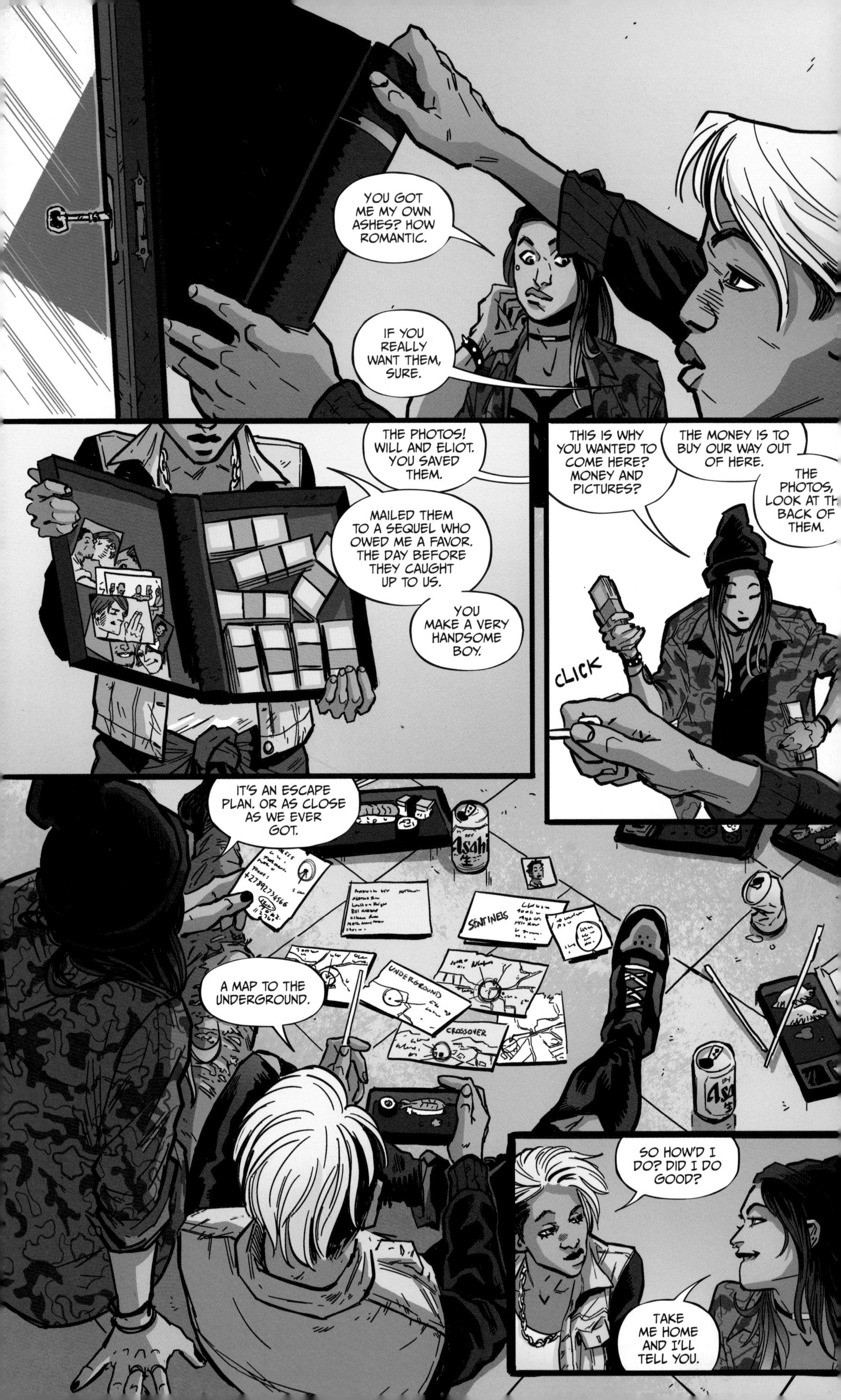
YOU GOT ME MY OWN ASHES? HOW ROMANTIC.
IF YOU REALLY WANT THEM, SURE.
THE PHOTOS! WILL AND ELIOT. YOU SAVED THEM.
MAILED THEM TO A SEQUEL WHO OWED ME A FAVOR. THE DAY BEFORE THEY CAUGHT UP TO US.
YOU MAKE A VERY HANDSOME BOY.
THIS IS WHY YOU WANTED TO COME HERE? MONEY AND PICTURES?
THE MONEY IS TO BUY OUR WAY OUT OF HERE.
THE PHOTOS, LOOK AT TH BACK OF THEM.
CLICK
IT'S AN ESCAPE PLAN. OR AS CLOSE AS WE EVER GOT.
A MAP TO THE UNDERGROUND.
SENTINELS
UNDERGROUND
CROSSOVER
SO HOW'D I DO? DID I DO GOOD?
TAKE ME HOME AND I'LL TELL YOU.

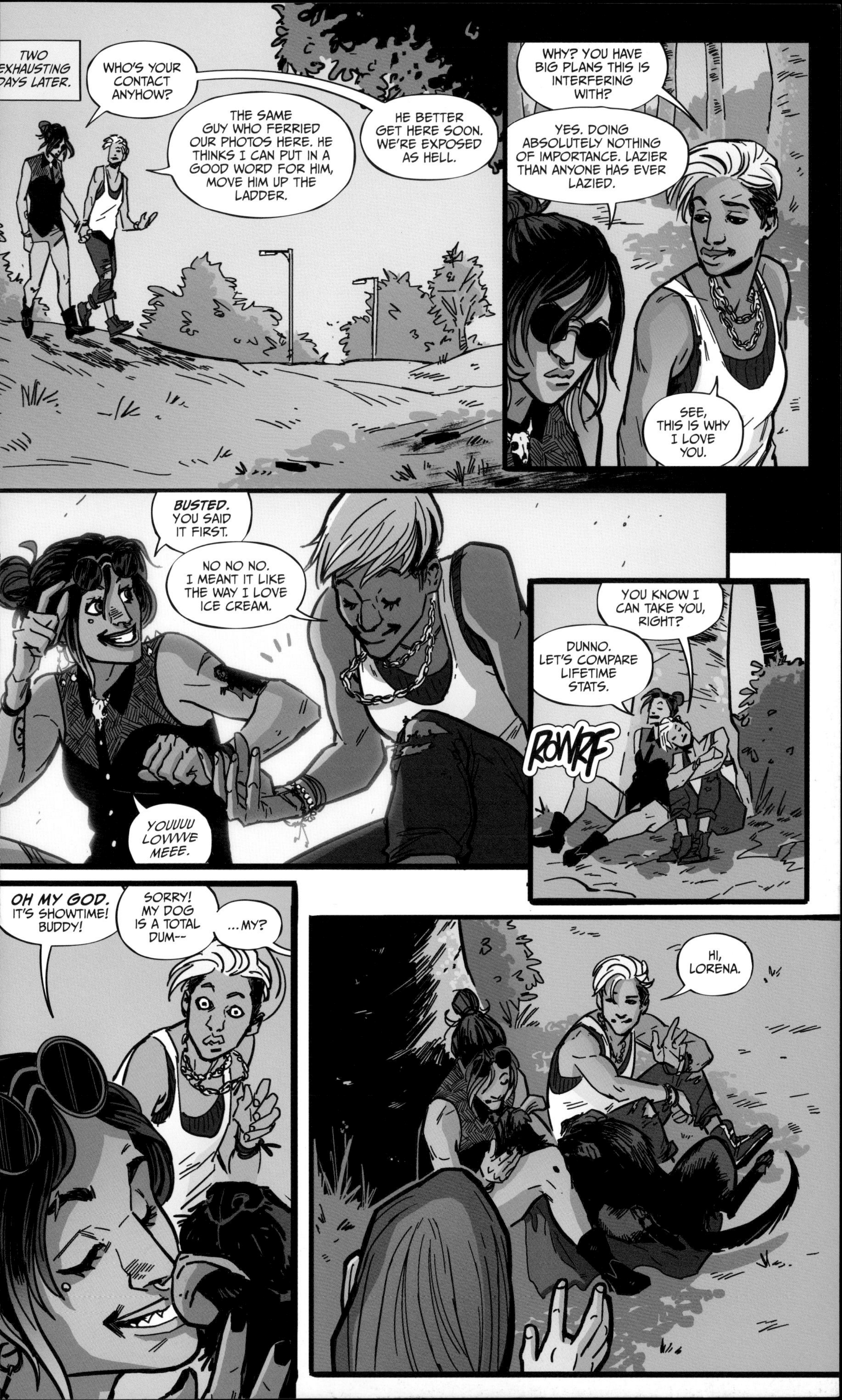

TWO EXHAUSTING DAYS LATER.
WHO'S YOUR CONTACT ANYHOW?
THE SAME GUY WHO FERRIED OUR PHOTOS HERE. HE THINKS I CAN PUT IN A GOOD WORD FOR HIM, MOVE HIM UP THE LADDER.
HE BETTER GET HERE SOON. WE'RE EXPOSED AS HELL.
WHY? YOU HAVE BIG PLANS THIS IS INTERFERING WITH?
YES. DOING ABSOLUTELY NOTHING OF IMPORTANCE. LAZIER THAN ANYONE HAS EVER LAZIED.
SEE, THIS IS WHY I LOVE YOU.
BUSTED. YOU SAID IT FIRST.
NO NO NO. I MEANT IT LIKE THE WAY I LOVE ICE CREAM.
YOUUUU LOVVVVE MEEE.
YOU KNOW I CAN TAKE YOU, RIGHT?
DUNNO. LET'S COMPARE LIFETIME STATS.
ROWRF
OH MY GOD. IT'S SHOWTIME! BUDDY!
SORRY! MY DOG IS A TOTAL DUM--
...MY?
HI, LORENA.

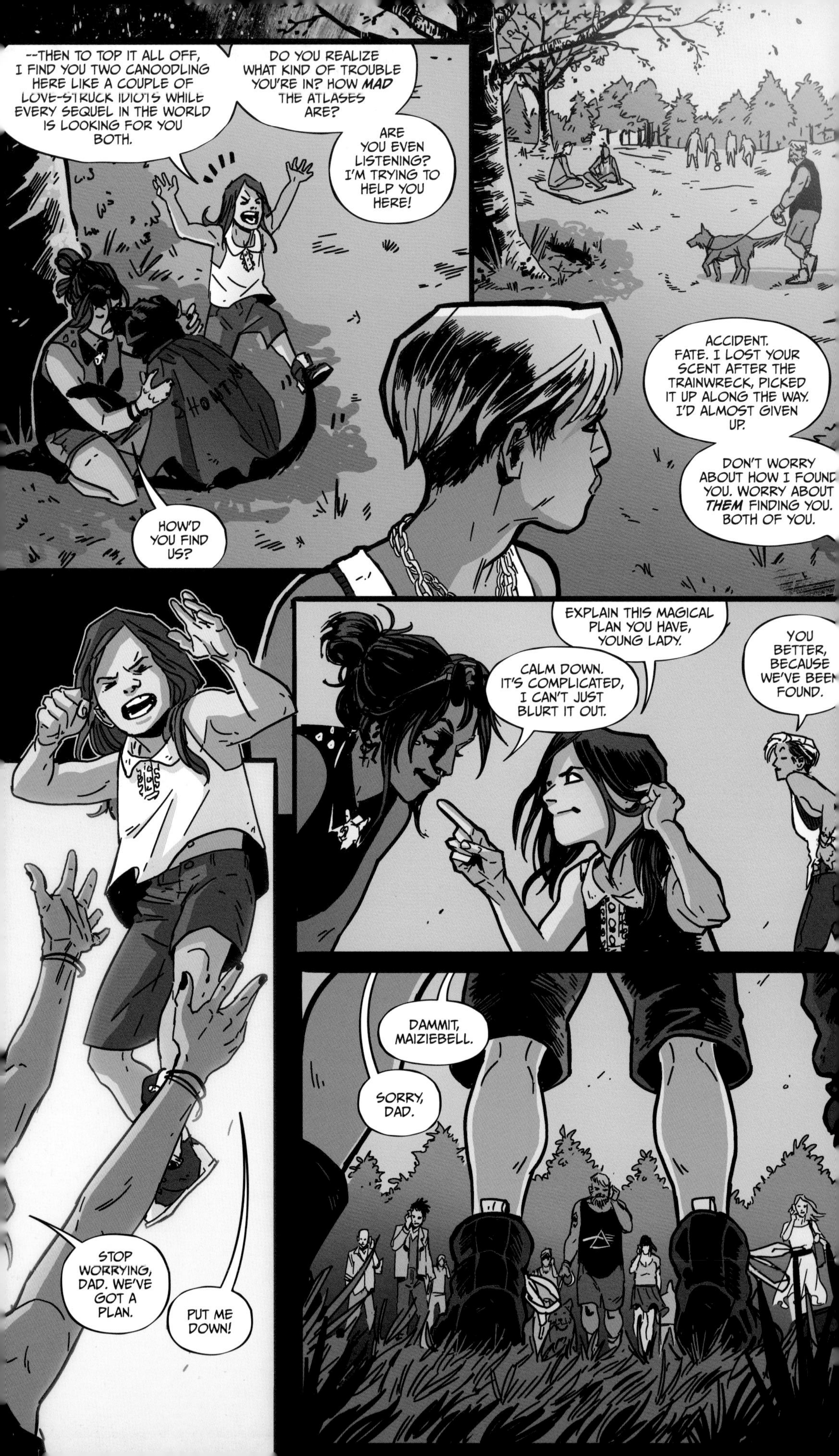
--THEN TO TOP IT ALL OFF, I FIND YOU TWO CANOODLING HERE LIKE A COUPLE OF LOVE-STRUCK IDIOTS WHILE EVERY SEQUEL IN THE WORLD IS LOOKING FOR YOU BOTH.
DO YOU REALIZE WHAT KIND OF TROUBLE YOU'RE IN? HOW MAD THE ATLASES ARE?
ARE YOU EVEN LISTENING? I'M TRYING TO HELP YOU HERE!
HOW'D YOU FIND US?
ACCIDENT. FATE. I LOST YOUR SCENT AFTER THE TRAINWRECK, PICKED IT UP ALONG THE WAY. I'D ALMOST GIVEN UP.
DON'T WORRY ABOUT HOW I FOUND YOU. WORRY ABOUT THEM FINDING YOU. BOTH OF YOU.
STOP WORRYING, DAD. WE'VE GOT A PLAN.
PUT ME DOWN!
EXPLAIN THIS MAGICAL PLAN YOU HAVE, YOUNG LADY.
CALM DOWN. IT'S COMPLICATED, I CAN'T JUST BLURT IT OUT.
YOU BETTER, BECAUSE WE'VE BEEN FOUND.
DAMMIT, MAIZIEBELL.
SORRY, DAD.

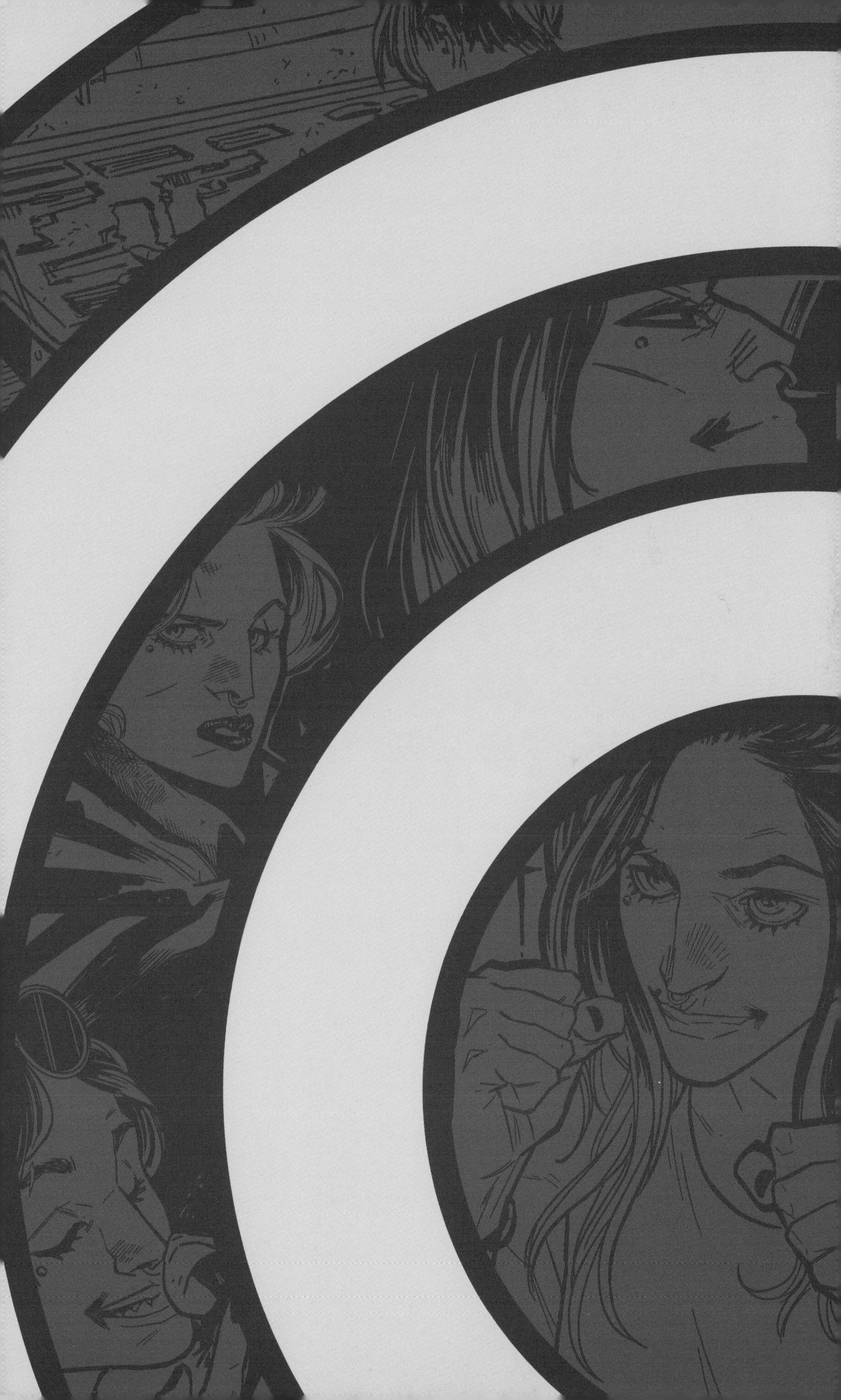

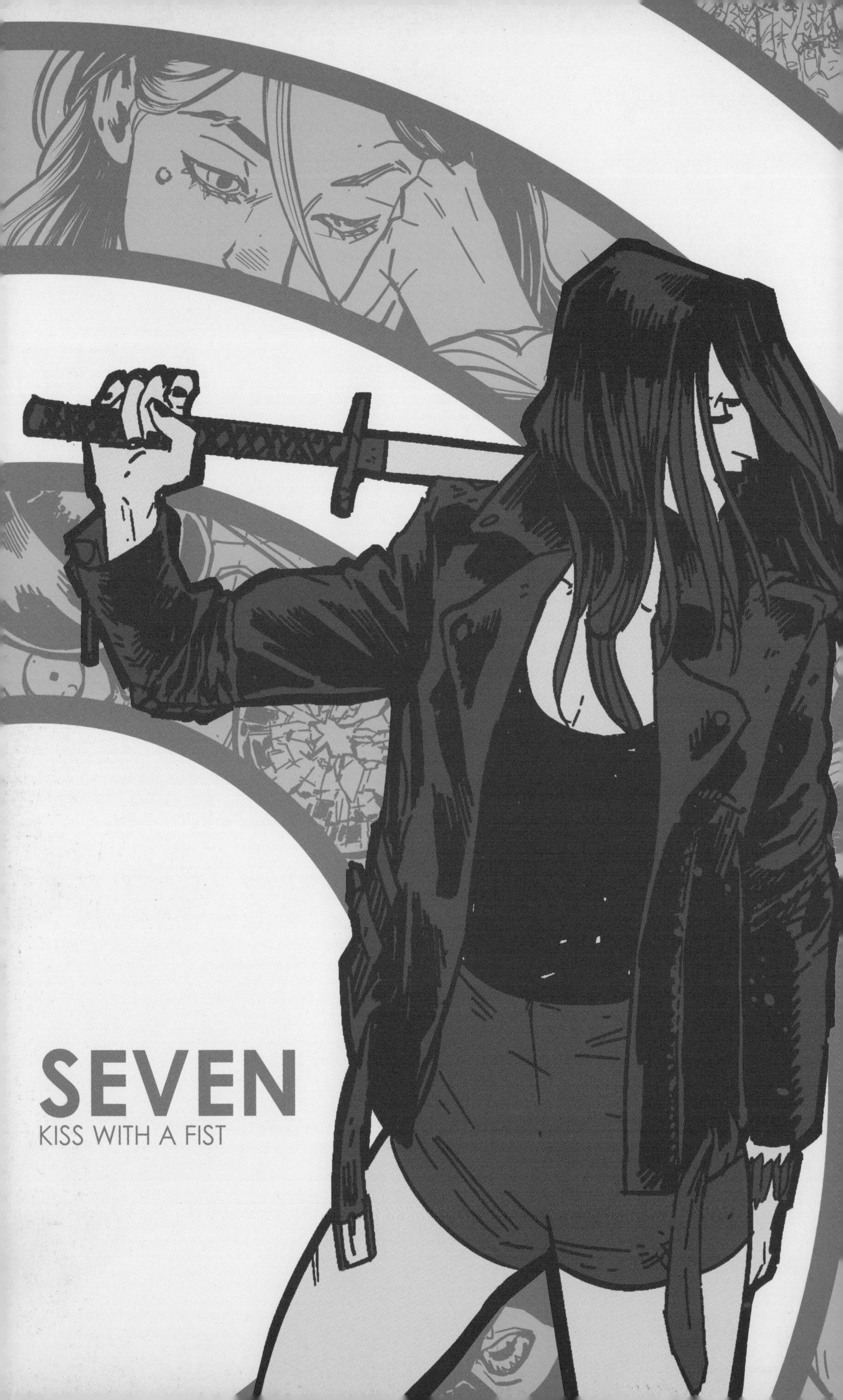

SEVEN
KISS WITH A FIST

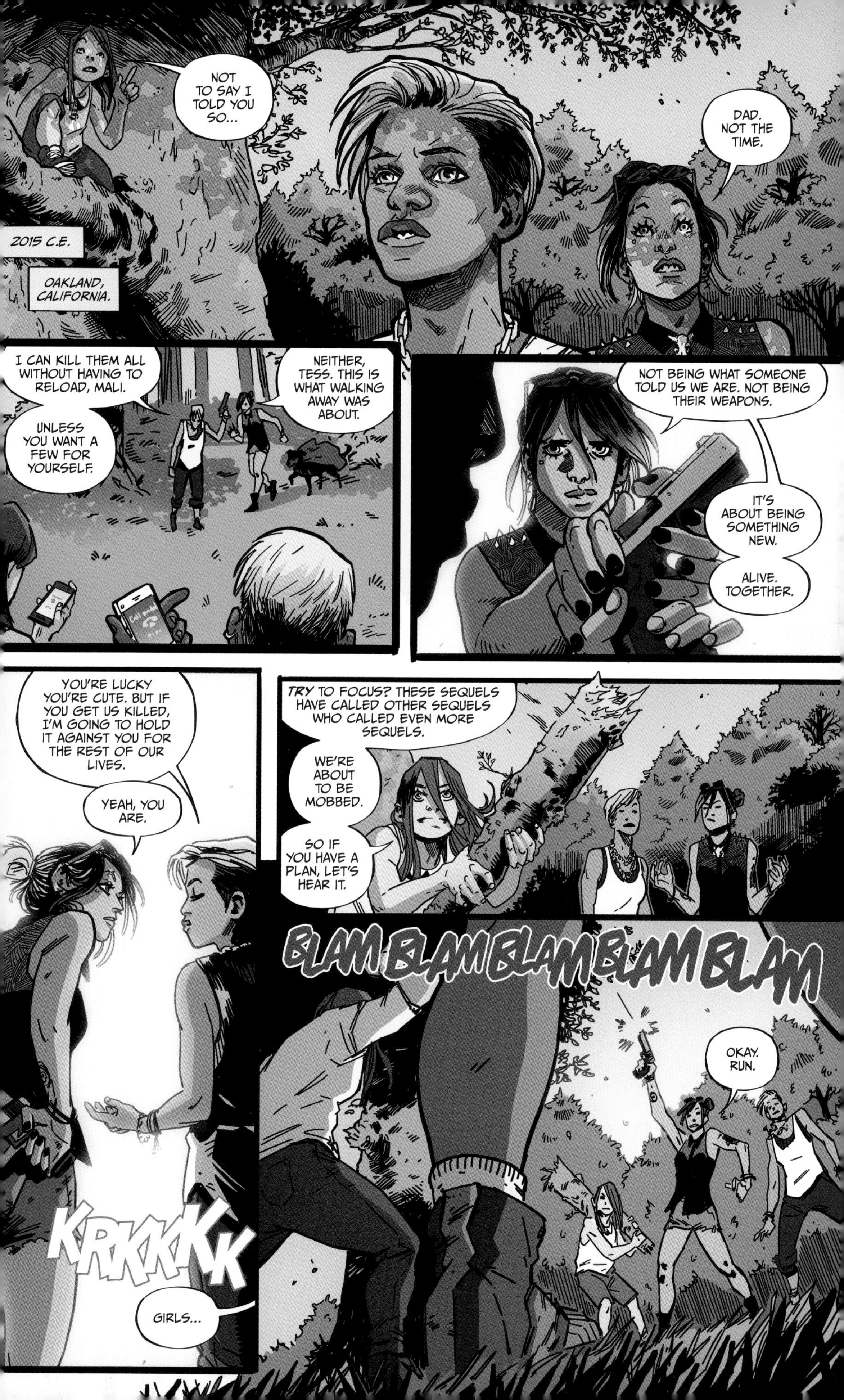
NOT TO SAY I TOLD YOU SO...
DAD. NOT THE TIME.
2015 C.E.
OAKLAND, CALIFORNIA.
I CAN KILL THEM ALL WITHOUT HAVING TO RELOAD, MALI.
UNLESS YOU WANT A FEW FOR YOURSELF.
NEITHER, TESS. THIS IS WHAT WALKING AWAY WAS ABOUT.
NOT BEING WHAT SOMEONE TOLD US WE ARE. NOT BEING THEIR WEAPONS.
IT'S ABOUT BEING SOMETHING NEW.
ALIVE. TOGETHER.
YOU'RE LUCKY YOU'RE CUTE. BUT IF YOU GET US KILLED, I'M GOING TO HOLD IT AGAINST YOU FOR THE REST OF OUR LIVES.
YEAH, YOU ARE.
TRY TO FOCUS? THESE SEQUELS HAVE CALLED OTHER SEQUELS WHO CALLED EVEN MORE SEQUELS.
WE'RE ABOUT TO BE MOBBED.
SO IF YOU HAVE A PLAN, LET'S HEAR IT.
BLAM BLAM BLAM BLAM BLAM
OKAY. RUN.
KRKKKKK
GIRLS...

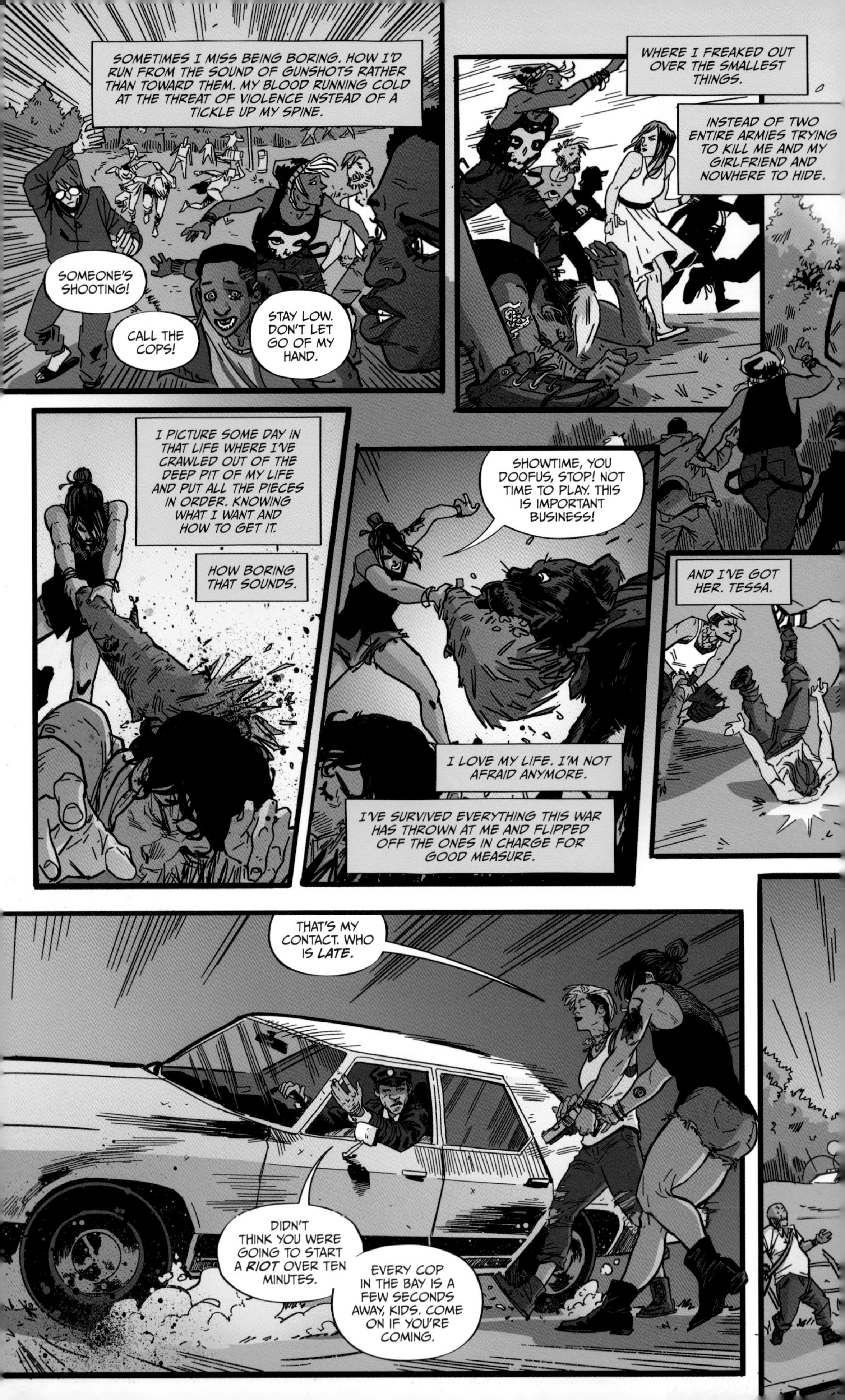
SOMETIMES I MISS BEING BORING. HOW I'D RUN FROM THE SOUND OF GUNSHOTS RATHER THAN TOWARD THEM. MY BLOOD RUNNING COLD AT THE THREAT OF VIOLENCE INSTEAD OF A TICKLE UP MY SPINE.
SOMEONE'S SHOOTING!
CALL THE COPS!
STAY LOW. DON'T LET GO OF MY HAND.
WHERE I FREAKED OUT OVER THE SMALLEST THINGS.
INSTEAD OF TWO ENTIRE ARMIES TRYING TO KILL ME AND MY GIRLFRIEND AND NOWHERE TO HIDE.
I PICTURE SOME DAY IN THAT LIFE WHERE I'VE CRAWLED OUT OF THE DEEP PIT OF MY LIFE AND PUT ALL THE PIECES IN ORDER. KNOWING WHAT I WANT AND HOW TO GET IT.
HOW BORING THAT SOUNDS.
SHOWTIME, YOU DOOFUS, STOP! NOT TIME TO PLAY. THIS IS IMPORTANT BUSINESS!
I LOVE MY LIFE. I'M NOT AFRAID ANYMORE.
I'VE SURVIVED EVERYTHING THIS WAR HAS THROWN AT ME AND FLIPPED OFF THE ONES IN CHARGE FOR GOOD MEASURE.
AND I'VE GOT HER. TESSA.
THAT'S MY CONTACT. WHO IS LATE.
DIDN'T THINK YOU WERE GOING TO START A RIOT OVER TEN MINUTES.
EVERY COP IN THE BAY IS A FEW SECONDS AWAY, KIDS. COME ON IF YOU'RE COMING.

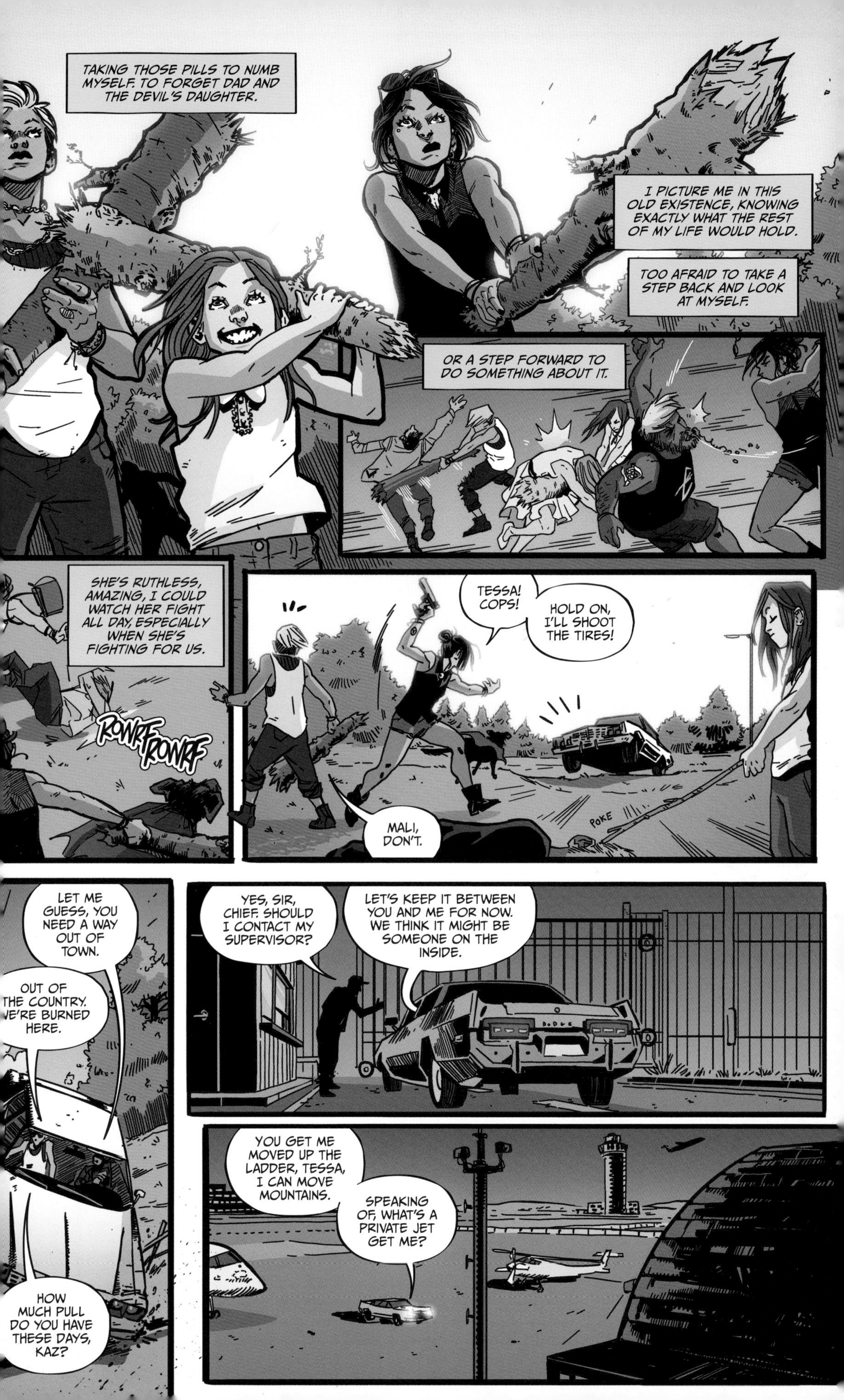

TAKING THOSE PILLS TO NUMB MYSELF. TO FORGET DAD AND THE DEVIL'S DAUGHTER.
I PICTURE ME IN THIS OLD EXISTENCE, KNOWING EXACTLY WHAT THE REST OF MY LIFE WOULD HOLD.
TOO AFRAID TO TAKE A STEP BACK AND LOOK AT MYSELF.
OR A STEP FORWARD TO DO SOMETHING ABOUT IT.
SHE'S RUTHLESS, AMAZING, I COULD WATCH HER FIGHT ALL DAY, ESPECIALLY WHEN SHE'S FIGHTING FOR US.
ROWRF ROWRF
TESSA! COPS!
HOLD ON, I'LL SHOOT THE TIRES!
MALI, DON'T.
POKE
LET ME GUESS, YOU NEED A WAY OUT OF TOWN.
OUT OF THE COUNTRY. WE'RE BURNED HERE.
HOW MUCH PULL DO YOU HAVE THESE DAYS, KAZ?
YES, SIR, CHIEF. SHOULD I CONTACT MY SUPERVISOR?
LET'S KEEP IT BETWEEN YOU AND ME FOR NOW. WE THINK IT MIGHT BE SOMEONE ON THE INSIDE.
YOU GET ME MOVED UP THE LADDER, TESSA, I CAN MOVE MOUNTAINS.
SPEAKING OF, WHAT'S A PRIVATE JET GET ME?

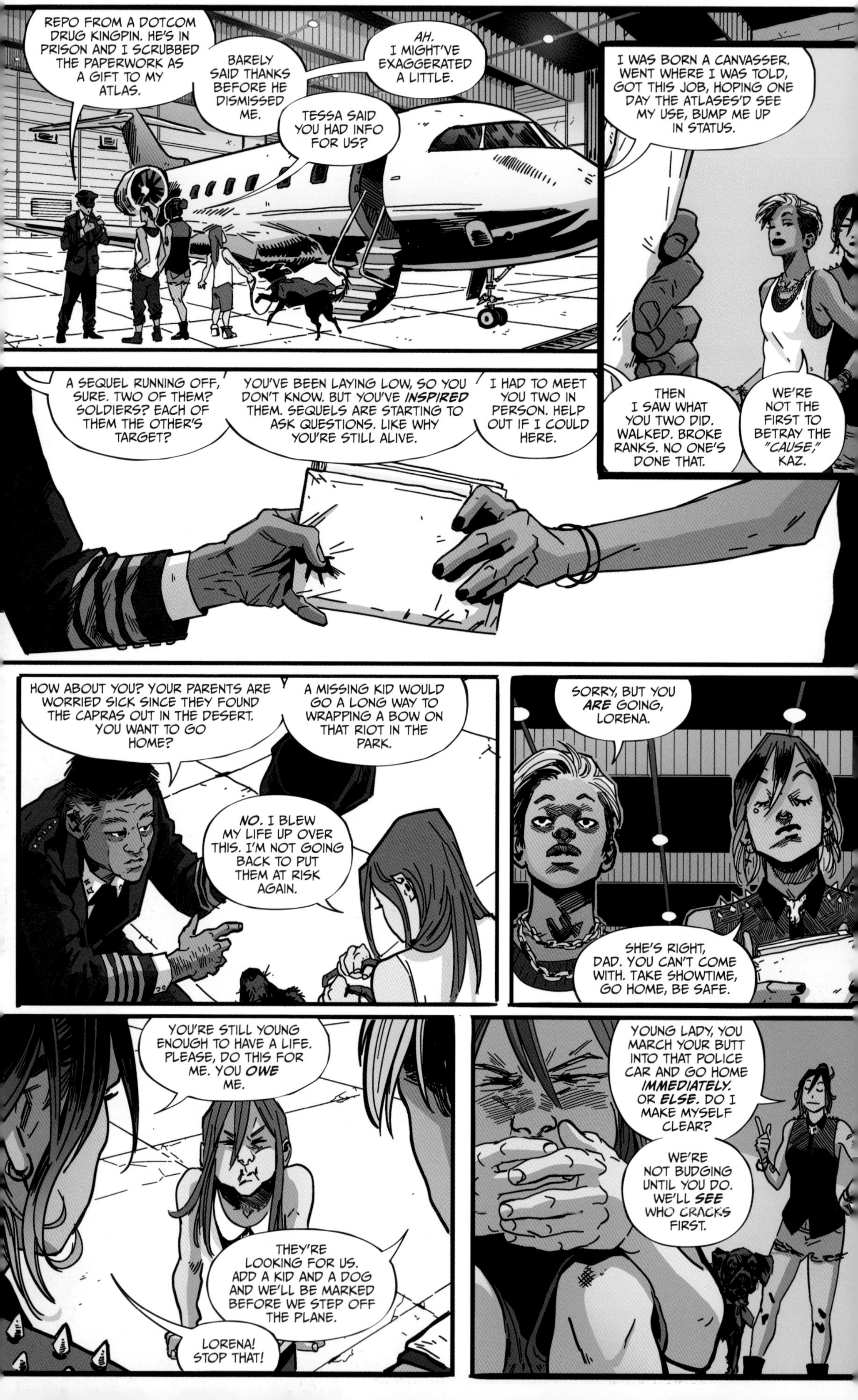

REPO FROM A DOTCOM DRUG KINGPIN. HE'S IN PRISON AND I SCRUBBED THE PAPERWORK AS A GIFT TO MY ATLAS.
BARELY SAID THANKS BEFORE HE DISMISSED ME.
AH. I MIGHT'VE EXAGGERATED A LITTLE.
TESSA SAID YOU HAD INFO FOR US?
I WAS BORN A CANVASSER. WENT WHERE I WAS TOLD, GOT THIS JOB, HOPING ONE DAY THE ATLASES'D SEE MY USE, BUMP ME UP IN STATUS.
THEN I SAW WHAT YOU TWO DID. WALKED. BROKE RANKS. NO ONE'S DONE THAT.
WE'RE NOT THE FIRST TO BETRAY THE "CAUSE," KAZ.
A SEQUEL RUNNING OFF, SURE. TWO OF THEM? SOLDIERS? EACH OF THEM THE OTHER'S TARGET?
YOU'VE BEEN LAYING LOW, SO YOU DON'T KNOW. BUT YOU'VE *INSPIRED* THEM. SEQUELS ARE STARTING TO ASK QUESTIONS. LIKE WHY YOU'RE STILL ALIVE.
I HAD TO MEET YOU TWO IN PERSON. HELP OUT IF I COULD HERE.
HOW ABOUT YOU? YOUR PARENTS ARE WORRIED SICK SINCE THEY FOUND THE CAPRAS OUT IN THE DESERT. YOU WANT TO GO HOME?
A MISSING KID WOULD GO A LONG WAY TO WRAPPING A BOW ON THAT RIOT IN THE PARK.
NO. I BLEW MY LIFE UP OVER THIS. I'M NOT GOING BACK TO PUT THEM AT RISK AGAIN.
SORRY, BUT YOU *ARE* GOING, LORENA.
SHE'S RIGHT, DAD. YOU CAN'T COME WITH. TAKE SHOWTIME, GO HOME, BE SAFE.
YOU'RE STILL YOUNG ENOUGH TO HAVE A LIFE. PLEASE, DO THIS FOR ME. YOU *OWE* ME.
THEY'RE LOOKING FOR US. ADD A KID AND A DOG AND WE'LL BE MARKED BEFORE WE STEP OFF THE PLANE.
LORENA! STOP THAT!
YOUNG LADY, YOU MARCH YOUR BUTT INTO THAT POLICE CAR AND GO HOME *IMMEDIATELY.* OR *ELSE.* DO I MAKE MYSELF CLEAR?
WE'RE NOT BUDGING UNTIL YOU DO. WE'LL *SEE* WHO CRACKS FIRST.

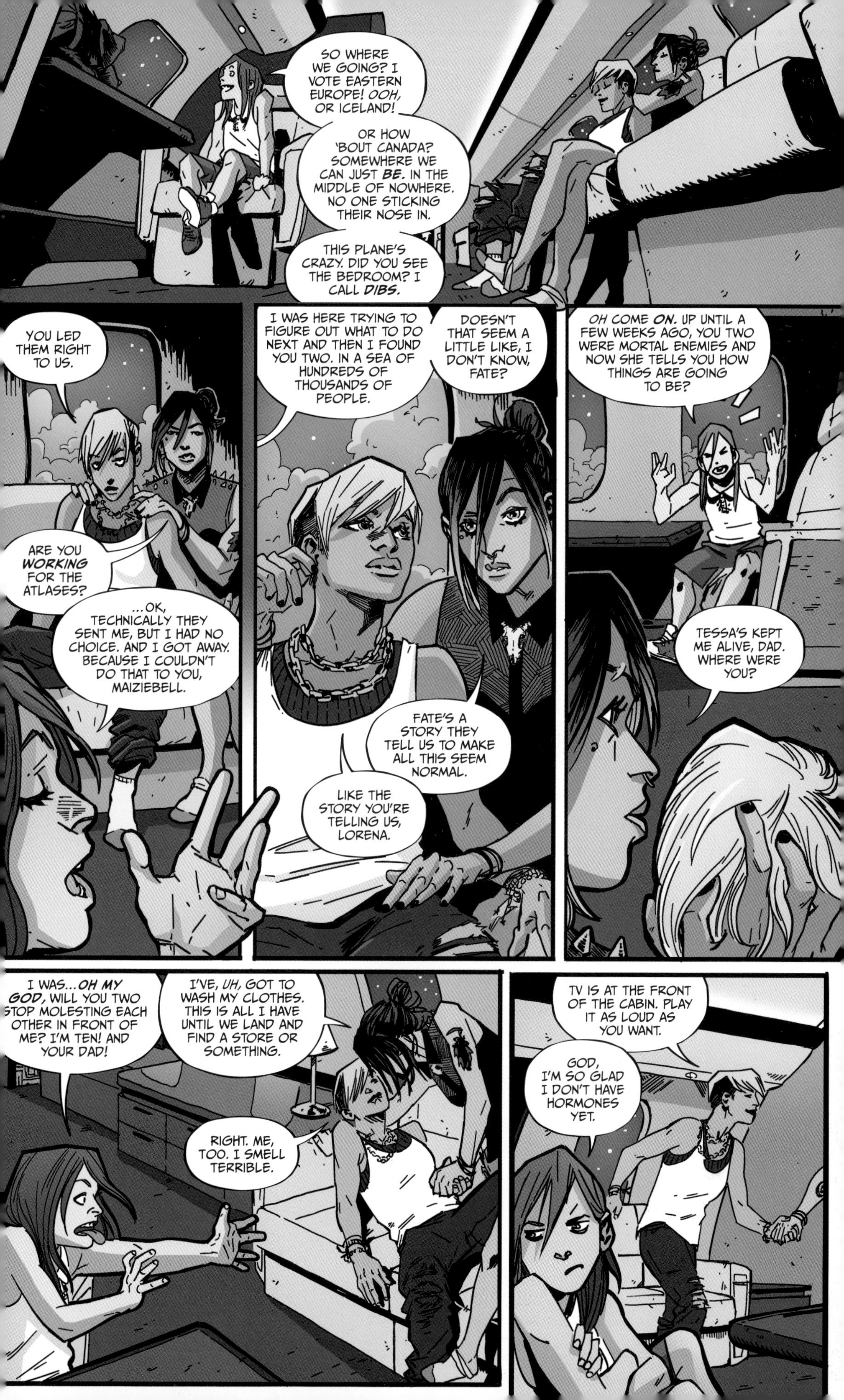
SO WHERE WE GOING? I VOTE EASTERN EUROPE! OOH, OR ICELAND!
OR HOW 'BOUT CANADA? SOMEWHERE WE CAN JUST BE. IN THE MIDDLE OF NOWHERE. NO ONE STICKING THEIR NOSE IN.
THIS PLANE'S CRAZY. DID YOU SEE THE BEDROOM? I CALL DIBS.
YOU LED THEM RIGHT TO US.
ARE YOU WORKING FOR THE ATLASES?
...OK, TECHNICALLY THEY SENT ME, BUT I HAD NO CHOICE. AND I GOT AWAY. BECAUSE I COULDN'T DO THAT TO YOU, MAIZIEBELL.
I WAS HERE TRYING TO FIGURE OUT WHAT TO DO NEXT AND THEN I FOUND YOU TWO. IN A SEA OF HUNDREDS OF THOUSANDS OF PEOPLE.
DOESN'T THAT SEEM A LITTLE LIKE, I DON'T KNOW, FATE?
FATE'S A STORY THEY TELL US TO MAKE ALL THIS SEEM NORMAL.
LIKE THE STORY YOU'RE TELLING US, LORENA.
OH COME ON. UP UNTIL A FEW WEEKS AGO, YOU TWO WERE MORTAL ENEMIES AND NOW SHE TELLS YOU HOW THINGS ARE GOING TO BE?
TESSA'S KEPT ME ALIVE, DAD. WHERE WERE YOU?
I WAS...OH MY GOD, WILL YOU TWO STOP MOLESTING EACH OTHER IN FRONT OF ME? I'M TEN! AND YOUR DAD!
I'VE, UH, GOT TO WASH MY CLOTHES. THIS IS ALL I HAVE UNTIL WE LAND AND FIND A STORE OR SOMETHING.
RIGHT. ME, TOO. I SMELL TERRIBLE.
TV IS AT THE FRONT OF THE CABIN. PLAY IT AS LOUD AS YOU WANT.
GOD, I'M SO GLAD I DON'T HAVE HORMONES YET.

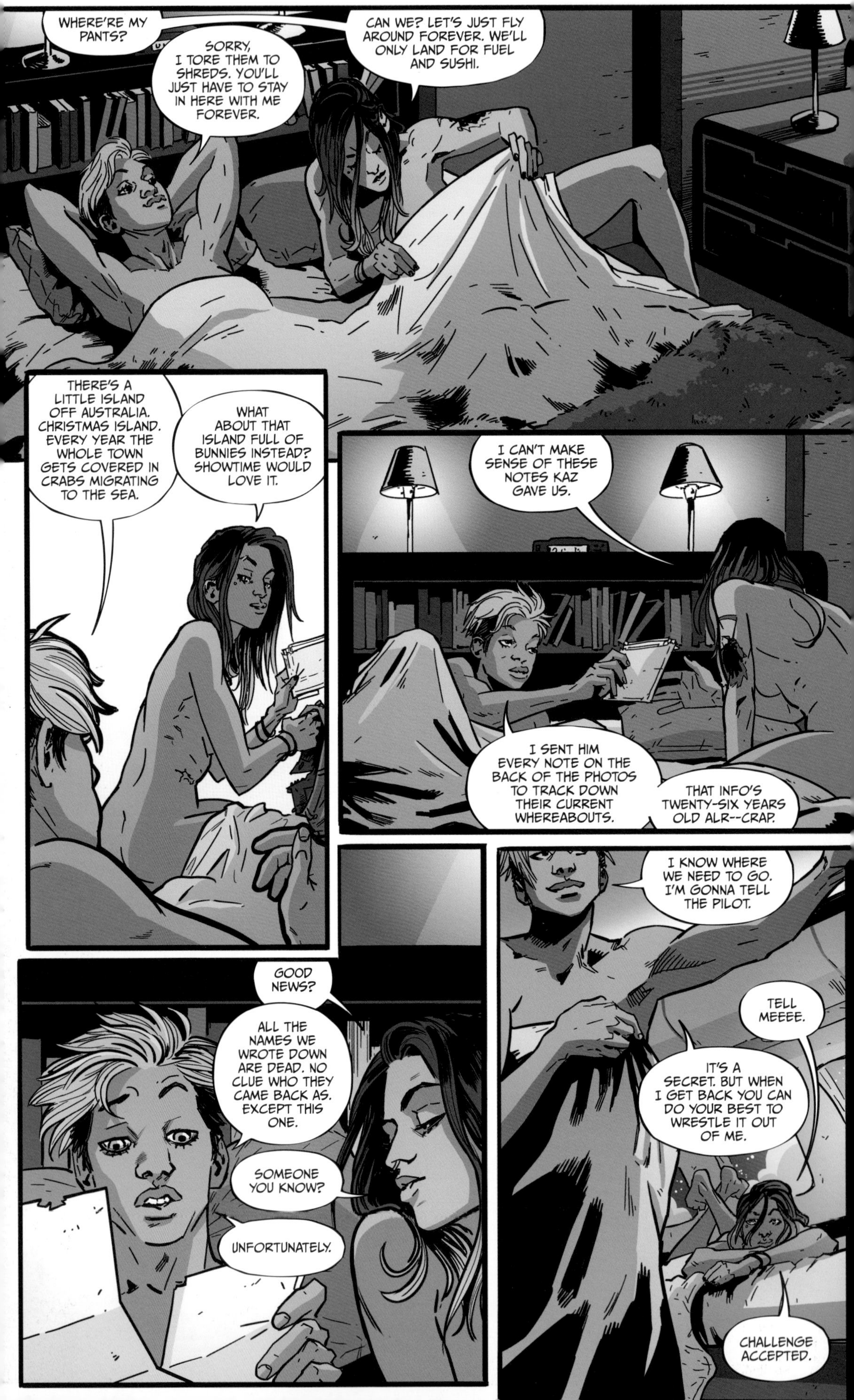
WHERE'RE MY PANTS?
SORRY, I TORE THEM TO SHREDS. YOU'LL JUST HAVE TO STAY IN HERE WITH ME FOREVER.
CAN WE? LET'S JUST FLY AROUND FOREVER. WE'LL ONLY LAND FOR FUEL AND SUSHI.
THERE'S A LITTLE ISLAND OFF AUSTRALIA. CHRISTMAS ISLAND. EVERY YEAR THE WHOLE TOWN GETS COVERED IN CRABS MIGRATING TO THE SEA.
WHAT ABOUT THAT ISLAND FULL OF BUNNIES INSTEAD? SHOWTIME WOULD LOVE IT.
I CAN'T MAKE SENSE OF THESE NOTES KAZ GAVE US.
I SENT HIM EVERY NOTE ON THE BACK OF THE PHOTOS TO TRACK DOWN THEIR CURRENT WHEREABOUTS.
THAT INFO'S TWENTY-SIX YEARS OLD ALR--CRAP.
GOOD NEWS?
ALL THE NAMES WE WROTE DOWN ARE DEAD. NO CLUE WHO THEY CAME BACK AS. EXCEPT THIS ONE.
SOMEONE YOU KNOW?
UNFORTUNATELY.
I KNOW WHERE WE NEED TO GO. I'M GONNA TELL THE PILOT.
TELL MEEEE.
IT'S A SECRET. BUT WHEN I GET BACK YOU CAN DO YOUR BEST TO WRESTLE IT OUT OF ME.
CHALLENGE ACCEPTED.

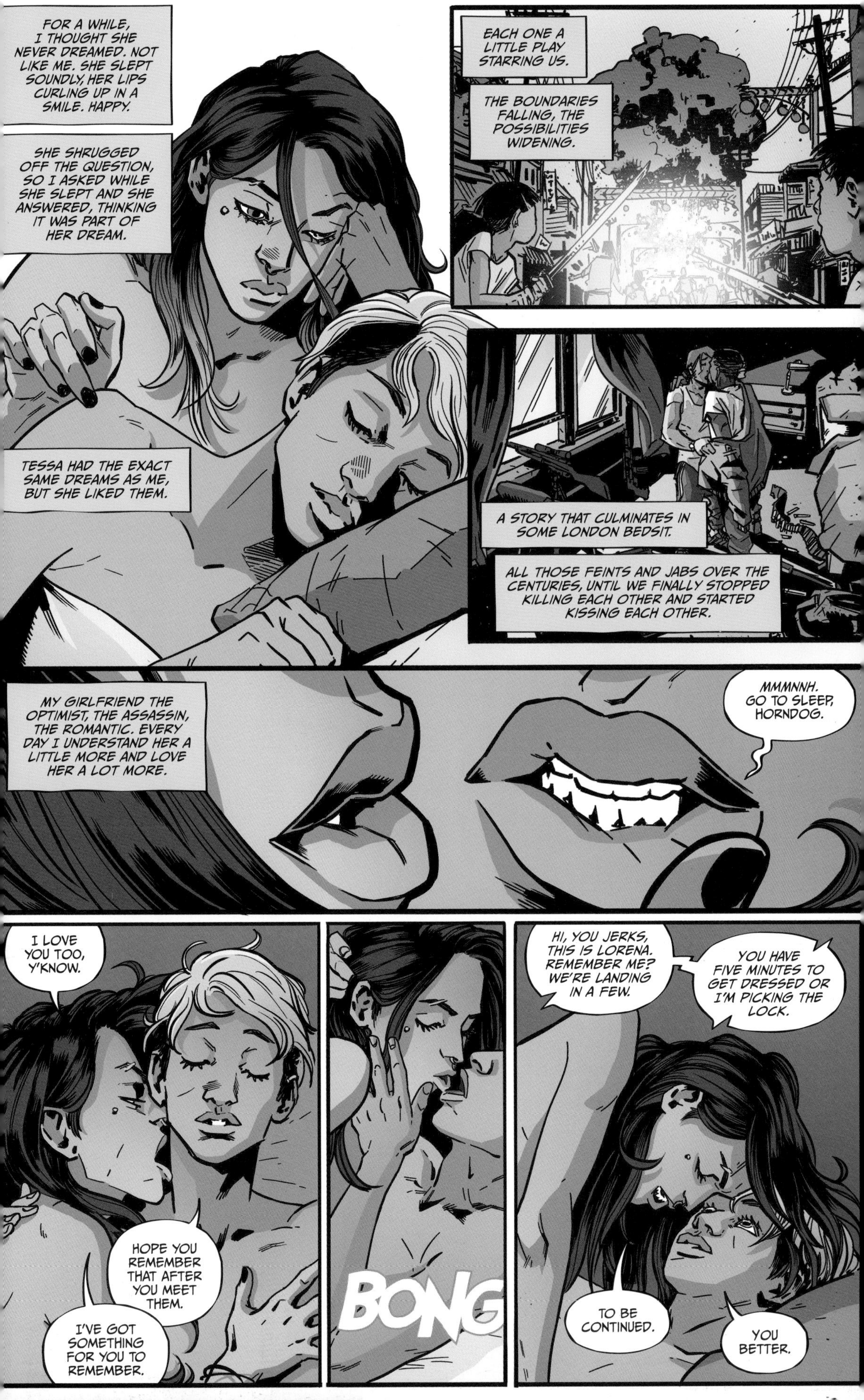
FOR A WHILE, I THOUGHT SHE NEVER DREAMED. NOT LIKE ME. SHE SLEPT SOUNDLY, HER LIPS CURLING UP IN A SMILE. HAPPY.
SHE SHRUGGED OFF THE QUESTION, SO I ASKED WHILE SHE SLEPT AND SHE ANSWERED, THINKING IT WAS PART OF HER DREAM.
TESSA HAD THE EXACT SAME DREAMS AS ME, BUT SHE LIKED THEM.
EACH ONE A LITTLE PLAY STARRING US.
THE BOUNDARIES FALLING, THE POSSIBILITIES WIDENING.
A STORY THAT CULMINATES IN SOME LONDON BEDSIT.
ALL THOSE FEINTS AND JABS OVER THE CENTURIES, UNTIL WE FINALLY STOPPED KILLING EACH OTHER AND STARTED KISSING EACH OTHER.
MY GIRLFRIEND THE OPTIMIST, THE ASSASSIN, THE ROMANTIC. EVERY DAY I UNDERSTAND HER A LITTLE MORE AND LOVE HER A LOT MORE.
MMMNNH. GO TO SLEEP, HORNDOG.
I LOVE YOU TOO, Y'KNOW.
HOPE YOU REMEMBER THAT AFTER YOU MEET THEM.
I'VE GOT SOMETHING FOR YOU TO REMEMBER.
BONG
HI, YOU JERKS, THIS IS LORENA. REMEMBER ME? WE'RE LANDING IN A FEW.
YOU HAVE FIVE MINUTES TO GET DRESSED OR I'M PICKING THE LOCK.
TO BE CONTINUED.
YOU BETTER.

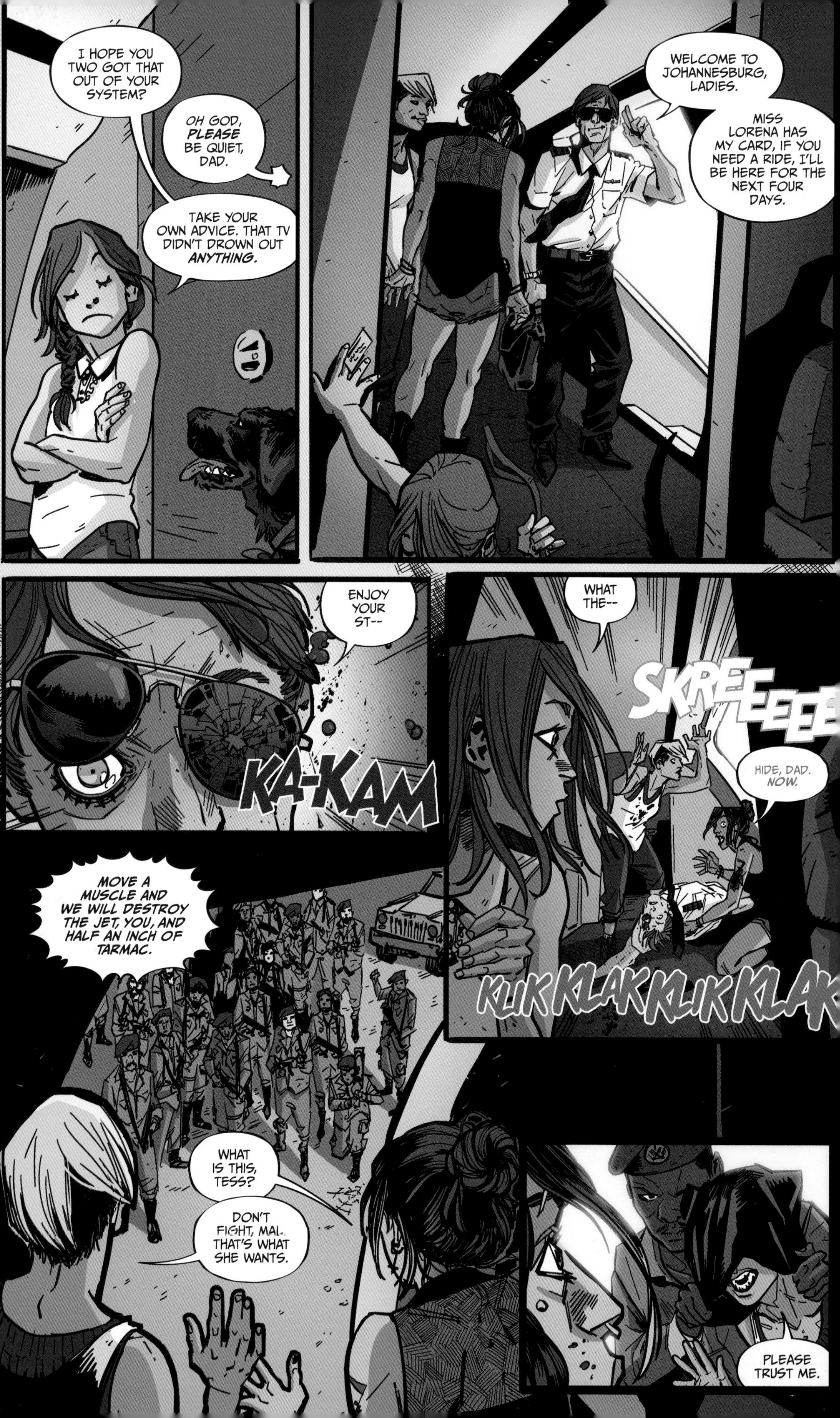

I HOPE YOU TWO GOT THAT OUT OF YOUR SYSTEM?
OH GOD, PLEASE BE QUIET, DAD.
TAKE YOUR OWN ADVICE. THAT TV DIDN'T DROWN OUT ANYTHING.
WELCOME TO JOHANNESBURG, LADIES.
MISS LORENA HAS MY CARD, IF YOU NEED A RIDE, I'LL BE HERE FOR THE NEXT FOUR DAYS.
ENJOY YOUR ST--
KA-KAM
WHAT THE--
SKREEEEEE
HIDE, DAD. NOW.
KLIK KLAK KLIK KLAK
MOVE A MUSCLE AND WE WILL DESTROY THE JET, YOU, AND HALF AN INCH OF TARMAC.
WHAT IS THIS, TESS?
DON'T FIGHT, MAL. THAT'S WHAT SHE WANTS.
PLEASE TRUST ME.

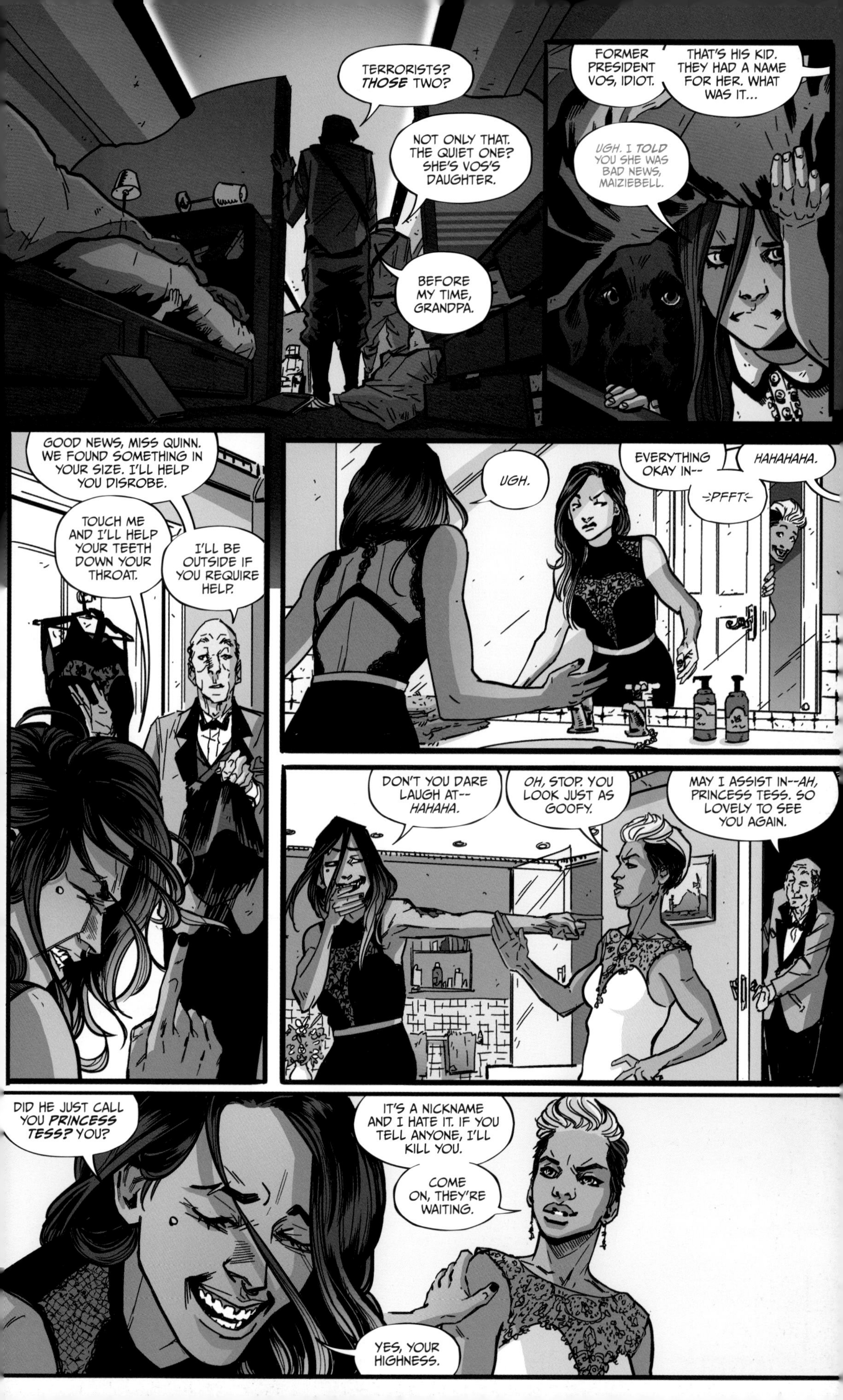
TERRORISTS? THOSE TWO?
NOT ONLY THAT. THE QUIET ONE? SHE'S VOS'S DAUGHTER.
BEFORE MY TIME, GRANDPA.
FORMER PRESIDENT VOS, IDIOT.
THAT'S HIS KID. THEY HAD A NAME FOR HER. WHAT WAS IT...
UGH. I TOLD YOU SHE WAS BAD NEWS, MAIZIEBELL.
GOOD NEWS, MISS QUINN. WE FOUND SOMETHING IN YOUR SIZE. I'LL HELP YOU DISROBE.
TOUCH ME AND I'LL HELP YOUR TEETH DOWN YOUR THROAT.
I'LL BE OUTSIDE IF YOU REQUIRE HELP.
UGH.
EVERYTHING OKAY IN--
PFFT
HAHAHAHA.
DON'T YOU DARE LAUGH AT-- HAHAHA.
OH, STOP. YOU LOOK JUST AS GOOFY.
MAY I ASSIST IN--AH, PRINCESS TESS. SO LOVELY TO SEE YOU AGAIN.
DID HE JUST CALL YOU PRINCESS TESS? YOU?
IT'S A NICKNAME AND I HATE IT. IF YOU TELL ANYONE, I'LL KILL YOU.
COME ON, THEY'RE WAITING.
YES, YOUR HIGHNESS.

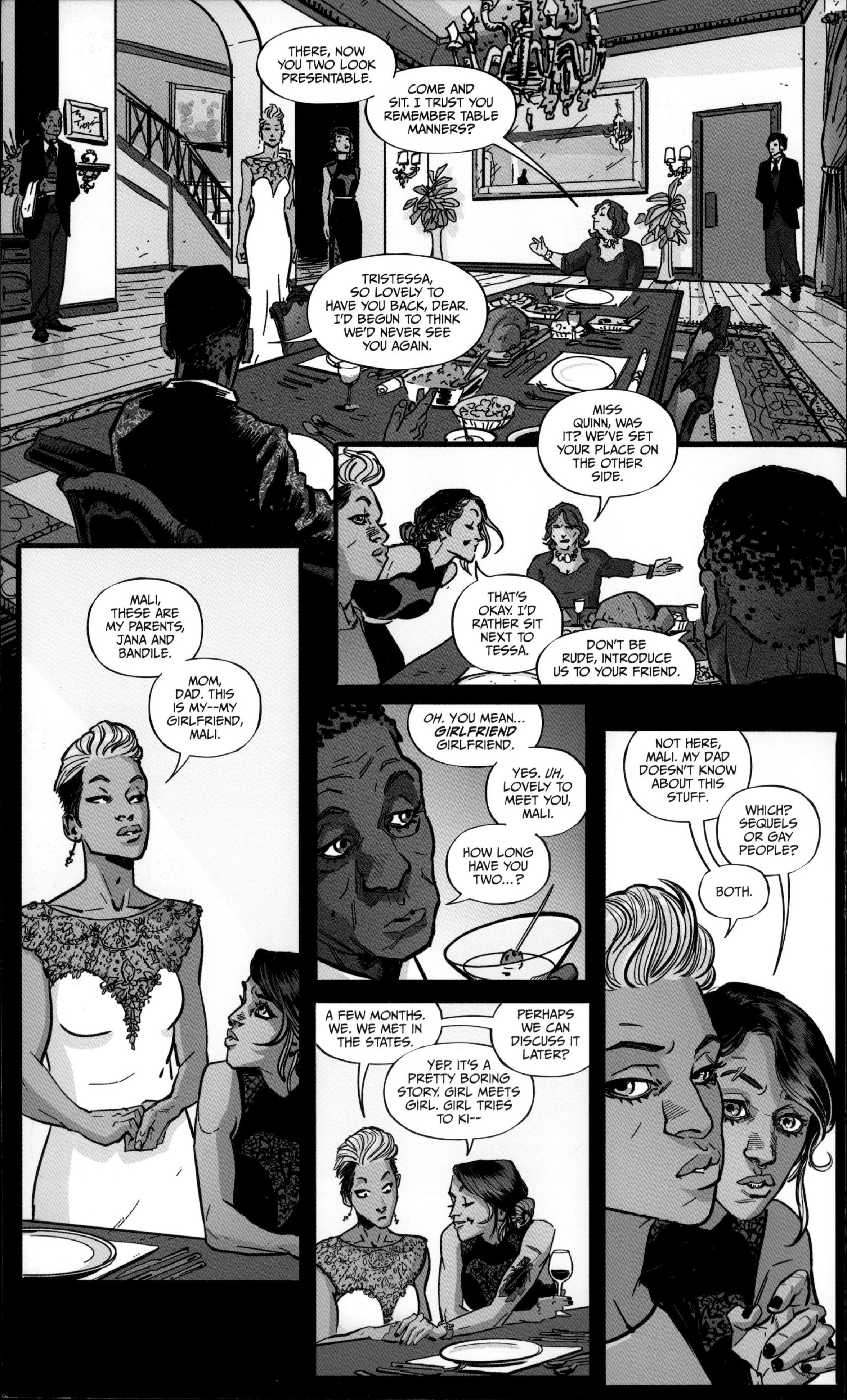
THERE, NOW YOU TWO LOOK PRESENTABLE.
COME AND SIT. I TRUST YOU REMEMBER TABLE MANNERS?
TRISTESSA, SO LOVELY TO HAVE YOU BACK, DEAR. I'D BEGUN TO THINK WE'D NEVER SEE YOU AGAIN.
MISS QUINN, WAS IT? WE'VE SET YOUR PLACE ON THE OTHER SIDE.
THAT'S OKAY. I'D RATHER SIT NEXT TO TESSA.
DON'T BE RUDE, INTRODUCE US TO YOUR FRIEND.
MALI, THESE ARE MY PARENTS, JANA AND BANDILE.
MOM, DAD. THIS IS MY--MY GIRLFRIEND, MALI.
OH. YOU MEAN... ***GIRLFRIEND*** GIRLFRIEND.
YES. *UH,* LOVELY TO MEET YOU, MALI.
HOW LONG HAVE YOU TWO...?
A FEW MONTHS. WE. WE MET IN THE STATES.
PERHAPS WE CAN DISCUSS IT LATER?
YEP. IT'S A PRETTY BORING STORY. GIRL MEETS GIRL. GIRL TRIES TO KI--
NOT HERE, MALI. MY DAD DOESN'T KNOW ABOUT THIS STUFF.
WHICH? SEQUELS OR GAY PEOPLE?
BOTH.

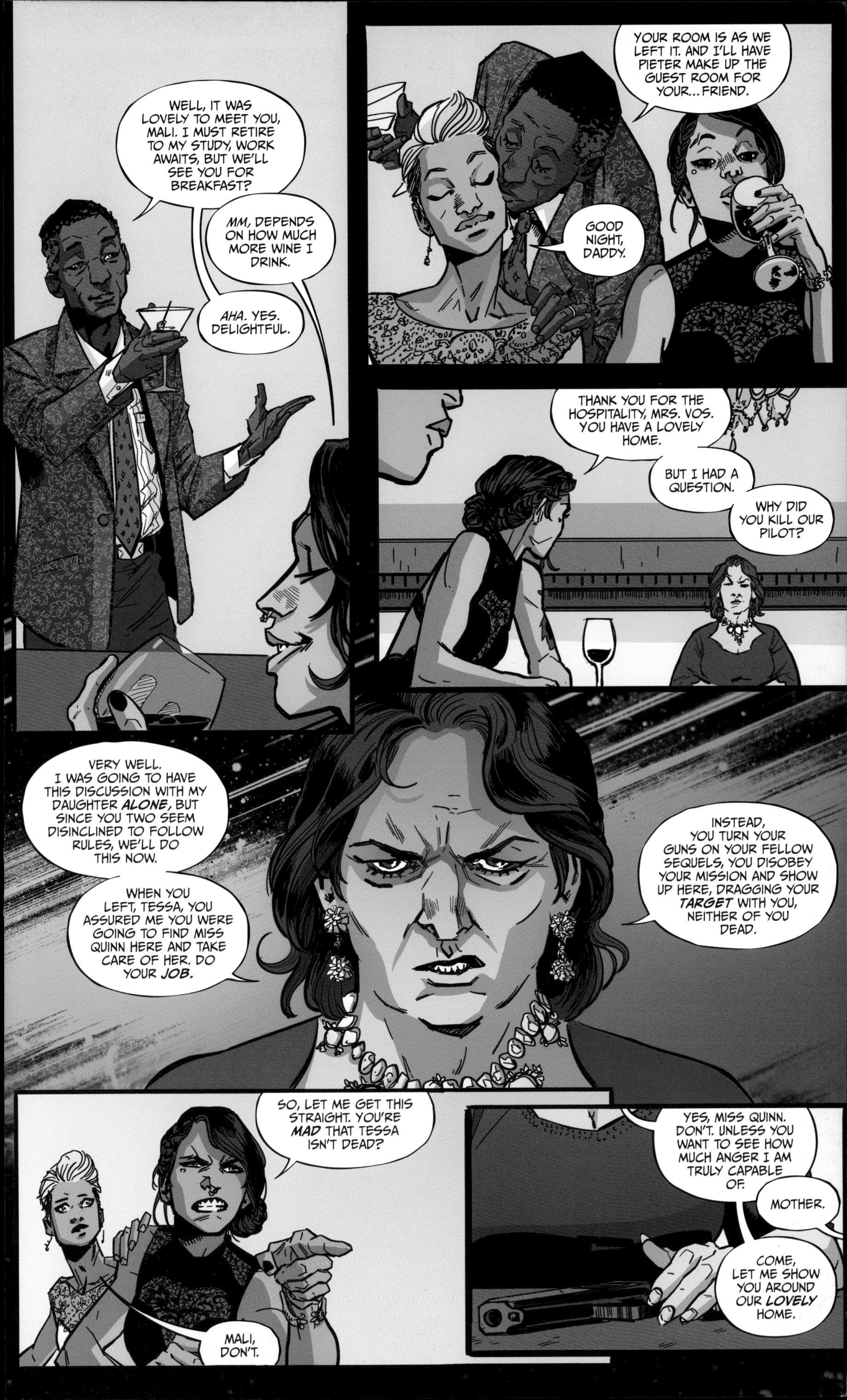
WELL, IT WAS LOVELY TO MEET YOU, MALI. I MUST RETIRE TO MY STUDY, WORK AWAITS, BUT WE'LL SEE YOU FOR BREAKFAST?
MM, DEPENDS ON HOW MUCH MORE WINE I DRINK.
AHA. YES. DELIGHTFUL.
YOUR ROOM IS AS WE LEFT IT. AND I'LL HAVE PIETER MAKE UP THE GUEST ROOM FOR YOUR...FRIEND.
GOOD NIGHT, DADDY.
THANK YOU FOR THE HOSPITALITY, MRS. VOS. YOU HAVE A LOVELY HOME.
BUT I HAD A QUESTION.
WHY DID YOU KILL OUR PILOT?
VERY WELL. I WAS GOING TO HAVE THIS DISCUSSION WITH MY DAUGHTER ALONE, BUT SINCE YOU TWO SEEM DISINCLINED TO FOLLOW RULES, WE'LL DO THIS NOW.
WHEN YOU LEFT, TESSA, YOU ASSURED ME YOU WERE GOING TO FIND MISS QUINN HERE AND TAKE CARE OF HER. DO YOUR JOB.
INSTEAD, YOU TURN YOUR GUNS ON YOUR FELLOW SEQUELS, YOU DISOBEY YOUR MISSION AND SHOW UP HERE, DRAGGING YOUR TARGET WITH YOU, NEITHER OF YOU DEAD.
SO, LET ME GET THIS STRAIGHT. YOU'RE MAD THAT TESSA ISN'T DEAD?
MALI, DON'T.
YES, MISS QUINN. DON'T. UNLESS YOU WANT TO SEE HOW MUCH ANGER I AM TRULY CAPABLE OF.
MOTHER.
COME, LET ME SHOW YOU AROUND OUR LOVELY HOME.

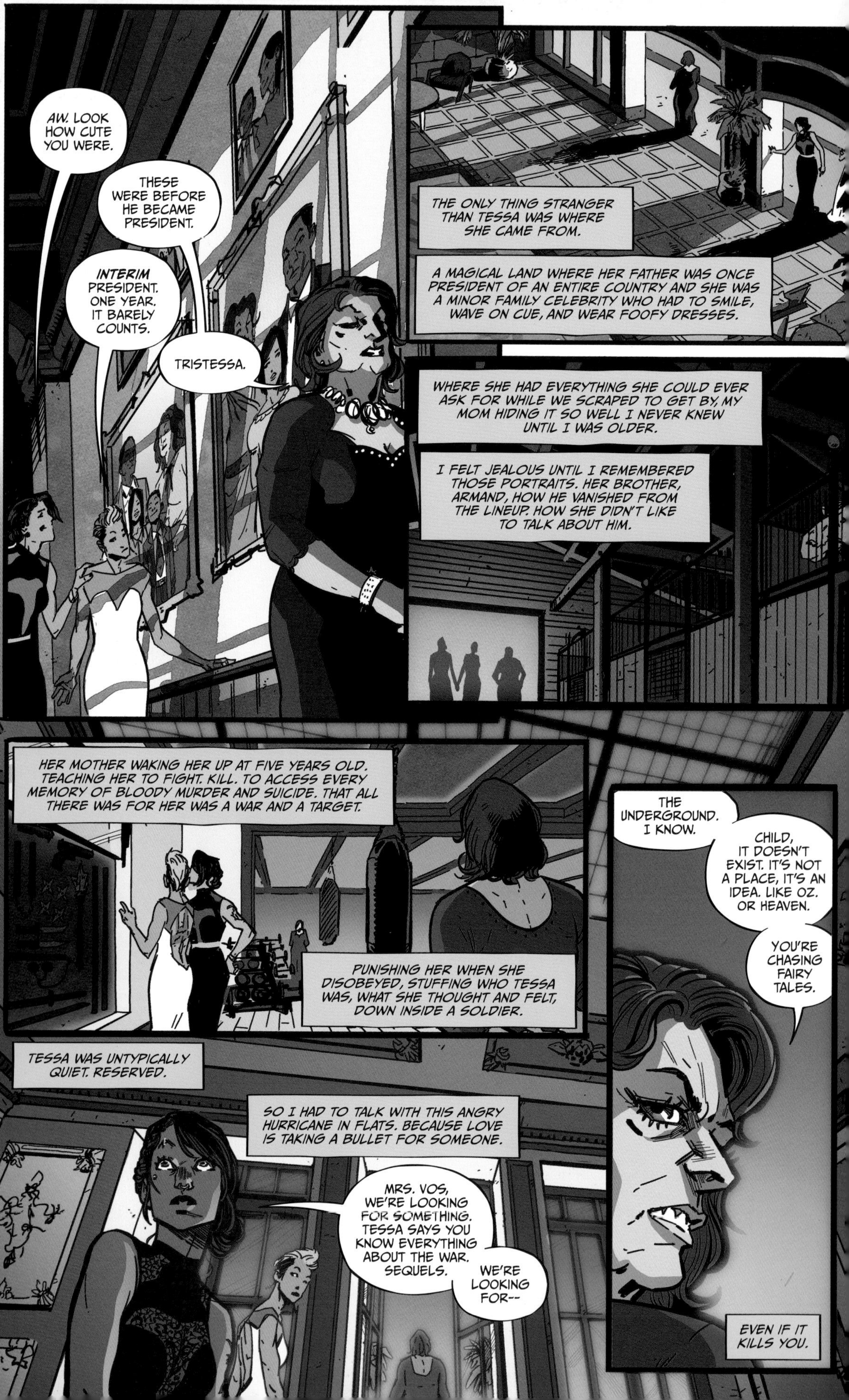
AW. LOOK HOW CUTE YOU WERE.
THESE WERE BEFORE HE BECAME PRESIDENT.
INTERIM PRESIDENT. ONE YEAR. IT BARELY COUNTS.
TRISTESSA.
THE ONLY THING STRANGER THAN TESSA WAS WHERE SHE CAME FROM.
A MAGICAL LAND WHERE HER FATHER WAS ONCE PRESIDENT OF AN ENTIRE COUNTRY AND SHE WAS A MINOR FAMILY CELEBRITY WHO HAD TO SMILE, WAVE ON CUE, AND WEAR FOOFY DRESSES.
WHERE SHE HAD EVERYTHING SHE COULD EVER ASK FOR WHILE WE SCRAPED TO GET BY, MY MOM HIDING IT SO WELL I NEVER KNEW UNTIL I WAS OLDER.
I FELT JEALOUS UNTIL I REMEMBERED THOSE PORTRAITS. HER BROTHER, ARMAND, HOW HE VANISHED FROM THE LINEUP. HOW SHE DIDN'T LIKE TO TALK ABOUT HIM.
HER MOTHER WAKING HER UP AT FIVE YEARS OLD. TEACHING HER TO FIGHT. KILL. TO ACCESS EVERY MEMORY OF BLOODY MURDER AND SUICIDE. THAT ALL THERE WAS FOR HER WAS A WAR AND A TARGET.
PUNISHING HER WHEN SHE DISOBEYED, STUFFING WHO TESSA WAS, WHAT SHE THOUGHT AND FELT, DOWN INSIDE A SOLDIER.
TESSA WAS UNTYPICALLY QUIET. RESERVED.
SO I HAD TO TALK WITH THIS ANGRY HURRICANE IN FLATS. BECAUSE LOVE IS TAKING A BULLET FOR SOMEONE.
MRS. VOS, WE'RE LOOKING FOR SOMETHING. TESSA SAYS YOU KNOW EVERYTHING ABOUT THE WAR. SEQUELS.
WE'RE LOOKING FOR--
THE UNDERGROUND. I KNOW.
CHILD, IT DOESN'T EXIST. IT'S NOT A PLACE, IT'S AN IDEA. LIKE OZ. OR HEAVEN.
YOU'RE CHASING FAIRY TALES.
EVEN IF IT KILLS YOU.

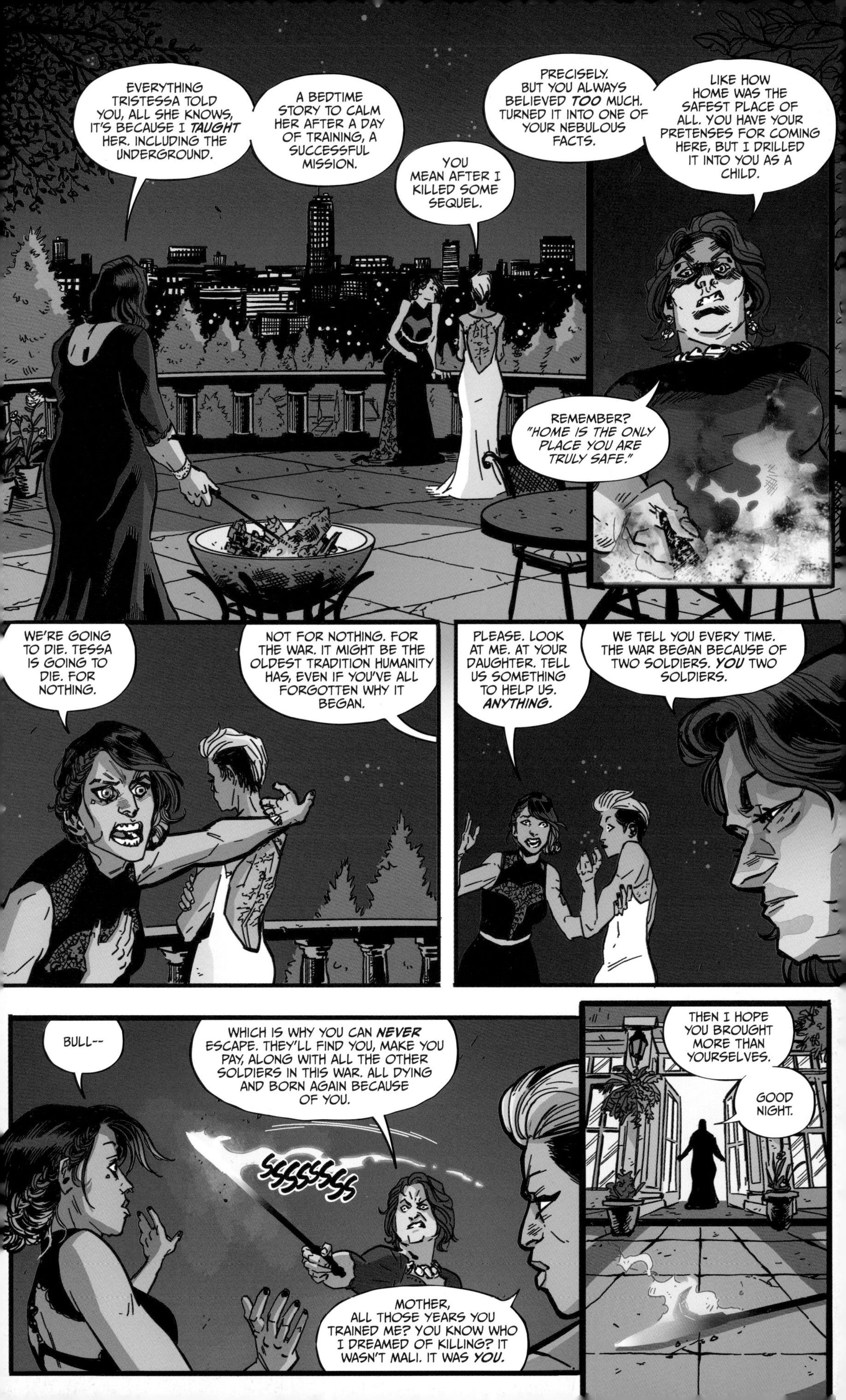
EVERYTHING TRISTESSA TOLD YOU, ALL SHE KNOWS, IT'S BECAUSE I TAUGHT HER. INCLUDING THE UNDERGROUND.
A BEDTIME STORY TO CALM HER AFTER A DAY OF TRAINING, A SUCCESSFUL MISSION.
YOU MEAN AFTER I KILLED SOME SEQUEL.
PRECISELY. BUT YOU ALWAYS BELIEVED TOO MUCH. TURNED IT INTO ONE OF YOUR NEBULOUS FACTS.
LIKE HOW HOME WAS THE SAFEST PLACE OF ALL. YOU HAVE YOUR PRETENSES FOR COMING HERE, BUT I DRILLED IT INTO YOU AS A CHILD.
REMEMBER? "HOME IS THE ONLY PLACE YOU ARE TRULY SAFE."
WE'RE GOING TO DIE. TESSA IS GOING TO DIE. FOR NOTHING.
NOT FOR NOTHING. FOR THE WAR. IT MIGHT BE THE OLDEST TRADITION HUMANITY HAS, EVEN IF YOU'VE ALL FORGOTTEN WHY IT BEGAN.
PLEASE. LOOK AT ME. AT YOUR DAUGHTER. TELL US SOMETHING TO HELP US. ANYTHING.
WE TELL YOU EVERY TIME. THE WAR BEGAN BECAUSE OF TWO SOLDIERS. YOU TWO SOLDIERS.
BULL--
WHICH IS WHY YOU CAN NEVER ESCAPE. THEY'LL FIND YOU, MAKE YOU PAY, ALONG WITH ALL THE OTHER SOLDIERS IN THIS WAR. ALL DYING AND BORN AGAIN BECAUSE OF YOU.
SSSSSSSS
MOTHER, ALL THOSE YEARS YOU TRAINED ME? YOU KNOW WHO I DREAMED OF KILLING? IT WASN'T MALI. IT WAS YOU.
THEN I HOPE YOU BROUGHT MORE THAN YOURSELVES.
GOOD NIGHT.

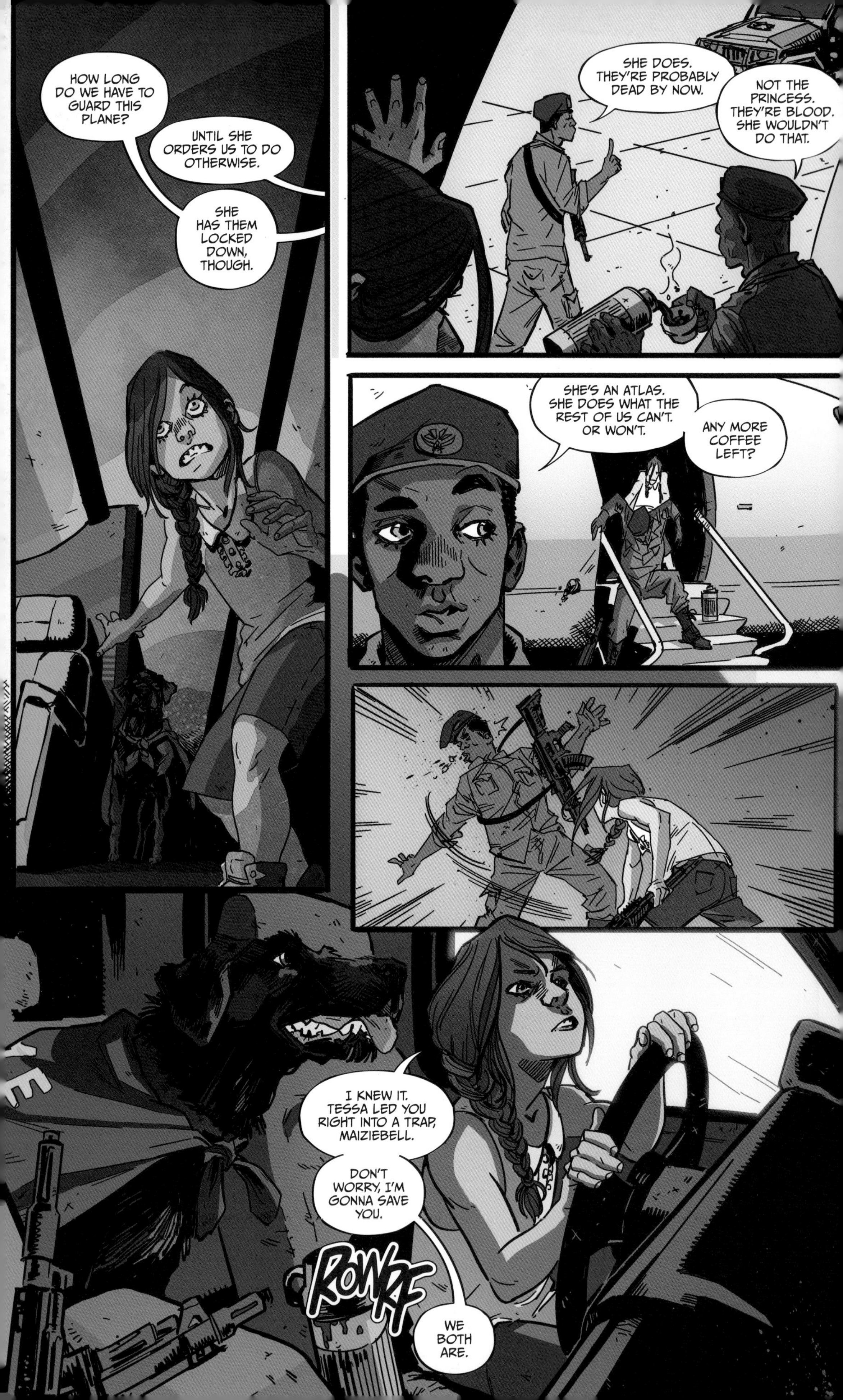
HOW LONG DO WE HAVE TO GUARD THIS PLANE?
UNTIL SHE ORDERS US TO DO OTHERWISE.
SHE HAS THEM LOCKED DOWN, THOUGH.
SHE DOES. THEY'RE PROBABLY DEAD BY NOW.
NOT THE PRINCESS. THEY'RE BLOOD. SHE WOULDN'T DO THAT.
SHE'S AN ATLAS. SHE DOES WHAT THE REST OF US CAN'T. OR WON'T.
ANY MORE COFFEE LEFT?
I KNEW IT. TESSA LED YOU RIGHT INTO A TRAP, MAIZIEBELL.
DON'T WORRY, I'M GONNA SAVE YOU.
ROWR
WE BOTH ARE.

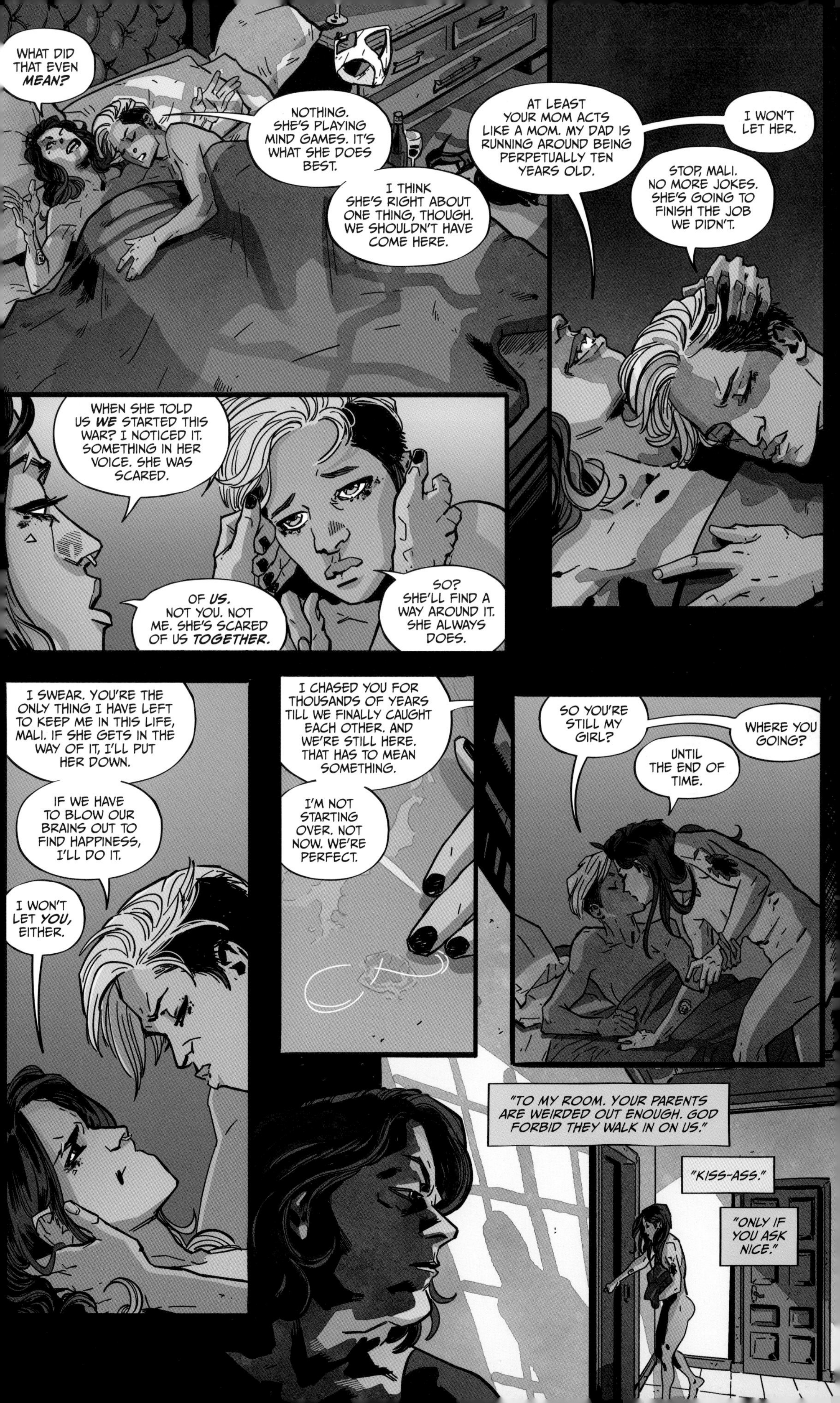

WHAT DID THAT EVEN *MEAN?*
NOTHING. SHE'S PLAYING MIND GAMES. IT'S WHAT SHE DOES BEST.
I THINK SHE'S RIGHT ABOUT ONE THING, THOUGH. WE SHOULDN'T HAVE COME HERE.
AT LEAST YOUR MOM ACTS LIKE A MOM. MY DAD IS RUNNING AROUND BEING PERPETUALLY TEN YEARS OLD.
I WON'T LET HER.
STOP, MALI. NO MORE JOKES. SHE'S GOING TO FINISH THE JOB WE DIDN'T.
WHEN SHE TOLD US *WE* STARTED THIS WAR? I NOTICED IT. SOMETHING IN HER VOICE. SHE WAS SCARED.
OF *US.* NOT YOU. NOT ME. SHE'S SCARED OF US *TOGETHER.*
SO? SHE'LL FIND A WAY AROUND IT. SHE ALWAYS DOES.
I SWEAR. YOU'RE THE ONLY THING I HAVE LEFT TO KEEP ME IN THIS LIFE, MALI. IF SHE GETS IN THE WAY OF IT, I'LL PUT HER DOWN.
IF WE HAVE TO BLOW OUR BRAINS OUT TO FIND HAPPINESS, I'LL DO IT.
I WON'T LET *YOU,* EITHER.
I CHASED YOU FOR THOUSANDS OF YEARS TILL WE FINALLY CAUGHT EACH OTHER. AND WE'RE STILL HERE. THAT HAS TO MEAN SOMETHING.
I'M NOT STARTING OVER. NOT NOW. WE'RE PERFECT.
SO YOU'RE STILL MY GIRL?
UNTIL THE END OF TIME.
WHERE YOU GOING?
"TO MY ROOM. YOUR PARENTS ARE WEIRDED OUT ENOUGH. GOD FORBID THEY WALK IN ON US."
"KISS-ASS."
"ONLY IF YOU ASK NICE."

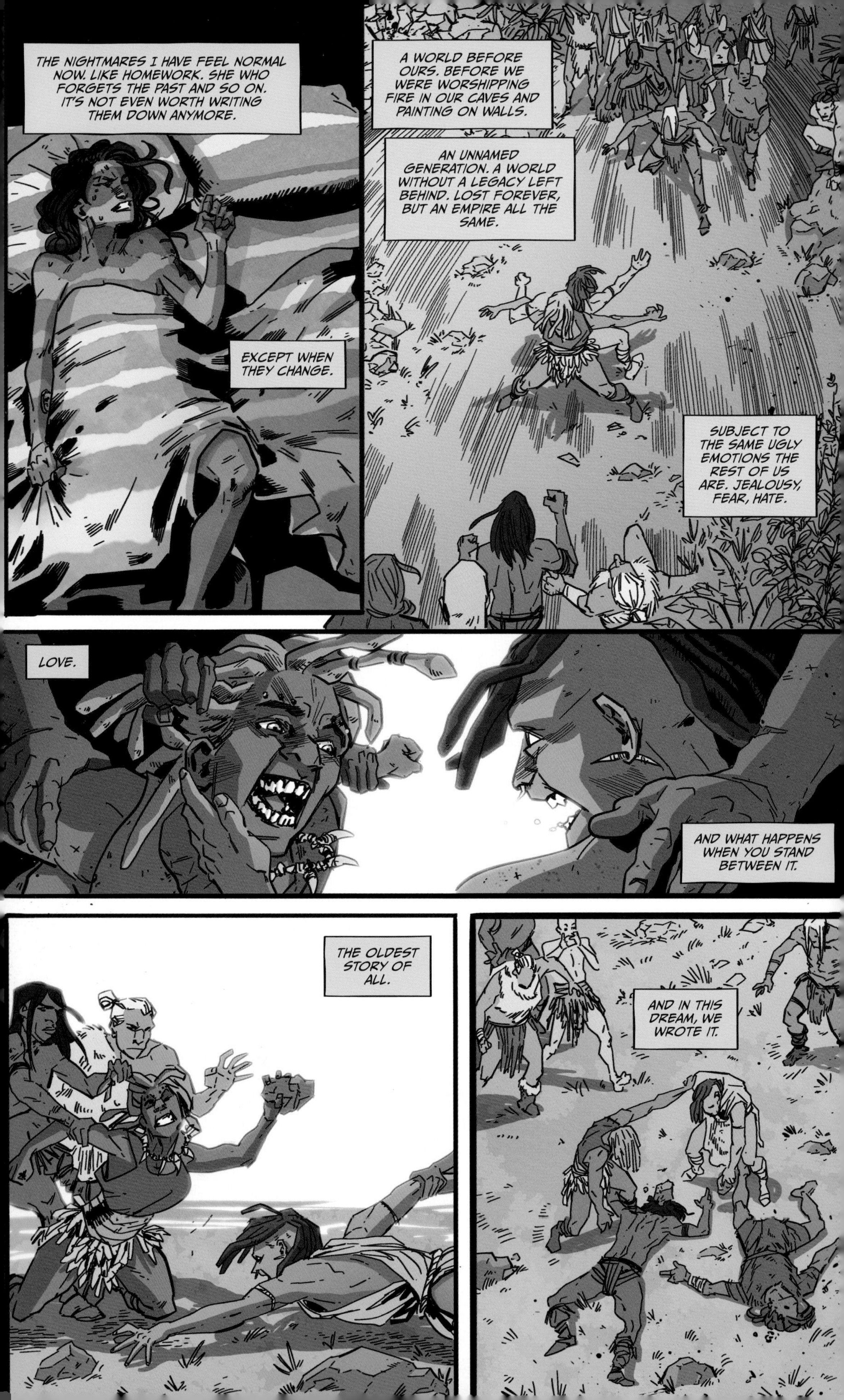
THE NIGHTMARES I HAVE FEEL NORMAL NOW. LIKE HOMEWORK. SHE WHO FORGETS THE PAST AND SO ON. IT'S NOT EVEN WORTH WRITING THEM DOWN ANYMORE.
EXCEPT WHEN THEY CHANGE.
A WORLD BEFORE OURS. BEFORE WE WERE WORSHIPPING FIRE IN OUR CAVES AND PAINTING ON WALLS.
AN UNNAMED GENERATION. A WORLD WITHOUT A LEGACY LEFT BEHIND. LOST FOREVER, BUT AN EMPIRE ALL THE SAME.
SUBJECT TO THE SAME UGLY EMOTIONS THE REST OF US ARE. JEALOUSY, FEAR, HATE.
LOVE.
AND WHAT HAPPENS WHEN YOU STAND BETWEEN IT.
THE OLDEST STORY OF ALL.
AND IN THIS DREAM, WE WROTE IT.

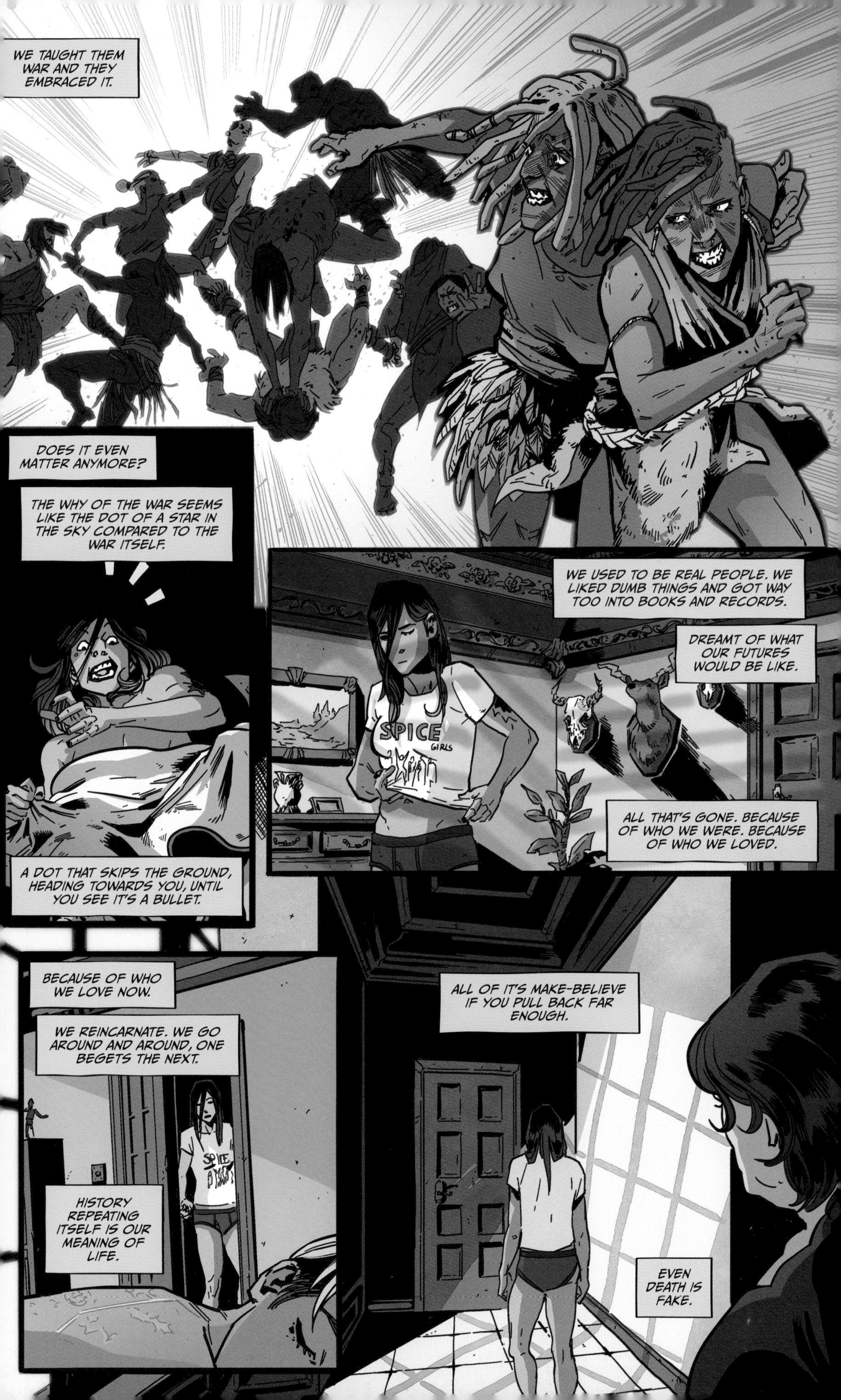
WE TAUGHT THEM WAR AND THEY EMBRACED IT.
DOES IT EVEN MATTER ANYMORE?
THE WHY OF THE WAR SEEMS LIKE THE DOT OF A STAR IN THE SKY COMPARED TO THE WAR ITSELF.
A DOT THAT SKIPS THE GROUND, HEADING TOWARDS YOU, UNTIL YOU SEE IT'S A BULLET.
WE USED TO BE REAL PEOPLE. WE LIKED DUMB THINGS AND GOT WAY TOO INTO BOOKS AND RECORDS.
DREAMT OF WHAT OUR FUTURES WOULD BE LIKE.
SPICE GIRLS
ALL THAT'S GONE. BECAUSE OF WHO WE WERE. BECAUSE OF WHO WE LOVED.
BECAUSE OF WHO WE LOVE NOW.
WE REINCARNATE. WE GO AROUND AND AROUND, ONE BEGETS THE NEXT.
HISTORY REPEATING ITSELF IS OUR MEANING OF LIFE.
ALL OF IT'S MAKE-BELIEVE IF YOU PULL BACK FAR ENOUGH.
EVEN DEATH IS FAKE.

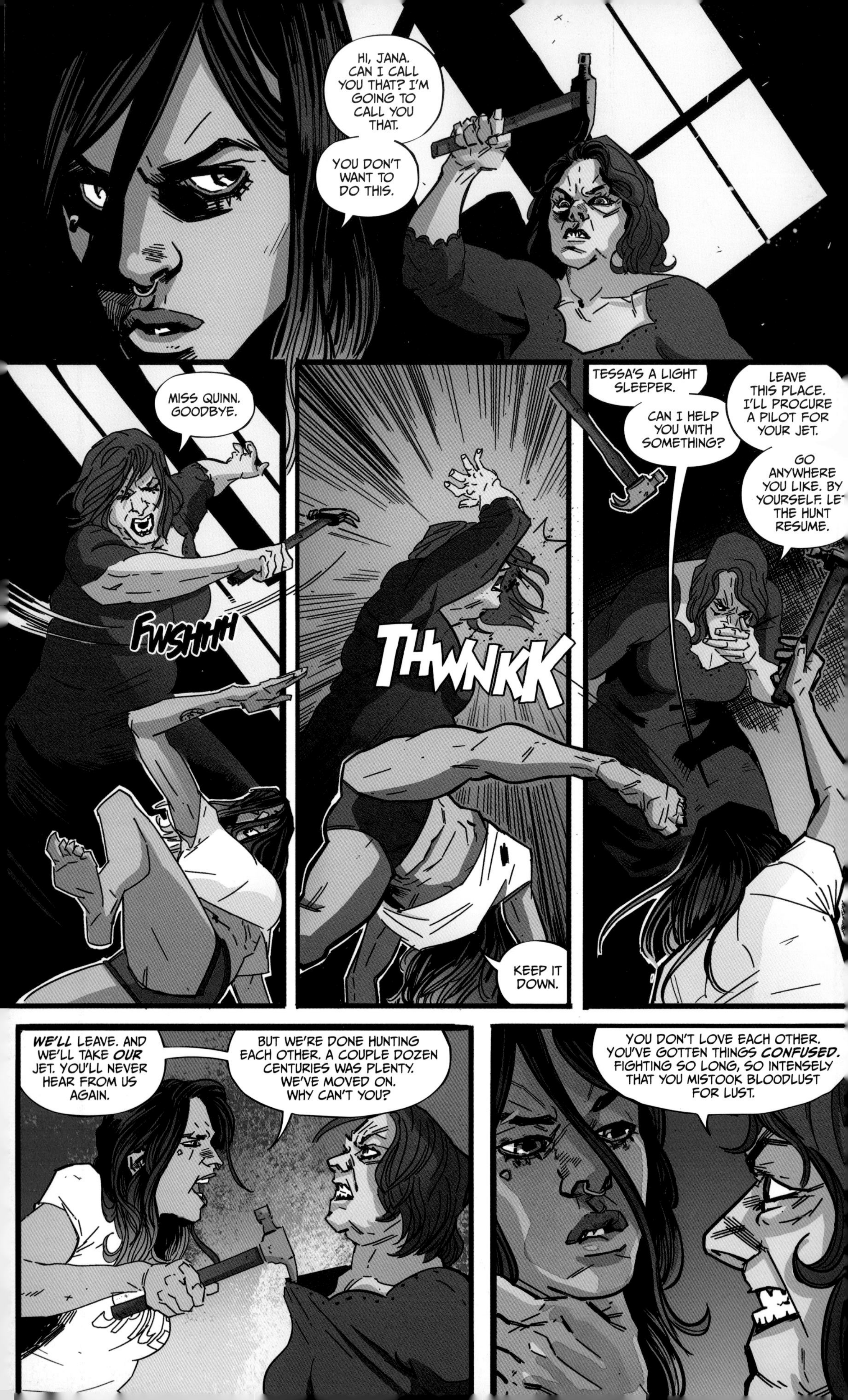

HI, JANA. CAN I CALL YOU THAT? I'M GOING TO CALL YOU THAT.
YOU DON'T WANT TO DO THIS.
MISS QUINN. GOODBYE.
FWSHHH
THWNKK
KEEP IT DOWN.
TESSA'S A LIGHT SLEEPER.
CAN I HELP YOU WITH SOMETHING?
LEAVE THIS PLACE. I'LL PROCURE A PILOT FOR YOUR JET.
GO ANYWHERE YOU LIKE. BY YOURSELF. LET THE HUNT RESUME.
WE'LL LEAVE. AND WE'LL TAKE OUR JET. YOU'LL NEVER HEAR FROM US AGAIN.
BUT WE'RE DONE HUNTING EACH OTHER. A COUPLE DOZEN CENTURIES WAS PLENTY. WE'VE MOVED ON. WHY CAN'T YOU?
YOU DON'T LOVE EACH OTHER. YOU'VE GOTTEN THINGS CONFUSED. FIGHTING SO LONG, SO INTENSELY THAT YOU MISTOOK BLOODLUST FOR LUST.

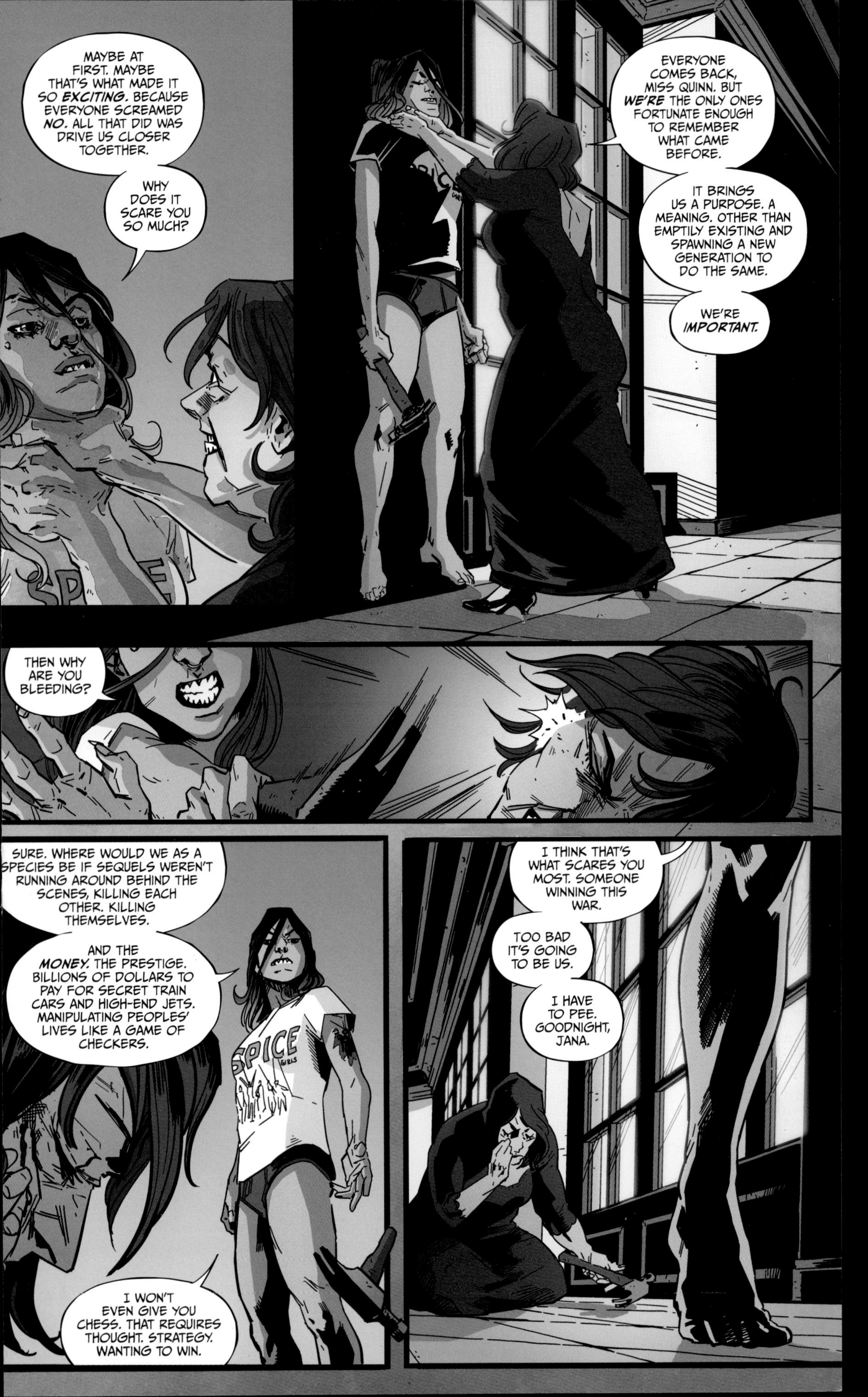
MAYBE AT FIRST. MAYBE THAT'S WHAT MADE IT SO EXCITING. BECAUSE EVERYONE SCREAMED NO. ALL THAT DID WAS DRIVE US CLOSER TOGETHER.
WHY DOES IT SCARE YOU SO MUCH?
EVERYONE COMES BACK, MISS QUINN. BUT WE'RE THE ONLY ONES FORTUNATE ENOUGH TO REMEMBER WHAT CAME BEFORE.
IT BRINGS US A PURPOSE. A MEANING. OTHER THAN EMPTILY EXISTING AND SPAWNING A NEW GENERATION TO DO THE SAME.
WE'RE IMPORTANT.
THEN WHY ARE YOU BLEEDING?
SURE. WHERE WOULD WE AS A SPECIES BE IF SEQUELS WEREN'T RUNNING AROUND BEHIND THE SCENES, KILLING EACH OTHER. KILLING THEMSELVES.
AND THE MONEY. THE PRESTIGE. BILLIONS OF DOLLARS TO PAY FOR SECRET TRAIN CARS AND HIGH-END JETS. MANIPULATING PEOPLES' LIVES LIKE A GAME OF CHECKERS.
I WON'T EVEN GIVE YOU CHESS. THAT REQUIRES THOUGHT. STRATEGY. WANTING TO WIN.
I THINK THAT'S WHAT SCARES YOU MOST. SOMEONE WINNING THIS WAR.
TOO BAD IT'S GOING TO BE US.
I HAVE TO PEE. GOODNIGHT, JANA.

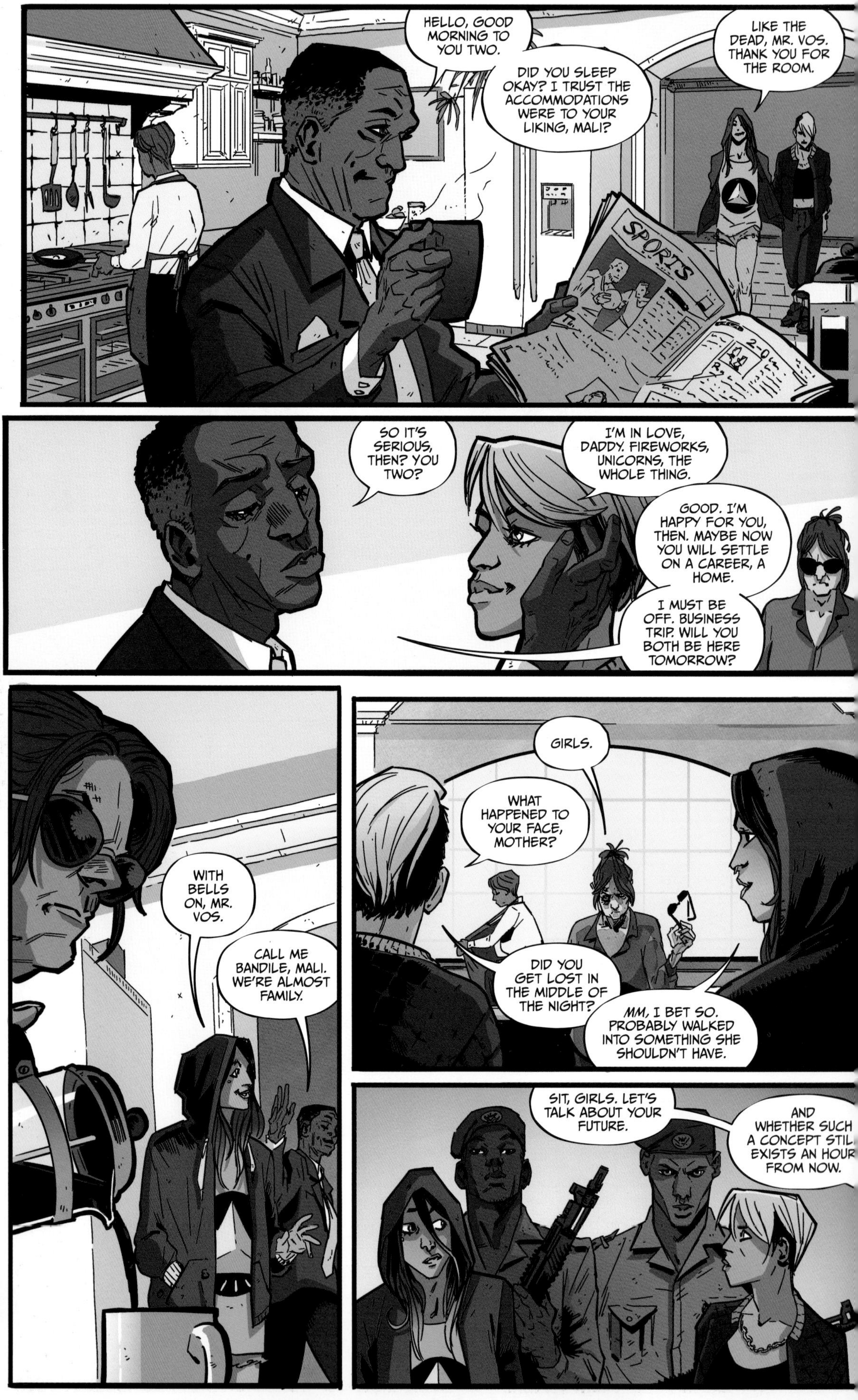
HELLO, GOOD MORNING TO YOU TWO.
DID YOU SLEEP OKAY? I TRUST THE ACCOMMODATIONS WERE TO YOUR LIKING, MALI?
LIKE THE DEAD, MR. VOS. THANK YOU FOR THE ROOM.
SPORTS
2-0
SO IT'S SERIOUS, THEN? YOU TWO?
I'M IN LOVE, DADDY. FIREWORKS, UNICORNS, THE WHOLE THING.
GOOD. I'M HAPPY FOR YOU, THEN. MAYBE NOW YOU WILL SETTLE ON A CAREER, A HOME.
I MUST BE OFF. BUSINESS TRIP. WILL YOU BOTH BE HERE TOMORROW?
WITH BELLS ON, MR. VOS.
CALL ME BANDILE, MALI. WE'RE ALMOST FAMILY.
GIRLS.
WHAT HAPPENED TO YOUR FACE, MOTHER?
DID YOU GET LOST IN THE MIDDLE OF THE NIGHT?
MM, I BET SO. PROBABLY WALKED INTO SOMETHING SHE SHOULDN'T HAVE.
SIT, GIRLS. LET'S TALK ABOUT YOUR FUTURE.
AND WHETHER SUCH A CONCEPT STIL EXISTS AN HOUR FROM NOW.

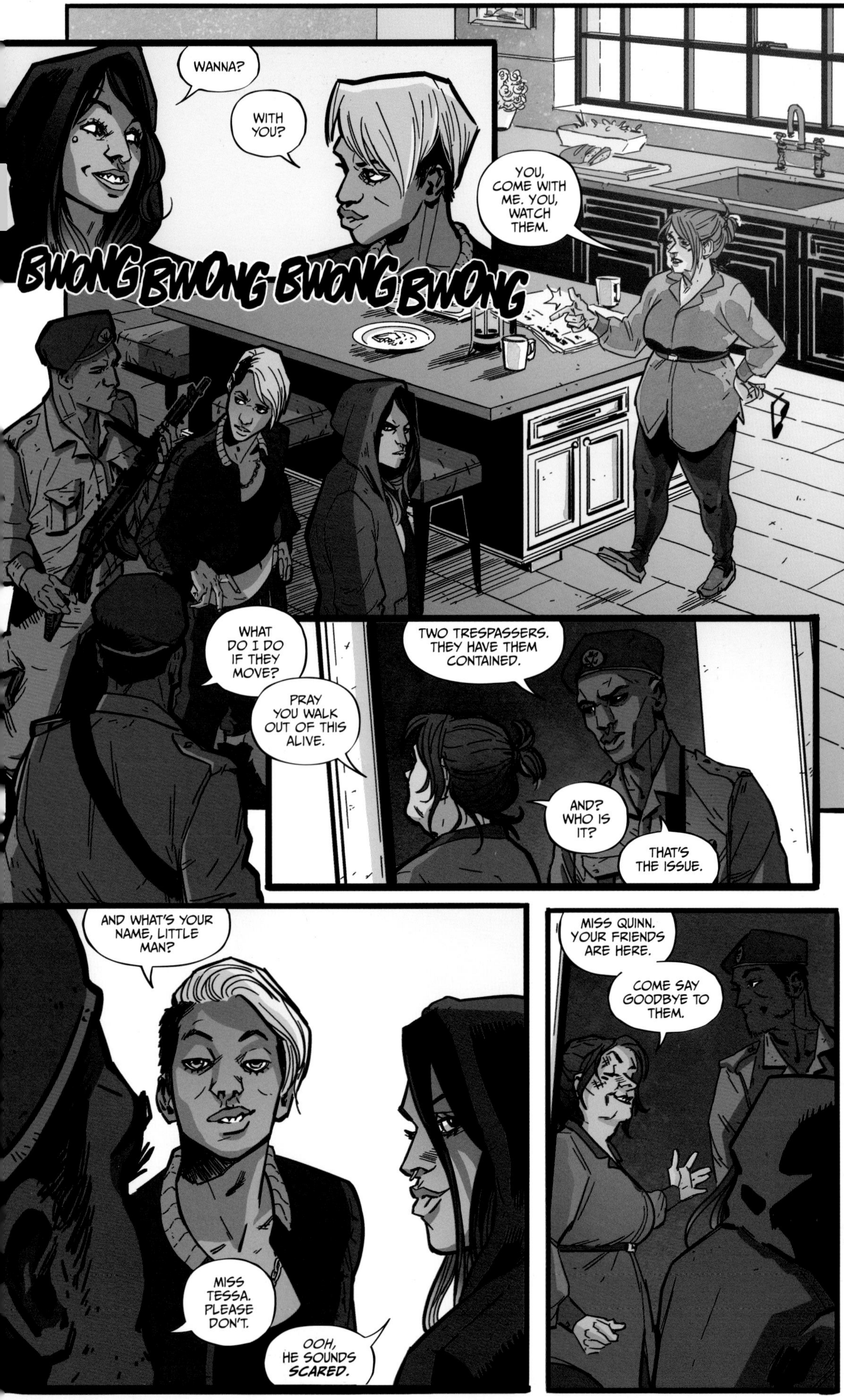

WANNA?
WITH YOU?
YOU, COME WITH ME. YOU, WATCH THEM.
BWONG BWONG BWONG BWONG
WHAT DO I DO IF THEY MOVE?
PRAY YOU WALK OUT OF THIS ALIVE.
TWO TRESPASSERS. THEY HAVE THEM CONTAINED.
AND? WHO IS IT?
THAT'S THE ISSUE.
AND WHAT'S YOUR NAME, LITTLE MAN?
MISS TESSA. PLEASE DON'T.
OOH, HE SOUNDS *SCARED.*
MISS QUINN. YOUR FRIENDS ARE HERE.
COME SAY GOODBYE TO THEM.

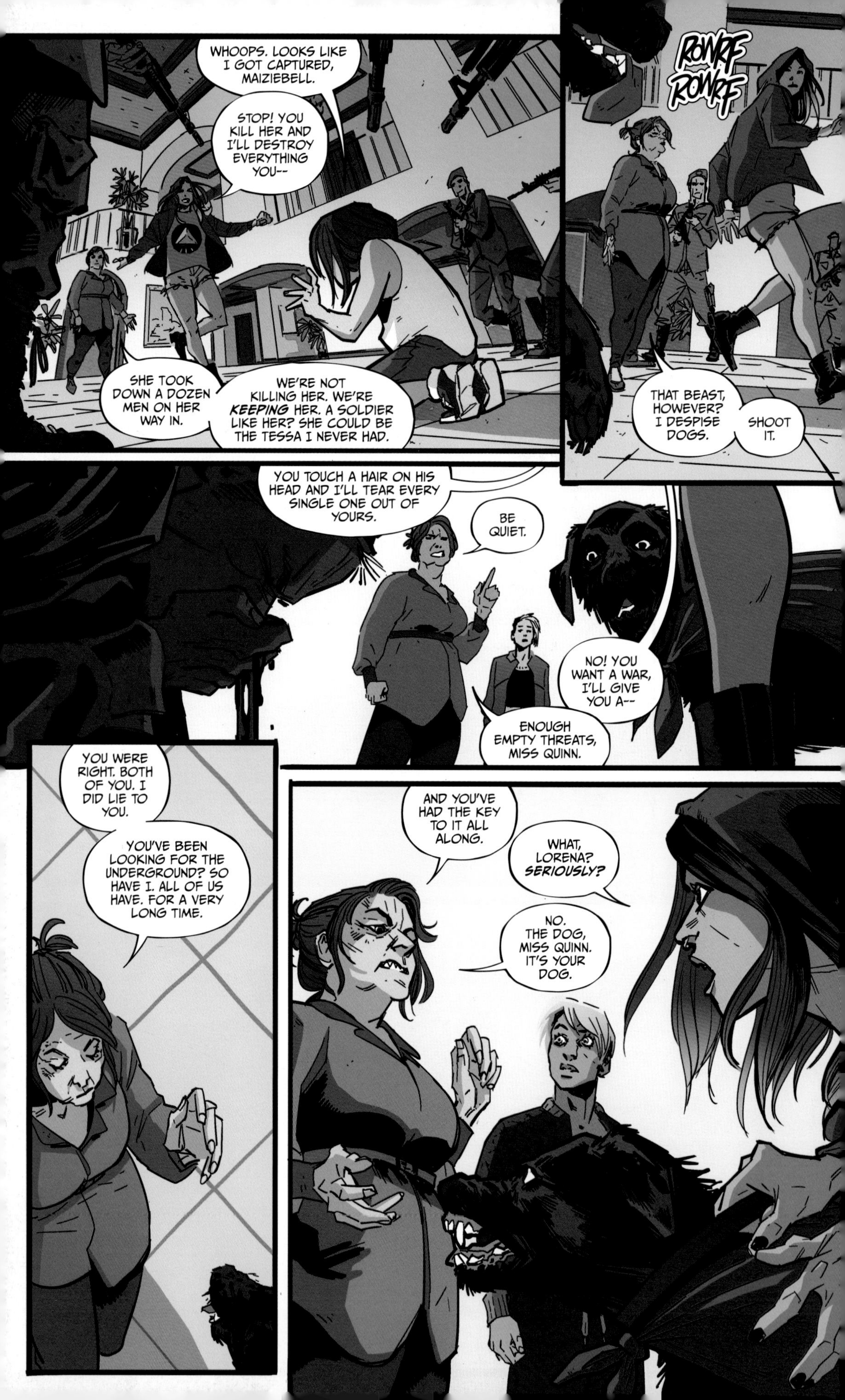
WHOOPS. LOOKS LIKE I GOT CAPTURED, MAIZIEBELL.
STOP! YOU KILL HER AND I'LL DESTROY EVERYTHING YOU--
SHE TOOK DOWN A DOZEN MEN ON HER WAY IN.
WE'RE NOT KILLING HER. WE'RE *KEEPING* HER. A SOLDIER LIKE HER? SHE COULD BE THE TESSA I NEVER HAD.
ROWRF ROWRF
THAT BEAST, HOWEVER? I DESPISE DOGS.
SHOOT IT.
YOU TOUCH A HAIR ON HIS HEAD AND I'LL TEAR EVERY SINGLE ONE OUT OF YOURS.
BE QUIET.
NO! YOU WANT A WAR, I'LL GIVE YOU A--
ENOUGH EMPTY THREATS, MISS QUINN.
YOU WERE RIGHT. BOTH OF YOU. I DID LIE TO YOU.
YOU'VE BEEN LOOKING FOR THE UNDERGROUND? SO HAVE I. ALL OF US HAVE. FOR A VERY LONG TIME.
AND YOU'VE HAD THE KEY TO IT ALL ALONG.
WHAT, LORENA? *SERIOUSLY?*
NO. THE DOG, MISS QUINN. IT'S YOUR DOG.

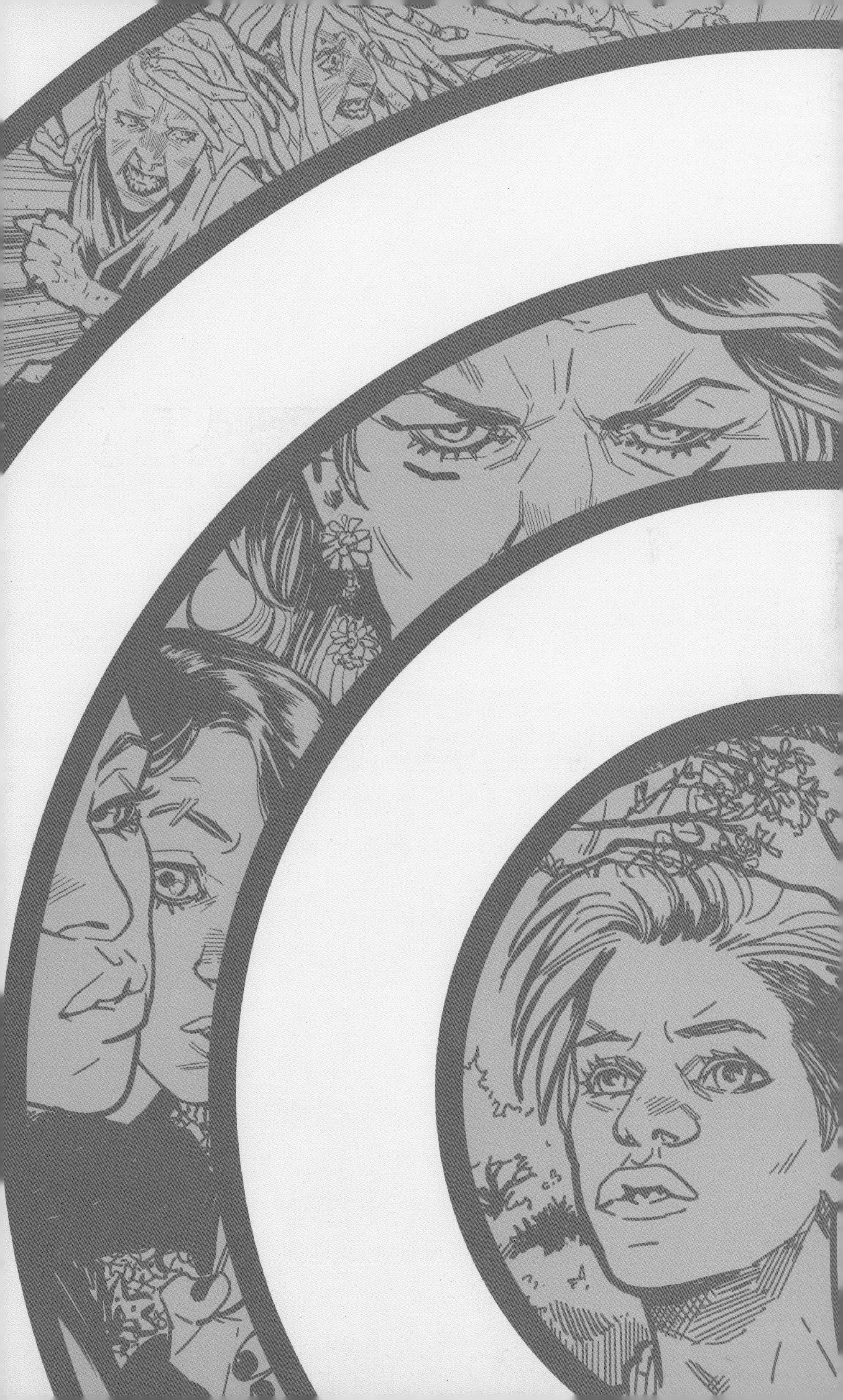

EIGHT
I KNOW PLACES

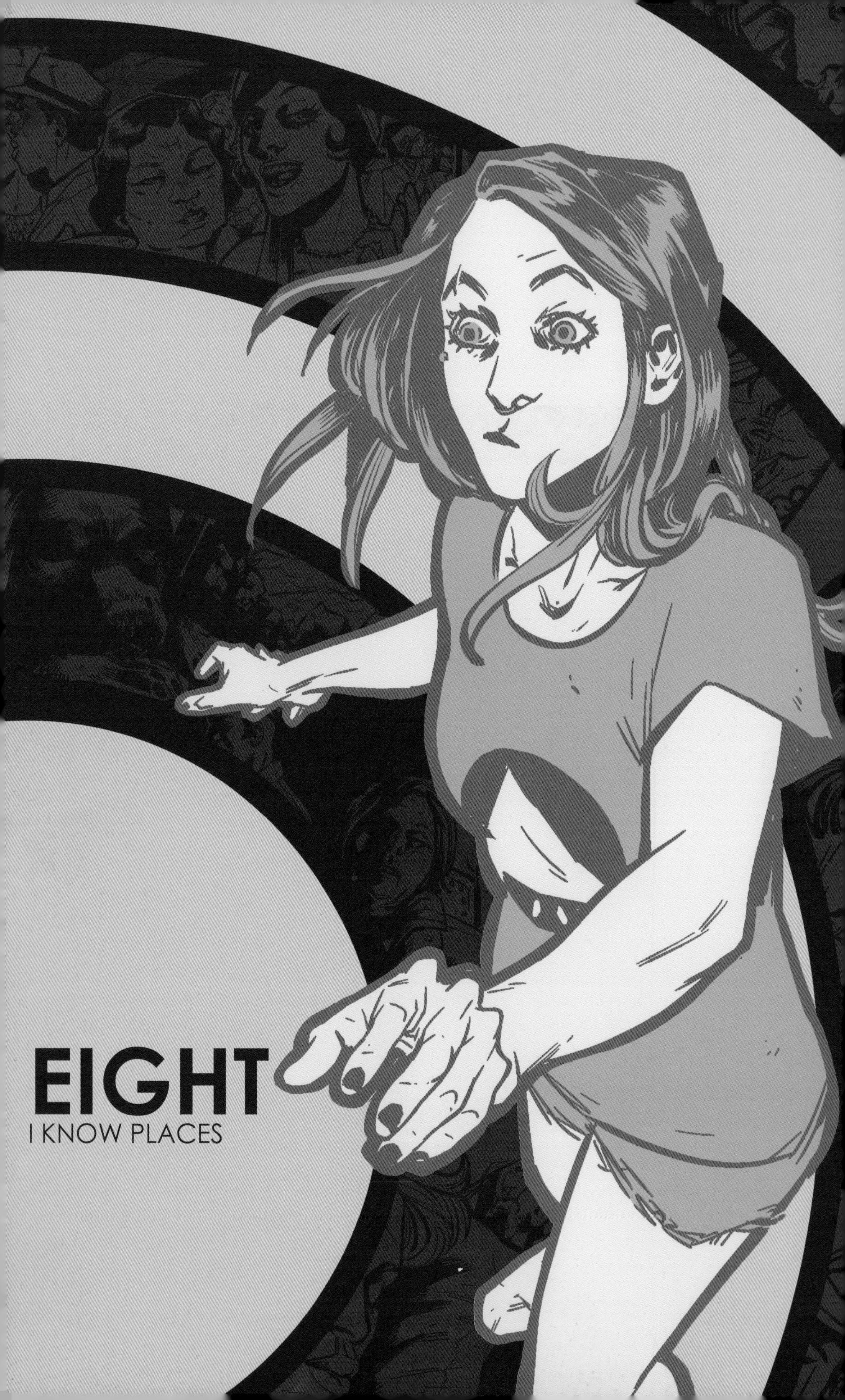

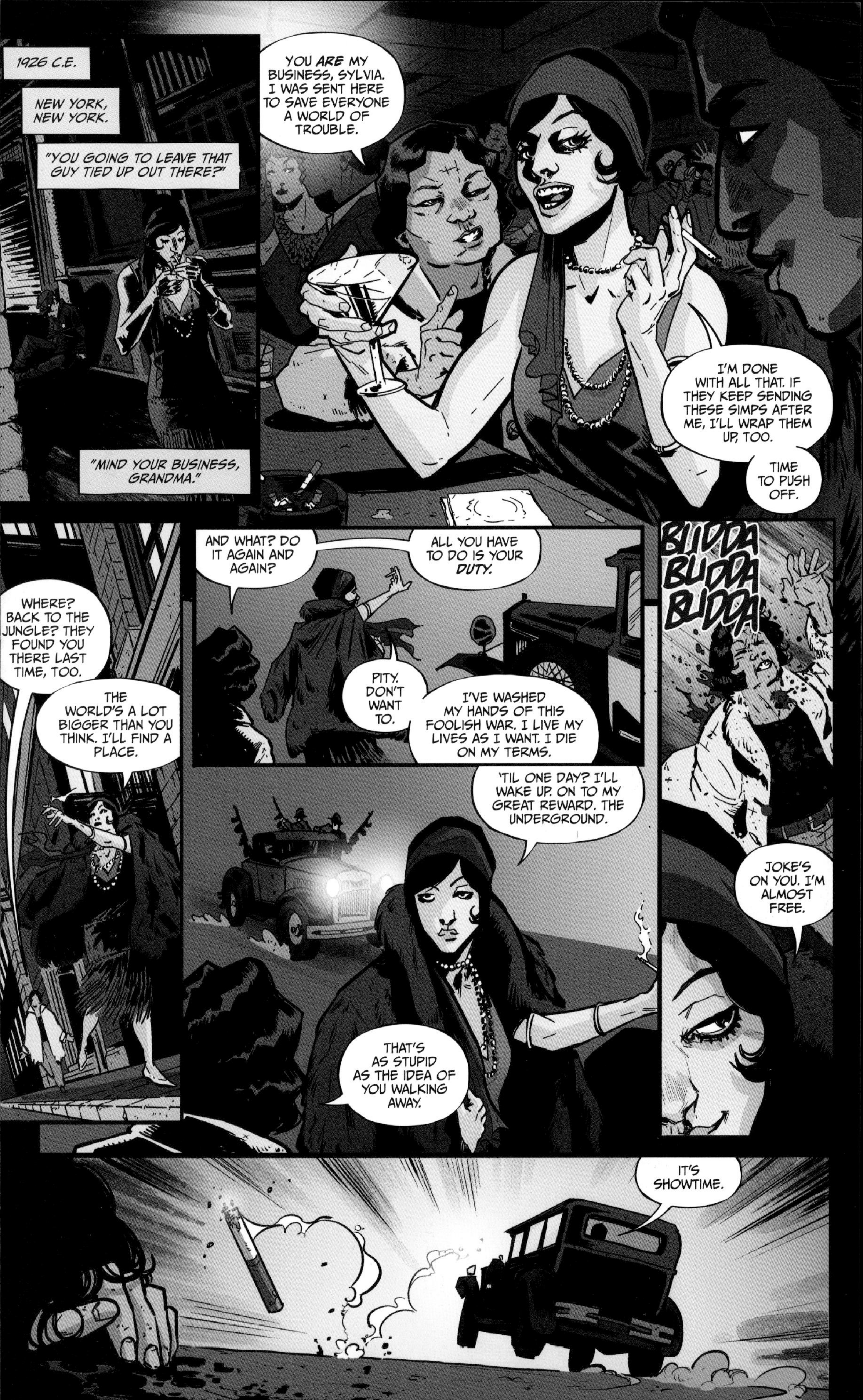
1926 C.E.
NEW YORK, NEW YORK.
"YOU GOING TO LEAVE THAT GUY TIED UP OUT THERE?"
"MIND YOUR BUSINESS, GRANDMA."
YOU ARE MY BUSINESS, SYLVIA. I WAS SENT HERE TO SAVE EVERYONE A WORLD OF TROUBLE.
I'M DONE WITH ALL THAT. IF THEY KEEP SENDING THESE SIMPS AFTER ME, I'LL WRAP THEM UP, TOO.
TIME TO PUSH OFF.
WHERE? BACK TO THE JUNGLE? THEY FOUND YOU THERE LAST TIME, TOO.
THE WORLD'S A LOT BIGGER THAN YOU THINK. I'LL FIND A PLACE.
AND WHAT? DO IT AGAIN AND AGAIN?
ALL YOU HAVE TO DO IS YOUR DUTY.
PITY. DON'T WANT TO.
I'VE WASHED MY HANDS OF THIS FOOLISH WAR. I LIVE MY LIVES AS I WANT. I DIE ON MY TERMS.
'TIL ONE DAY? I'LL WAKE UP. ON TO MY GREAT REWARD. THE UNDERGROUND.
THAT'S AS STUPID AS THE IDEA OF YOU WALKING AWAY.
BUDDA BUDDA BUDDA
JOKE'S ON YOU. I'M ALMOST FREE.
IT'S SHOWTIME.

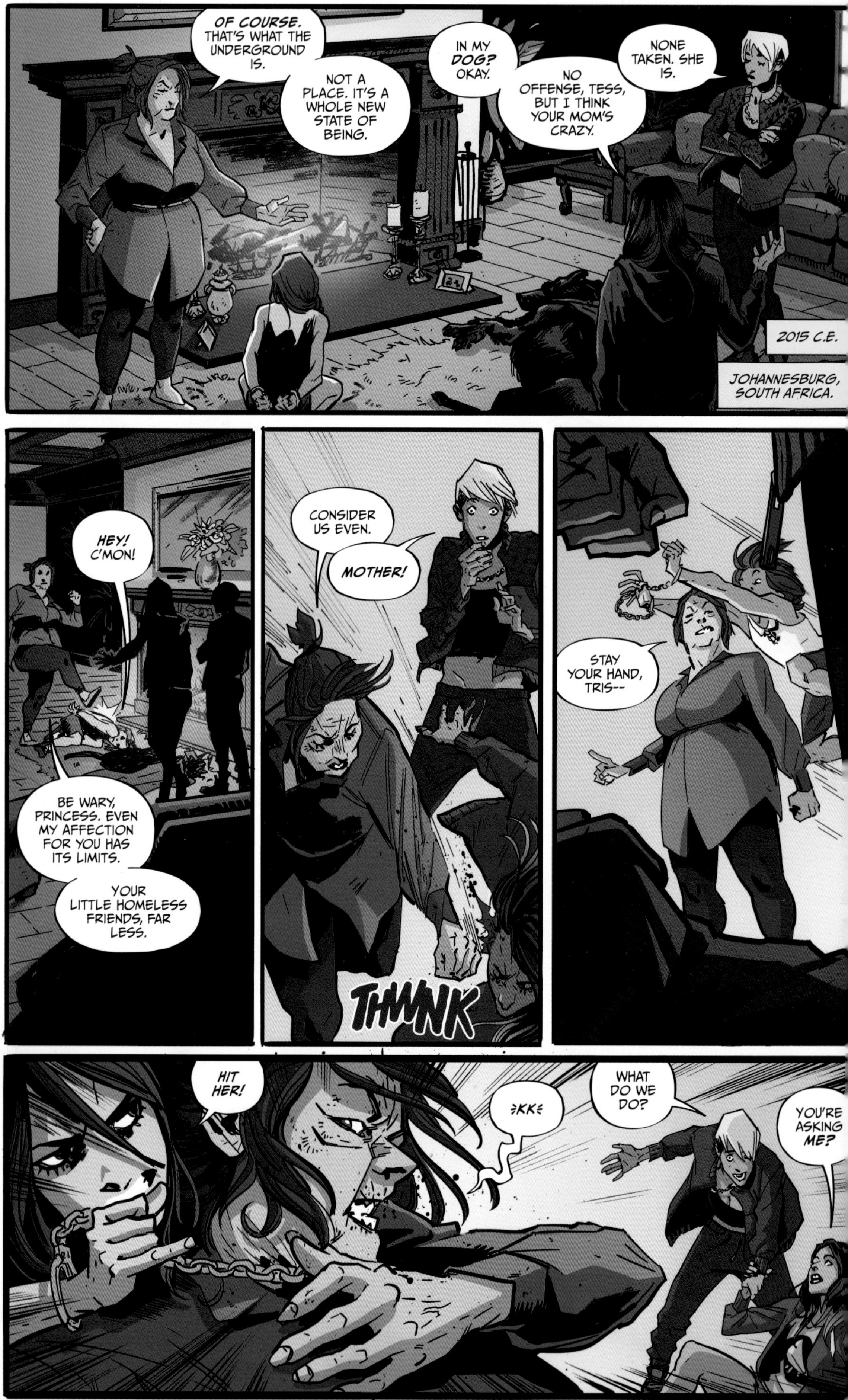
OF COURSE. THAT'S WHAT THE UNDERGROUND IS.
NOT A PLACE. IT'S A WHOLE NEW STATE OF BEING.
IN MY DOG? OKAY.
NO OFFENSE, TESS, BUT I THINK YOUR MOM'S CRAZY.
NONE TAKEN. SHE IS.
2015 C.E.
JOHANNESBURG, SOUTH AFRICA.
HEY! C'MON!
BE WARY, PRINCESS. EVEN MY AFFECTION FOR YOU HAS ITS LIMITS.
YOUR LITTLE HOMELESS FRIENDS, FAR LESS.
CONSIDER US EVEN.
MOTHER!
THWNK
STAY YOUR HAND, TRIS--
HIT HER!
KK
WHAT DO WE DO?
YOU'RE ASKING ME?

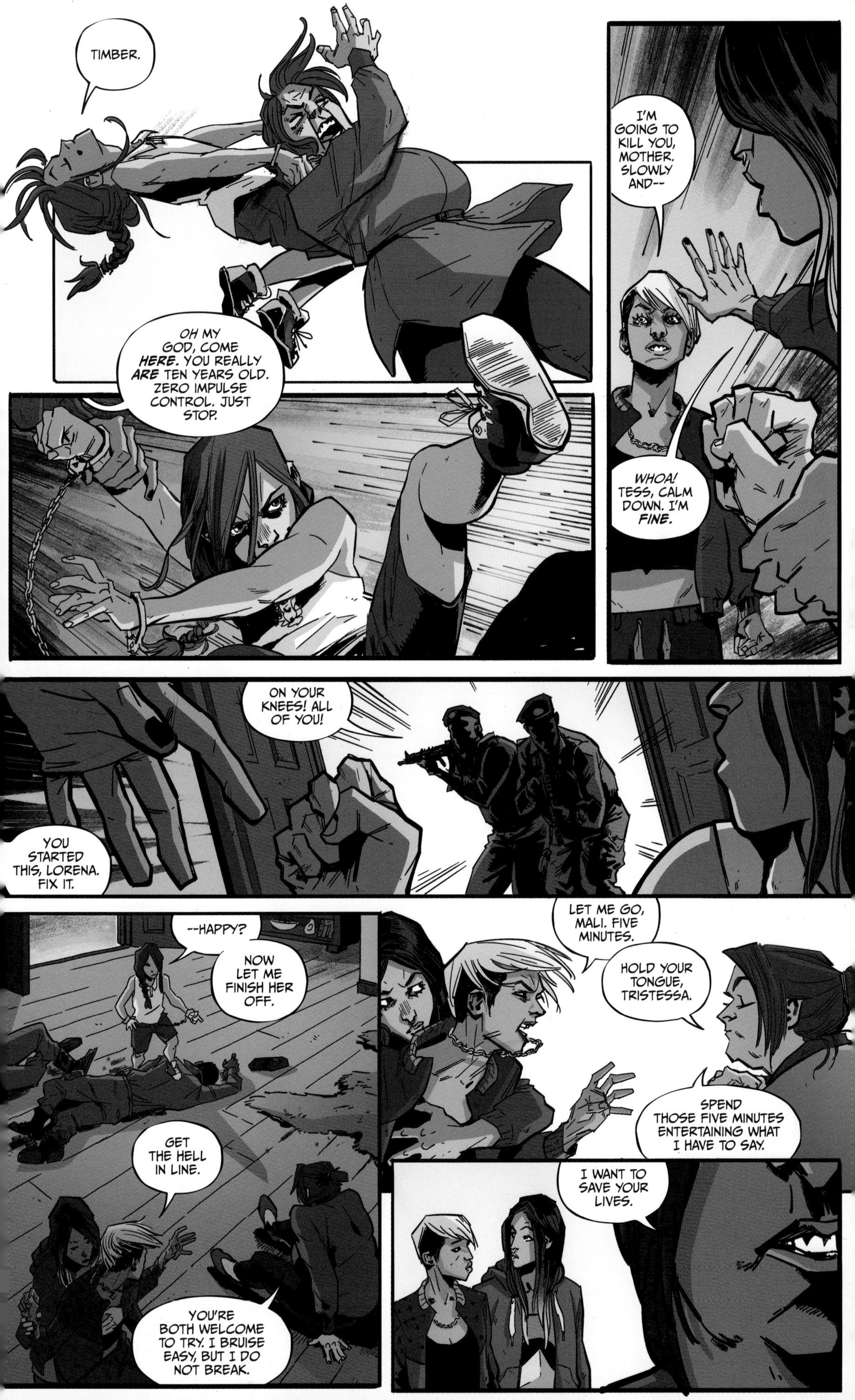
TIMBER.
I'M GOING TO KILL YOU, MOTHER. SLOWLY AND--
OH MY GOD, COME *HERE.* YOU REALLY *ARE* TEN YEARS OLD. ZERO IMPULSE CONTROL. JUST STOP.
WHOA! TESS, CALM DOWN. I'M *FINE.*
ON YOUR KNEES! ALL OF YOU!
YOU STARTED THIS, LORENA. FIX IT.
--HAPPY?
NOW LET ME FINISH HER OFF.
GET THE HELL IN LINE.
YOU'RE BOTH WELCOME TO TRY. I BRUISE EASY, BUT I DO NOT BREAK.
LET ME GO, MALI. FIVE MINUTES.
HOLD YOUR TONGUE, TRISTESSA.
SPEND THOSE FIVE MINUTES ENTERTAINING WHAT I HAVE TO SAY.
I WANT TO SAVE YOUR LIVES.

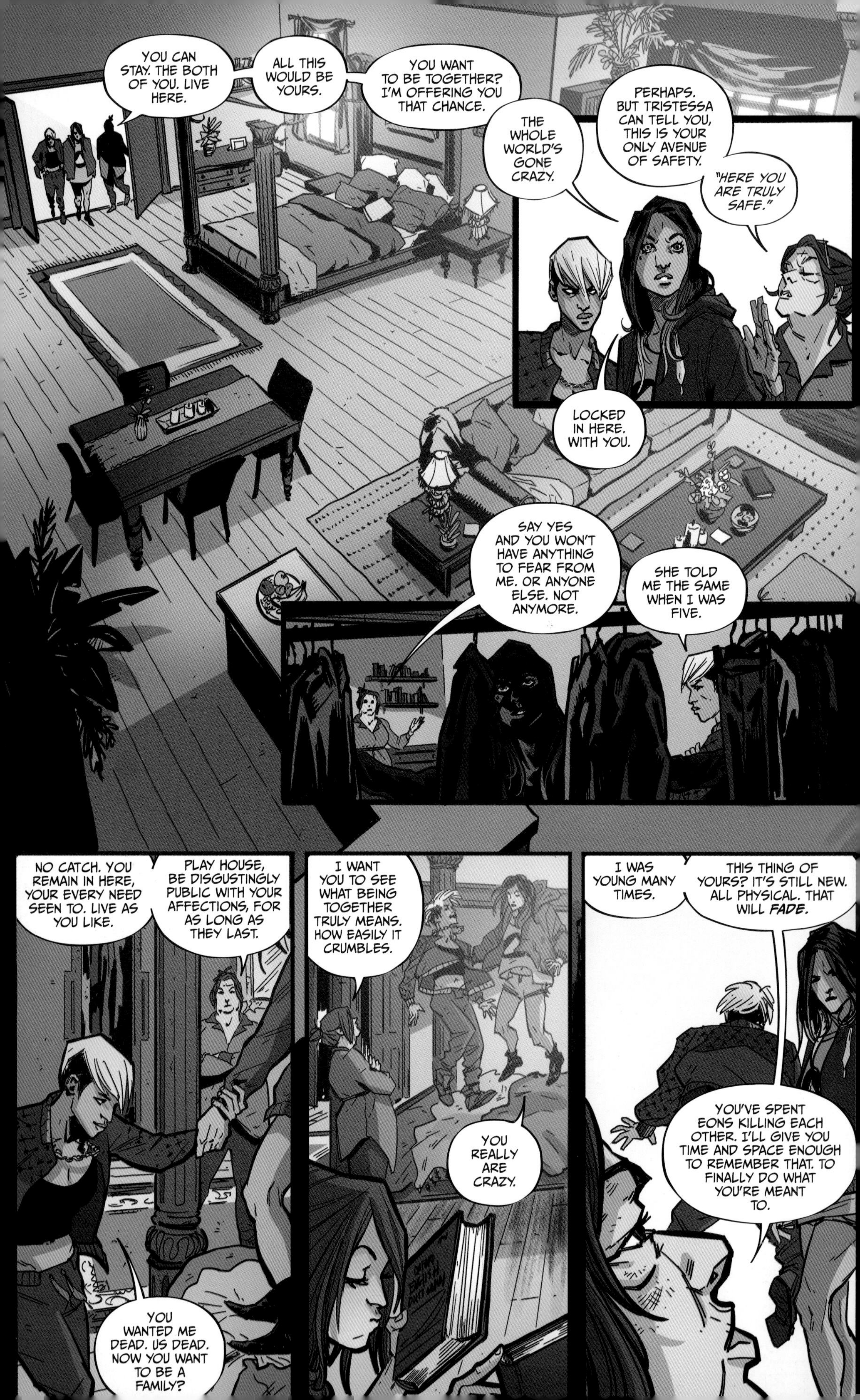
YOU CAN STAY. THE BOTH OF YOU. LIVE HERE.
ALL THIS WOULD BE YOURS.
YOU WANT TO BE TOGETHER? I'M OFFERING YOU THAT CHANCE.
THE WHOLE WORLD'S GONE CRAZY.
PERHAPS. BUT TRISTESSA CAN TELL YOU, THIS IS YOUR ONLY AVENUE OF SAFETY.
"HERE YOU ARE TRULY SAFE."
LOCKED IN HERE. WITH YOU.
SAY YES AND YOU WON'T HAVE ANYTHING TO FEAR FROM ME. OR ANYONE ELSE. NOT ANYMORE.
SHE TOLD ME THE SAME WHEN I WAS FIVE.
NO CATCH. YOU REMAIN IN HERE, YOUR EVERY NEED SEEN TO. LIVE AS YOU LIKE.
PLAY HOUSE, BE DISGUSTINGLY PUBLIC WITH YOUR AFFECTIONS, FOR AS LONG AS THEY LAST.
YOU WANTED ME DEAD. US DEAD. NOW YOU WANT TO BE A FAMILY?
I WANT YOU TO SEE WHAT BEING TOGETHER TRULY MEANS. HOW EASILY IT CRUMBLES.
YOU REALLY ARE CRAZY.
I WAS YOUNG MANY TIMES.
THIS THING OF YOURS? IT'S STILL NEW. ALL PHYSICAL. THAT WILL *FADE.*
YOU'VE SPENT EONS KILLING EACH OTHER. I'LL GIVE YOU TIME AND SPACE ENOUGH TO REMEMBER THAT. TO FINALLY DO WHAT YOU'RE MEANT TO.

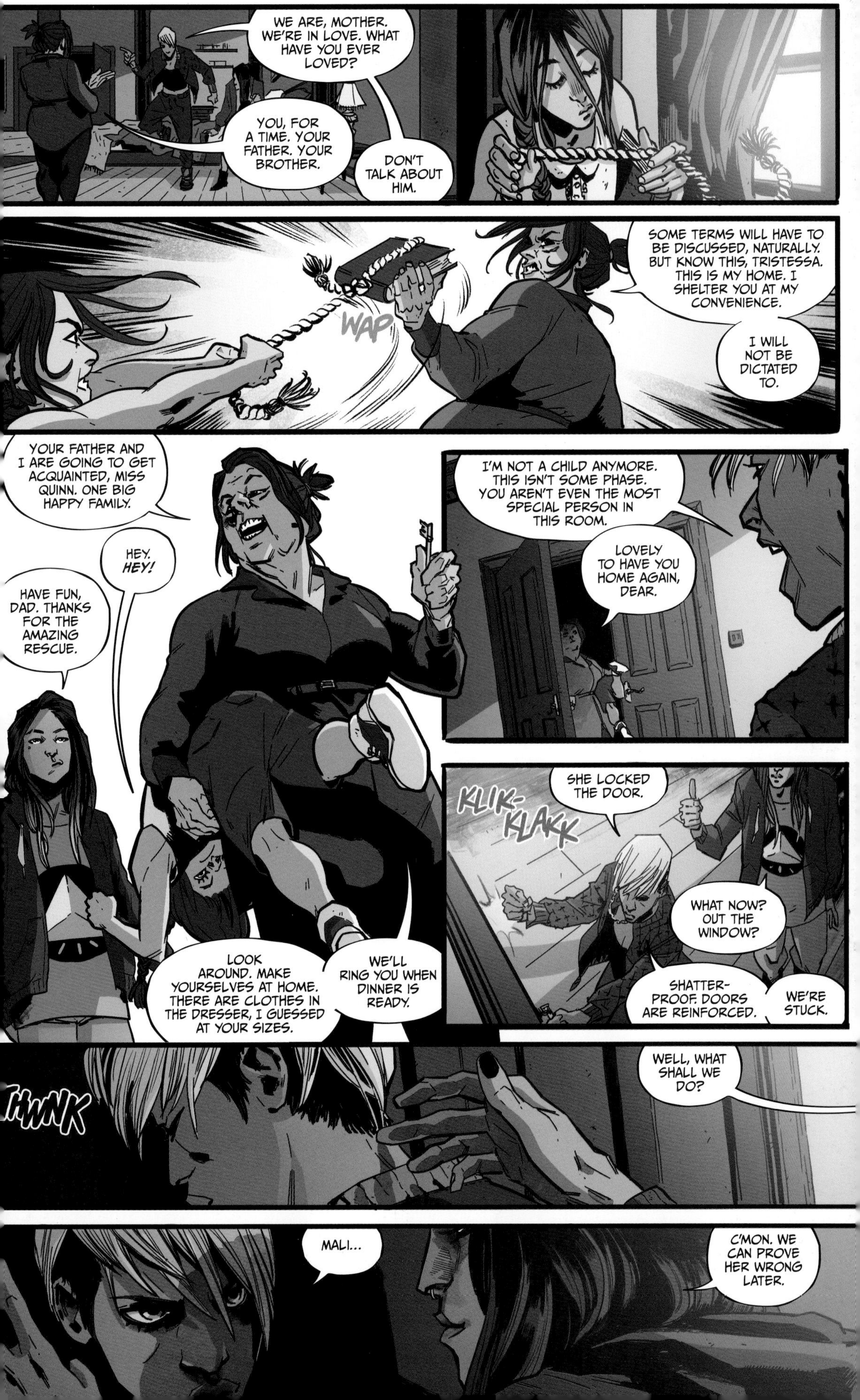
WE ARE, MOTHER. WE'RE IN LOVE. WHAT HAVE YOU EVER LOVED?
YOU, FOR A TIME. YOUR FATHER. YOUR BROTHER.
DON'T TALK ABOUT HIM.
WAP
SOME TERMS WILL HAVE TO BE DISCUSSED, NATURALLY. BUT KNOW THIS, TRISTESSA. THIS IS MY HOME. I SHELTER YOU AT MY CONVENIENCE.
I WILL NOT BE DICTATED TO.
YOUR FATHER AND I ARE GOING TO GET ACQUAINTED, MISS QUINN. ONE BIG HAPPY FAMILY.
HEY. HEY!
HAVE FUN, DAD. THANKS FOR THE AMAZING RESCUE.
LOOK AROUND. MAKE YOURSELVES AT HOME. THERE ARE CLOTHES IN THE DRESSER, I GUESSED AT YOUR SIZES.
WE'LL RING YOU WHEN DINNER IS READY.
I'M NOT A CHILD ANYMORE. THIS ISN'T SOME PHASE. YOU AREN'T EVEN THE MOST SPECIAL PERSON IN THIS ROOM.
LOVELY TO HAVE YOU HOME AGAIN, DEAR.
KLIK-KLAKK
SHE LOCKED THE DOOR.
WHAT NOW? OUT THE WINDOW?
SHATTER-PROOF. DOORS ARE REINFORCED.
WE'RE STUCK.
THWNK
WELL, WHAT SHALL WE DO?
MALI...
C'MON. WE CAN PROVE HER WRONG LATER.

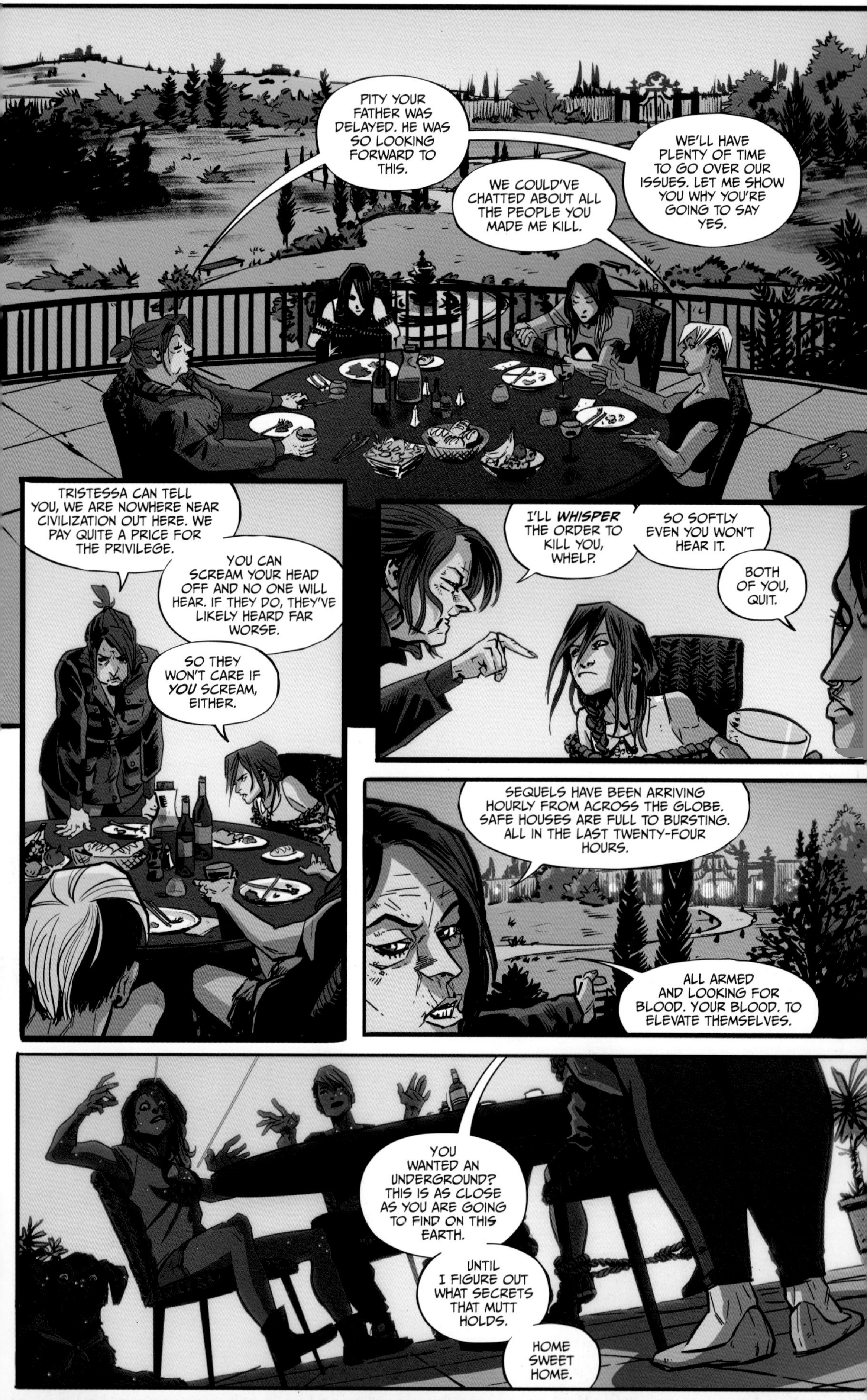
PITY YOUR FATHER WAS DELAYED. HE WAS SO LOOKING FORWARD TO THIS.
WE COULD'VE CHATTED ABOUT ALL THE PEOPLE YOU MADE ME KILL.
WE'LL HAVE PLENTY OF TIME TO GO OVER OUR ISSUES. LET ME SHOW YOU WHY YOU'RE GOING TO SAY YES.
TRISTESSA CAN TELL YOU, WE ARE NOWHERE NEAR CIVILIZATION OUT HERE. WE PAY QUITE A PRICE FOR THE PRIVILEGE.
YOU CAN SCREAM YOUR HEAD OFF AND NO ONE WILL HEAR. IF THEY DO, THEY'VE LIKELY HEARD FAR WORSE.
SO THEY WON'T CARE IF *YOU* SCREAM, EITHER.
I'LL *WHISPER* THE ORDER TO KILL YOU, WHELP.
SO SOFTLY EVEN YOU WON'T HEAR IT.
BOTH OF YOU, QUIT.
SEQUELS HAVE BEEN ARRIVING HOURLY FROM ACROSS THE GLOBE. SAFE HOUSES ARE FULL TO BURSTING. ALL IN THE LAST TWENTY-FOUR HOURS.
ALL ARMED AND LOOKING FOR BLOOD. YOUR BLOOD. TO ELEVATE THEMSELVES.
YOU WANTED AN UNDERGROUND? THIS IS AS CLOSE AS YOU ARE GOING TO FIND ON THIS EARTH.
UNTIL I FIGURE OUT WHAT SECRETS THAT MUTT HOLDS.
HOME SWEET HOME.

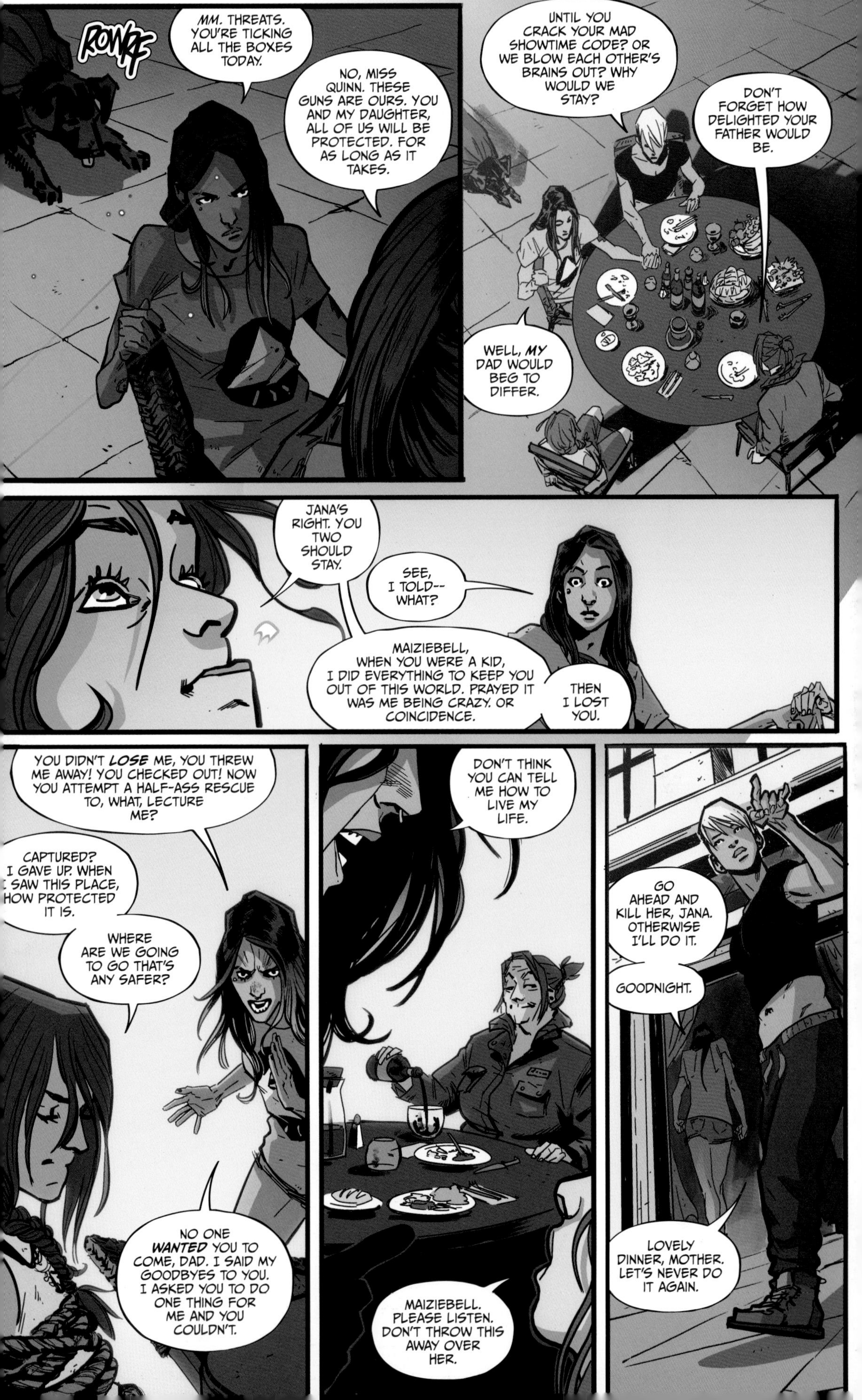
ROWF
MM. THREATS. YOU'RE TICKING ALL THE BOXES TODAY.
NO, MISS QUINN. THESE GUNS ARE OURS. YOU AND MY DAUGHTER, ALL OF US WILL BE PROTECTED. FOR AS LONG AS IT TAKES.
UNTIL YOU CRACK YOUR MAD SHOWTIME CODE? OR WE BLOW EACH OTHER'S BRAINS OUT? WHY WOULD WE STAY?
DON'T FORGET HOW DELIGHTED YOUR FATHER WOULD BE.
WELL, MY DAD WOULD BEG TO DIFFER.
JANA'S RIGHT. YOU TWO SHOULD STAY.
SEE, I TOLD-- WHAT?
MAIZIEBELL, WHEN YOU WERE A KID, I DID EVERYTHING TO KEEP YOU OUT OF THIS WORLD. PRAYED IT WAS ME BEING CRAZY. OR COINCIDENCE.
THEN I LOST YOU.
YOU DIDN'T LOSE ME, YOU THREW ME AWAY! YOU CHECKED OUT! NOW YOU ATTEMPT A HALF-ASS RESCUE TO, WHAT, LECTURE ME?
CAPTURED? I GAVE UP. WHEN I SAW THIS PLACE, HOW PROTECTED IT IS.
WHERE ARE WE GOING TO GO THAT'S ANY SAFER?
NO ONE WANTED YOU TO COME, DAD. I SAID MY GOODBYES TO YOU. I ASKED YOU TO DO ONE THING FOR ME AND YOU COULDN'T.
DON'T THINK YOU CAN TELL ME HOW TO LIVE MY LIFE.
MAIZIEBELL. PLEASE LISTEN. DON'T THROW THIS AWAY OVER HER.
GO AHEAD AND KILL HER, JANA. OTHERWISE I'LL DO IT.
GOODNIGHT.
LOVELY DINNER, MOTHER. LET'S NEVER DO IT AGAIN.

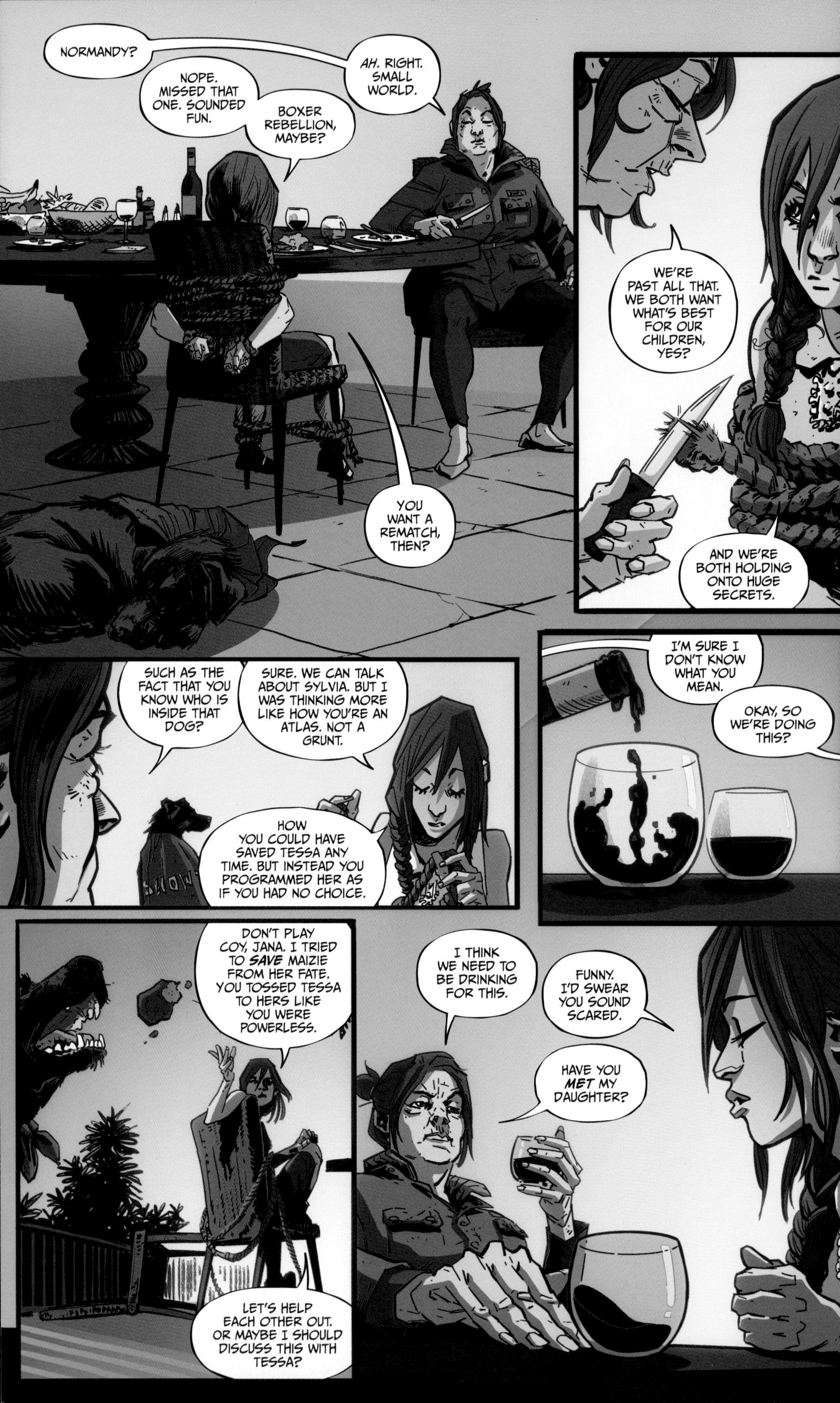

NORMANDY?
NOPE. MISSED THAT ONE. SOUNDED FUN.
BOXER REBELLION, MAYBE?
AH. RIGHT. SMALL WORLD.
YOU WANT A REMATCH, THEN?
WE'RE PAST ALL THAT. WE BOTH WANT WHAT'S BEST FOR OUR CHILDREN, YES?
AND WE'RE BOTH HOLDING ONTO HUGE SECRETS.
SUCH AS THE FACT THAT YOU KNOW WHO IS INSIDE THAT DOG?
SURE. WE CAN TALK ABOUT SYLVIA. BUT I WAS THINKING MORE LIKE HOW YOU'RE AN ATLAS. NOT A GRUNT.
HOW YOU COULD HAVE SAVED TESSA ANY TIME. BUT INSTEAD YOU PROGRAMMED HER AS IF YOU HAD NO CHOICE.
I'M SURE I DON'T KNOW WHAT YOU MEAN.
OKAY, SO WE'RE DOING THIS?
DON'T PLAY COY, JANA. I TRIED TO *SAVE* MAIZIE FROM HER FATE. YOU TOSSED TESSA TO HERS LIKE YOU WERE POWERLESS.
LET'S HELP EACH OTHER OUT. OR MAYBE I SHOULD DISCUSS THIS WITH TESSA?
I THINK WE NEED TO BE DRINKING FOR THIS.
FUNNY. I'D SWEAR YOU SOUND SCARED.
HAVE YOU *MET* MY DAUGHTER?

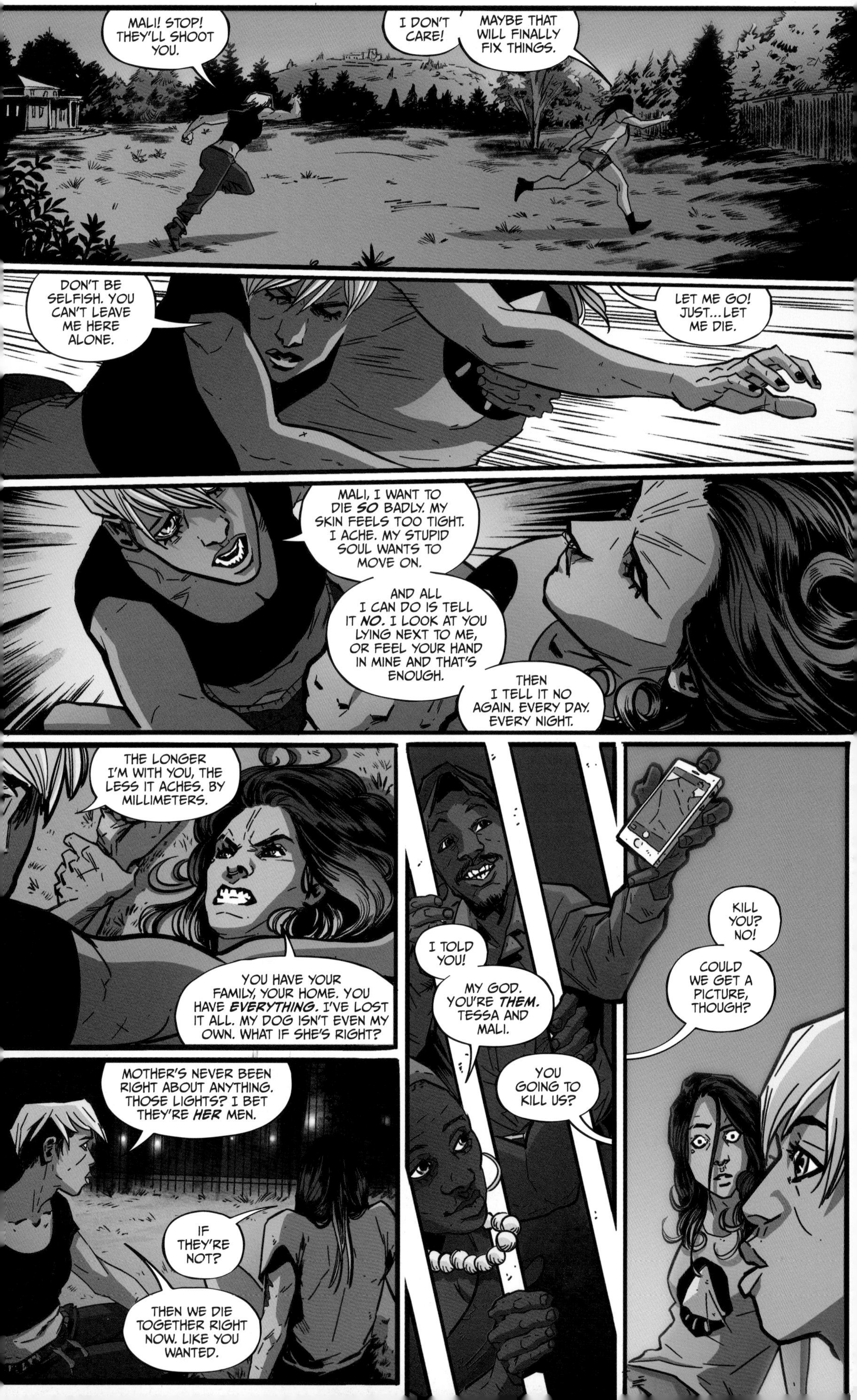
MALI! STOP! THEY'LL SHOOT YOU.
I DON'T CARE!
MAYBE THAT WILL FINALLY FIX THINGS.
DON'T BE SELFISH. YOU CAN'T LEAVE ME HERE ALONE.
LET ME GO! JUST... LET ME DIE.
MALI, I WANT TO DIE SO BADLY. MY SKIN FEELS TOO TIGHT. I ACHE. MY STUPID SOUL WANTS TO MOVE ON.
AND ALL I CAN DO IS TELL IT NO. I LOOK AT YOU LYING NEXT TO ME, OR FEEL YOUR HAND IN MINE AND THAT'S ENOUGH.
THEN I TELL IT NO AGAIN. EVERY DAY. EVERY NIGHT.
THE LONGER I'M WITH YOU, THE LESS IT ACHES. BY MILLIMETERS.
YOU HAVE YOUR FAMILY, YOUR HOME. YOU HAVE EVERYTHING. I'VE LOST IT ALL. MY DOG ISN'T EVEN MY OWN. WHAT IF SHE'S RIGHT?
MOTHER'S NEVER BEEN RIGHT ABOUT ANYTHING. THOSE LIGHTS? I BET THEY'RE HER MEN.
IF THEY'RE NOT?
THEN WE DIE TOGETHER RIGHT NOW. LIKE YOU WANTED.
I TOLD YOU!
MY GOD. YOU'RE THEM. TESSA AND MALI.
YOU GOING TO KILL US?
KILL YOU? NO!
COULD WE GET A PICTURE, THOUGH?

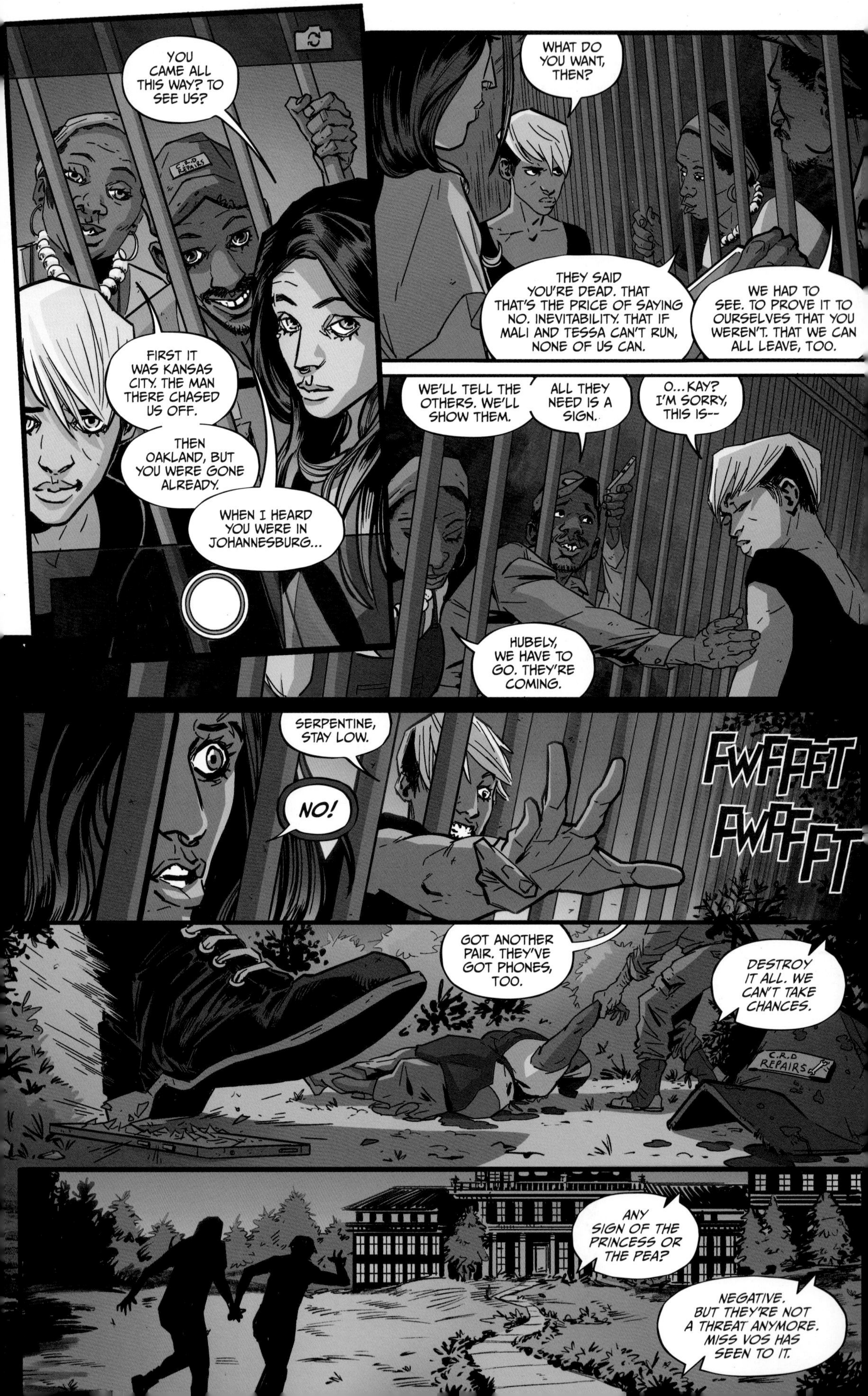

YOU CAME ALL THIS WAY? TO SEE US?
C.R.D REPAIRS
FIRST IT WAS KANSAS CITY. THE MAN THERE CHASED US OFF.
THEN OAKLAND, BUT YOU WERE GONE ALREADY.
WHEN I HEARD YOU WERE IN JOHANNESBURG...
WHAT DO YOU WANT, THEN?
THEY SAID YOU'RE DEAD. THAT THAT'S THE PRICE OF SAYING NO. INEVITABILITY. THAT IF MALI AND TESSA CAN'T RUN, NONE OF US CAN.
WE HAD TO SEE. TO PROVE IT TO OURSELVES THAT YOU WEREN'T. THAT WE CAN ALL LEAVE, TOO.
WE'LL TELL THE OTHERS. WE'LL SHOW THEM.
ALL THEY NEED IS A SIGN.
O...KAY? I'M SORRY, THIS IS--
HUBELY, WE HAVE TO GO. THEY'RE COMING.
SERPENTINE, STAY LOW.
NO!
FWFFFT
FWFFFT
GOT ANOTHER PAIR. THEY'VE GOT PHONES, TOO.
DESTROY IT ALL. WE CAN'T TAKE CHANCES.
C.R.D REPAIRS
ANY SIGN OF THE PRINCESS OR THE PEA?
NEGATIVE. BUT THEY'RE NOT A THREAT ANYMORE. MISS VOS HAS SEEN TO IT.

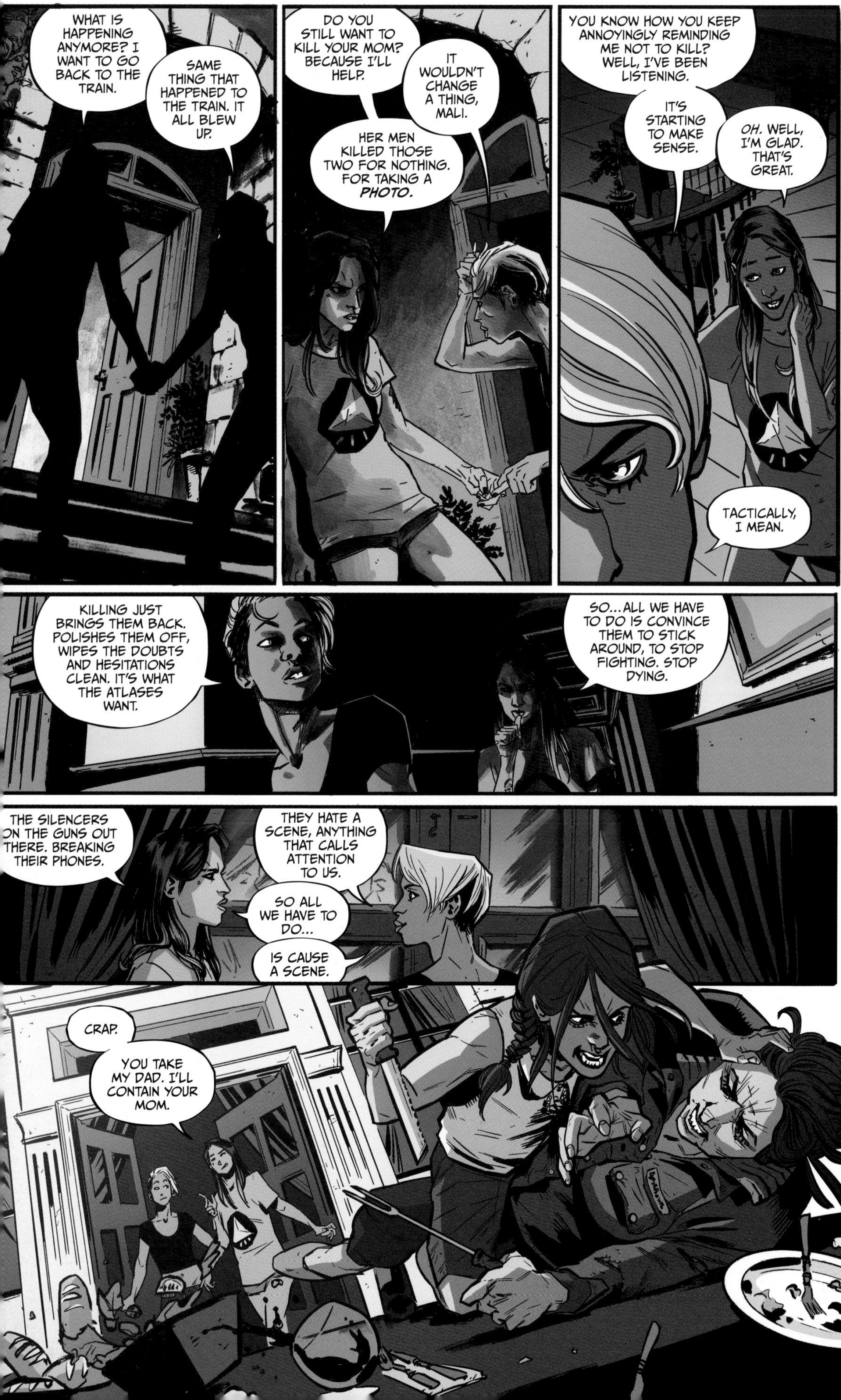
WHAT IS HAPPENING ANYMORE? I WANT TO GO BACK TO THE TRAIN.
SAME THING THAT HAPPENED TO THE TRAIN. IT ALL BLEW UP.
DO YOU STILL WANT TO KILL YOUR MOM? BECAUSE I'LL HELP.
IT WOULDN'T CHANGE A THING, MALI.
HER MEN KILLED THOSE TWO FOR NOTHING. FOR TAKING A PHOTO.
YOU KNOW HOW YOU KEEP ANNOYINGLY REMINDING ME NOT TO KILL? WELL, I'VE BEEN LISTENING.
IT'S STARTING TO MAKE SENSE.
OH. WELL, I'M GLAD. THAT'S GREAT.
TACTICALLY, I MEAN.
KILLING JUST BRINGS THEM BACK. POLISHES THEM OFF, WIPES THE DOUBTS AND HESITATIONS CLEAN. IT'S WHAT THE ATLASES WANT.
SO... ALL WE HAVE TO DO IS CONVINCE THEM TO STICK AROUND, TO STOP FIGHTING. STOP DYING.
THE SILENCERS ON THE GUNS OUT THERE. BREAKING THEIR PHONES.
THEY HATE A SCENE, ANYTHING THAT CALLS ATTENTION TO US.
SO ALL WE HAVE TO DO...
IS CAUSE A SCENE.
CRAP.
YOU TAKE MY DAD. I'LL CONTAIN YOUR MOM.

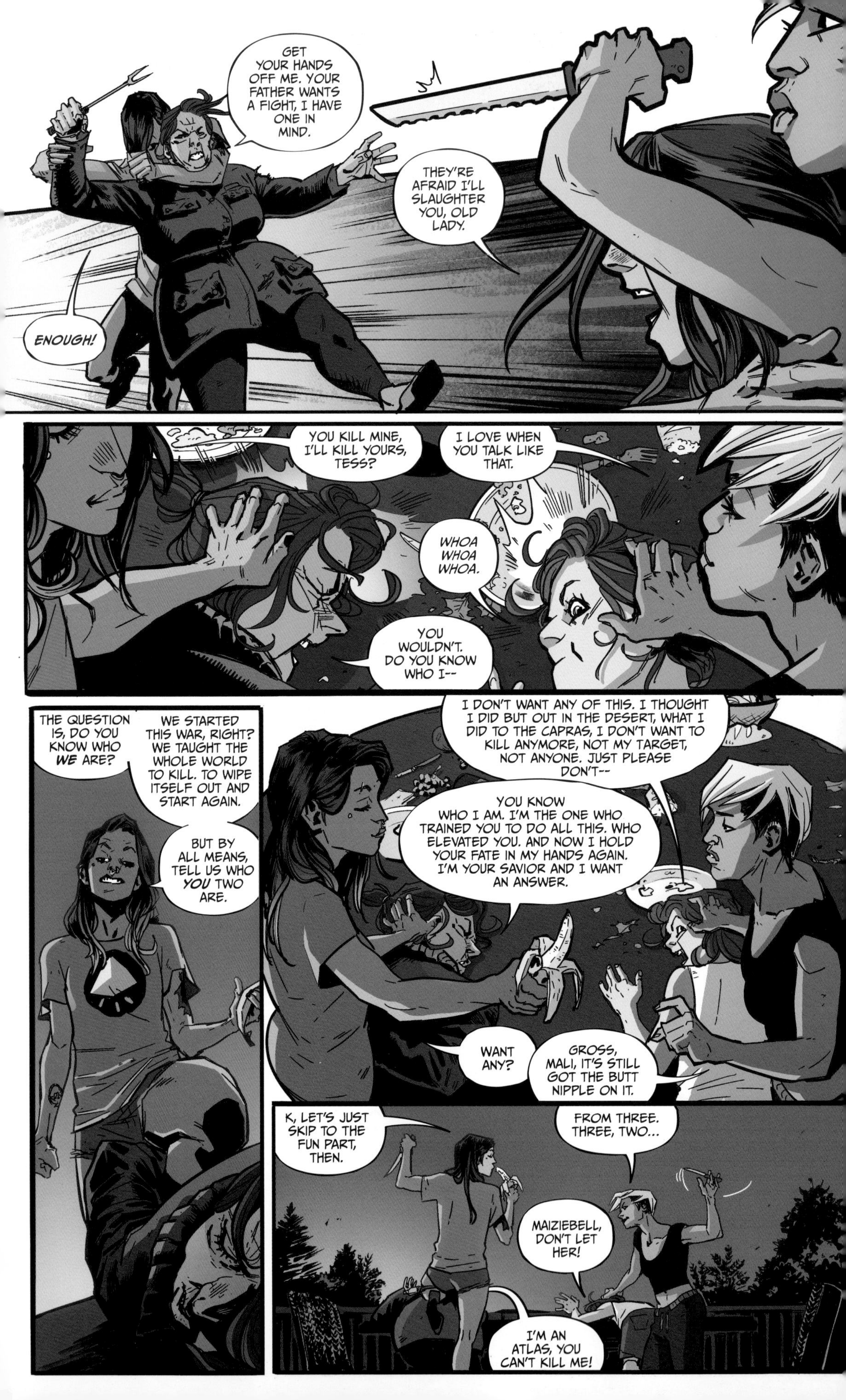
GET YOUR HANDS OFF ME. YOUR FATHER WANTS A FIGHT, I HAVE ONE IN MIND.
THEY'RE AFRAID I'LL SLAUGHTER YOU, OLD LADY.
ENOUGH!
YOU KILL MINE, I'LL KILL YOURS, TESS?
I LOVE WHEN YOU TALK LIKE THAT.
WHOA WHOA WHOA.
YOU WOULDN'T. DO YOU KNOW WHO I--
THE QUESTION IS, DO YOU KNOW WHO WE ARE?
WE STARTED THIS WAR, RIGHT? WE TAUGHT THE WHOLE WORLD TO KILL. TO WIPE ITSELF OUT AND START AGAIN.
BUT BY ALL MEANS, TELL US WHO YOU TWO ARE.
I DON'T WANT ANY OF THIS. I THOUGHT I DID BUT OUT IN THE DESERT, WHAT I DID TO THE CAPRAS, I DON'T WANT TO KILL ANYMORE, NOT MY TARGET, NOT ANYONE. JUST PLEASE DON'T--
YOU KNOW WHO I AM. I'M THE ONE WHO TRAINED YOU TO DO ALL THIS. WHO ELEVATED YOU. AND NOW I HOLD YOUR FATE IN MY HANDS AGAIN. I'M YOUR SAVIOR AND I WANT AN ANSWER.
WANT ANY?
GROSS, MALI, IT'S STILL GOT THE BUTT NIPPLE ON IT.
K, LET'S JUST SKIP TO THE FUN PART, THEN.
FROM THREE. THREE, TWO...
MAIZIEBELL, DON'T LET HER!
I'M AN ATLAS, YOU CAN'T KILL ME!

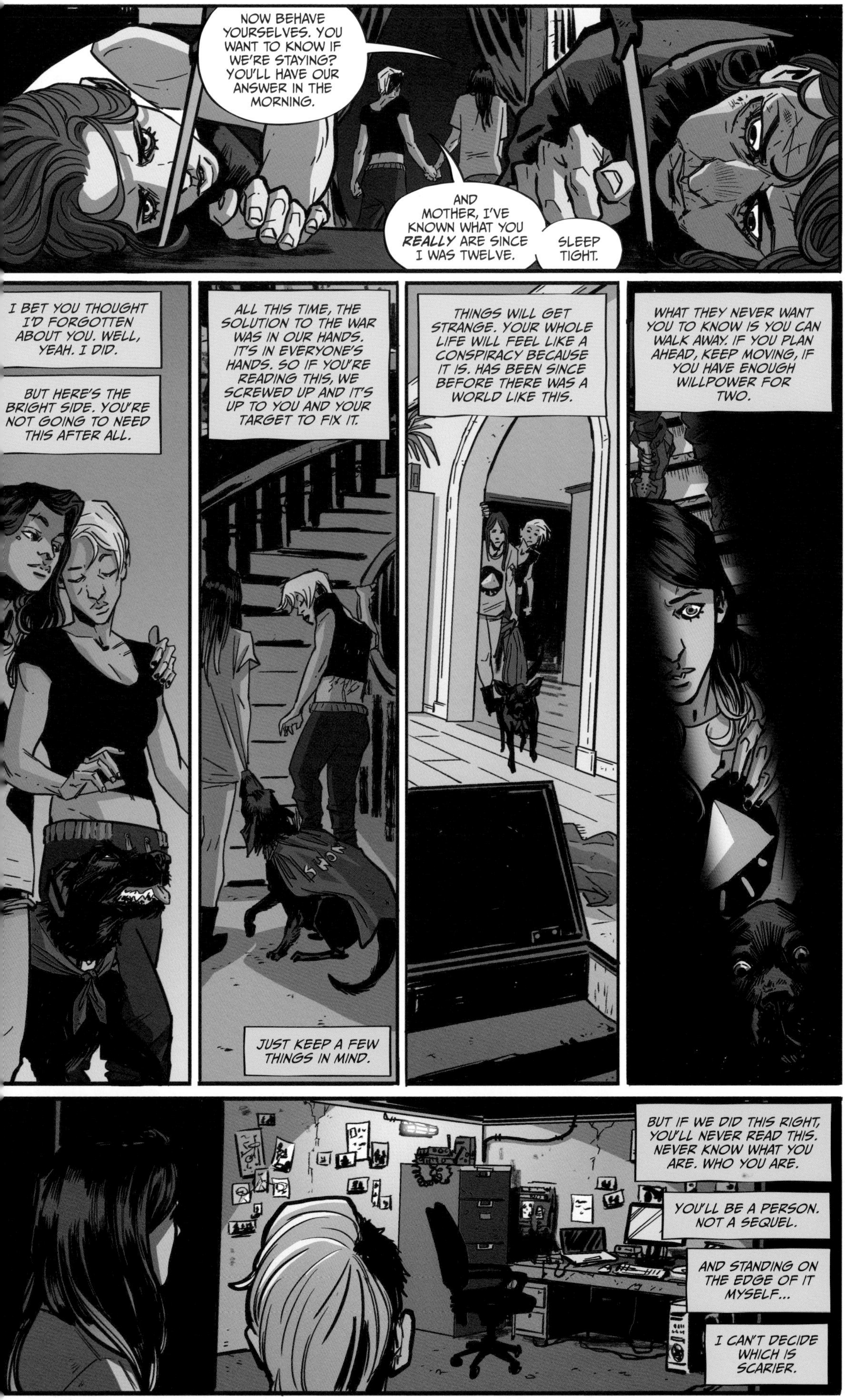
NOW BEHAVE YOURSELVES. YOU WANT TO KNOW IF WE'RE STAYING? YOU'LL HAVE OUR ANSWER IN THE MORNING.
AND MOTHER, I'VE KNOWN WHAT YOU REALLY ARE SINCE I WAS TWELVE.
SLEEP TIGHT.
I BET YOU THOUGHT I'D FORGOTTEN ABOUT YOU. WELL, YEAH. I DID.
BUT HERE'S THE BRIGHT SIDE. YOU'RE NOT GOING TO NEED THIS AFTER ALL.
ALL THIS TIME, THE SOLUTION TO THE WAR WAS IN OUR HANDS. IT'S IN EVERYONE'S HANDS. SO IF YOU'RE READING THIS, WE SCREWED UP AND IT'S UP TO YOU AND YOUR TARGET TO FIX IT.
JUST KEEP A FEW THINGS IN MIND.
THINGS WILL GET STRANGE. YOUR WHOLE LIFE WILL FEEL LIKE A CONSPIRACY BECAUSE IT IS. HAS BEEN SINCE BEFORE THERE WAS A WORLD LIKE THIS.
WHAT THEY NEVER WANT YOU TO KNOW IS YOU CAN WALK AWAY. IF YOU PLAN AHEAD, KEEP MOVING, IF YOU HAVE ENOUGH WILLPOWER FOR TWO.
BUT IF WE DID THIS RIGHT, YOU'LL NEVER READ THIS. NEVER KNOW WHAT YOU ARE. WHO YOU ARE.
YOU'LL BE A PERSON. NOT A SEQUEL.
AND STANDING ON THE EDGE OF IT MYSELF...
I CAN'T DECIDE WHICH IS SCARIER.

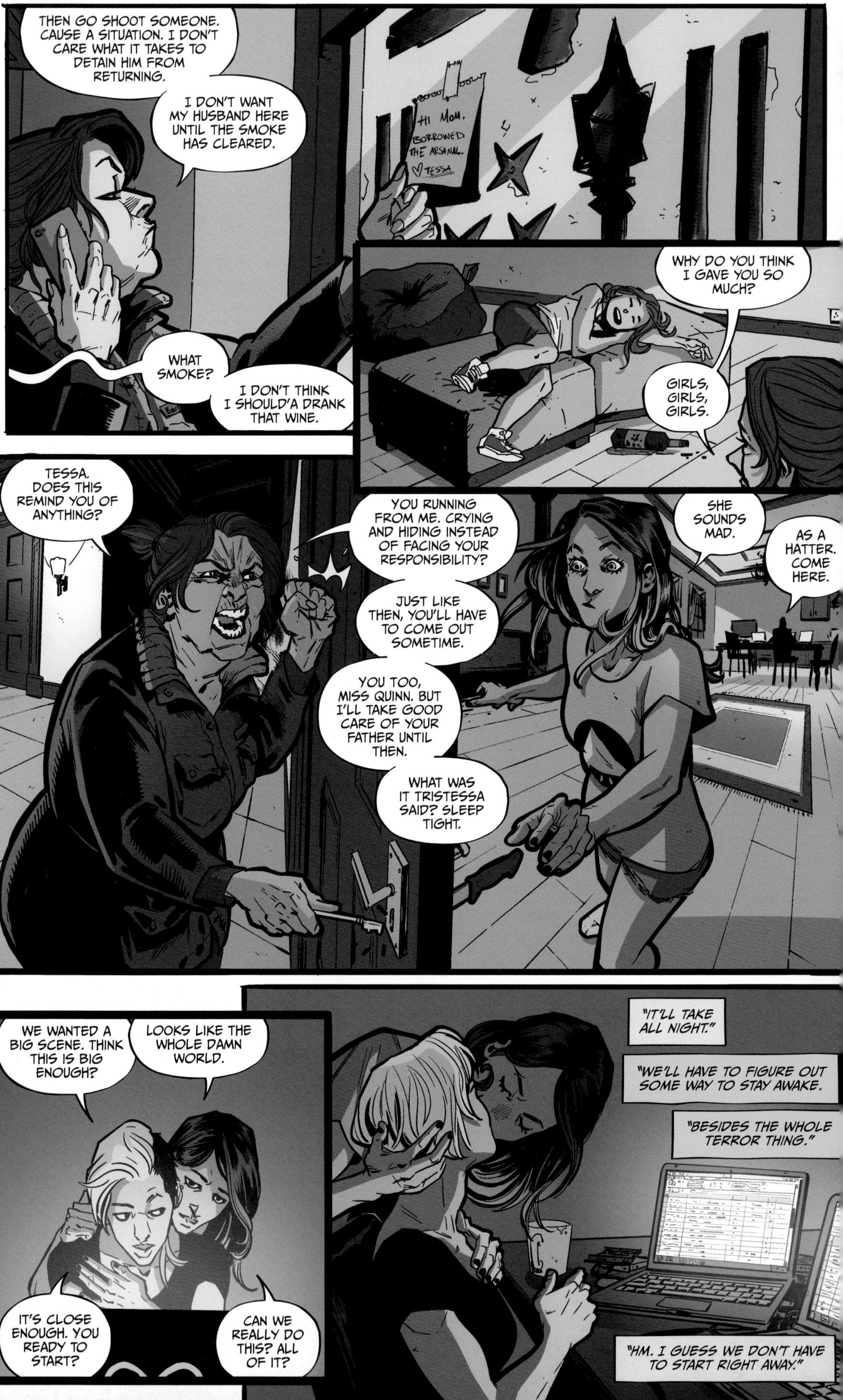
THEN GO SHOOT SOMEONE. CAUSE A SITUATION. I DON'T CARE WHAT IT TAKES TO DETAIN HIM FROM RETURNING.
I DON'T WANT MY HUSBAND HERE UNTIL THE SMOKE HAS CLEARED.
HI MOM. BORROWED THE ARSANAL. ♡ TESSA
WHAT SMOKE?
I DON'T THINK I SHOULD'A DRANK THAT WINE.
WHY DO YOU THINK I GAVE YOU SO MUCH?
GIRLS, GIRLS, GIRLS.
TESSA. DOES THIS REMIND YOU OF ANYTHING?
YOU RUNNING FROM ME. CRYING AND HIDING INSTEAD OF FACING YOUR RESPONSIBILITY?
JUST LIKE THEN, YOU'LL HAVE TO COME OUT SOMETIME.
YOU TOO, MISS QUINN. BUT I'LL TAKE GOOD CARE OF YOUR FATHER UNTIL THEN.
WHAT WAS IT TRISTESSA SAID? SLEEP TIGHT.
SHE SOUNDS MAD.
AS A HATTER. COME HERE.
WE WANTED A BIG SCENE. THINK THIS IS BIG ENOUGH?
LOOKS LIKE THE WHOLE DAMN WORLD.
IT'S CLOSE ENOUGH. YOU READY TO START?
CAN WE REALLY DO THIS? ALL OF IT?
"IT'LL TAKE ALL NIGHT."
"WE'LL HAVE TO FIGURE OUT SOME WAY TO STAY AWAKE."
"BESIDES THE WHOLE TERROR THING."
"HM. I GUESS WE DON'T HAVE TO START RIGHT AWAY."

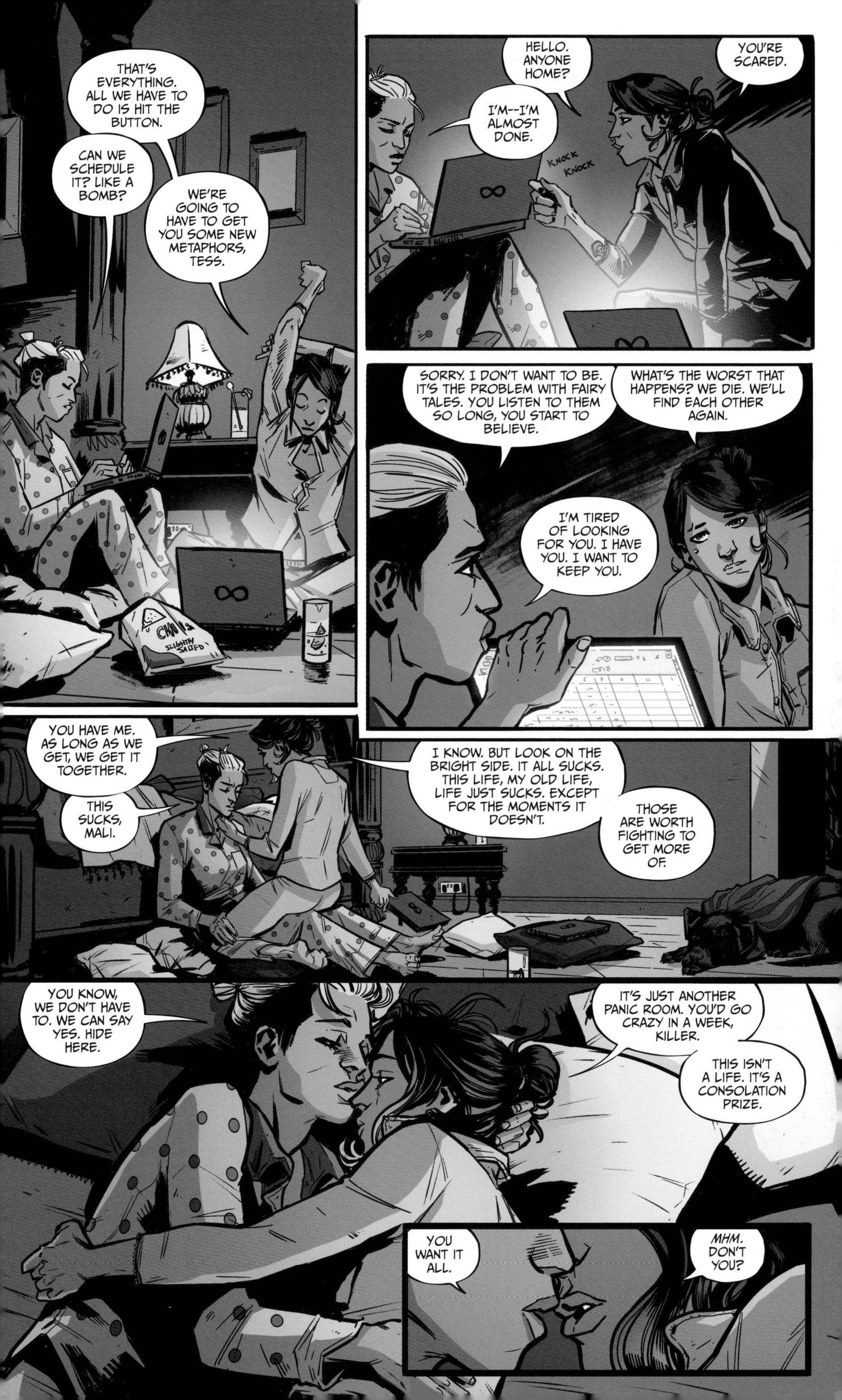

THAT'S EVERYTHING. ALL WE HAVE TO DO IS HIT THE BUTTON.
CAN WE SCHEDULE IT? LIKE A BOMB?
WE'RE GOING TO HAVE TO GET YOU SOME NEW METAPHORS, TESS.
CHIPS SLIGHTLY SALTED
HELLO. ANYONE HOME?
I'M--I'M ALMOST DONE.
KNOCK KNOCK
YOU'RE SCARED.
SORRY. I DON'T WANT TO BE. IT'S THE PROBLEM WITH FAIRY TALES. YOU LISTEN TO THEM SO LONG, YOU START TO BELIEVE.
WHAT'S THE WORST THAT HAPPENS? WE DIE. WE'LL FIND EACH OTHER AGAIN.
I'M TIRED OF LOOKING FOR YOU. I HAVE YOU. I WANT TO KEEP YOU.
YOU HAVE ME. AS LONG AS WE GET, WE GET IT TOGETHER.
THIS SUCKS, MALI.
I KNOW. BUT LOOK ON THE BRIGHT SIDE. IT ALL SUCKS. THIS LIFE, MY OLD LIFE, LIFE JUST SUCKS. EXCEPT FOR THE MOMENTS IT DOESN'T.
THOSE ARE WORTH FIGHTING TO GET MORE OF.
YOU KNOW, WE DON'T HAVE TO. WE CAN SAY YES. HIDE HERE.
IT'S JUST ANOTHER PANIC ROOM. YOU'D GO CRAZY IN A WEEK, KILLER.
THIS ISN'T A LIFE. IT'S A CONSOLATION PRIZE.
YOU WANT IT ALL.
MHM. DON'T YOU?

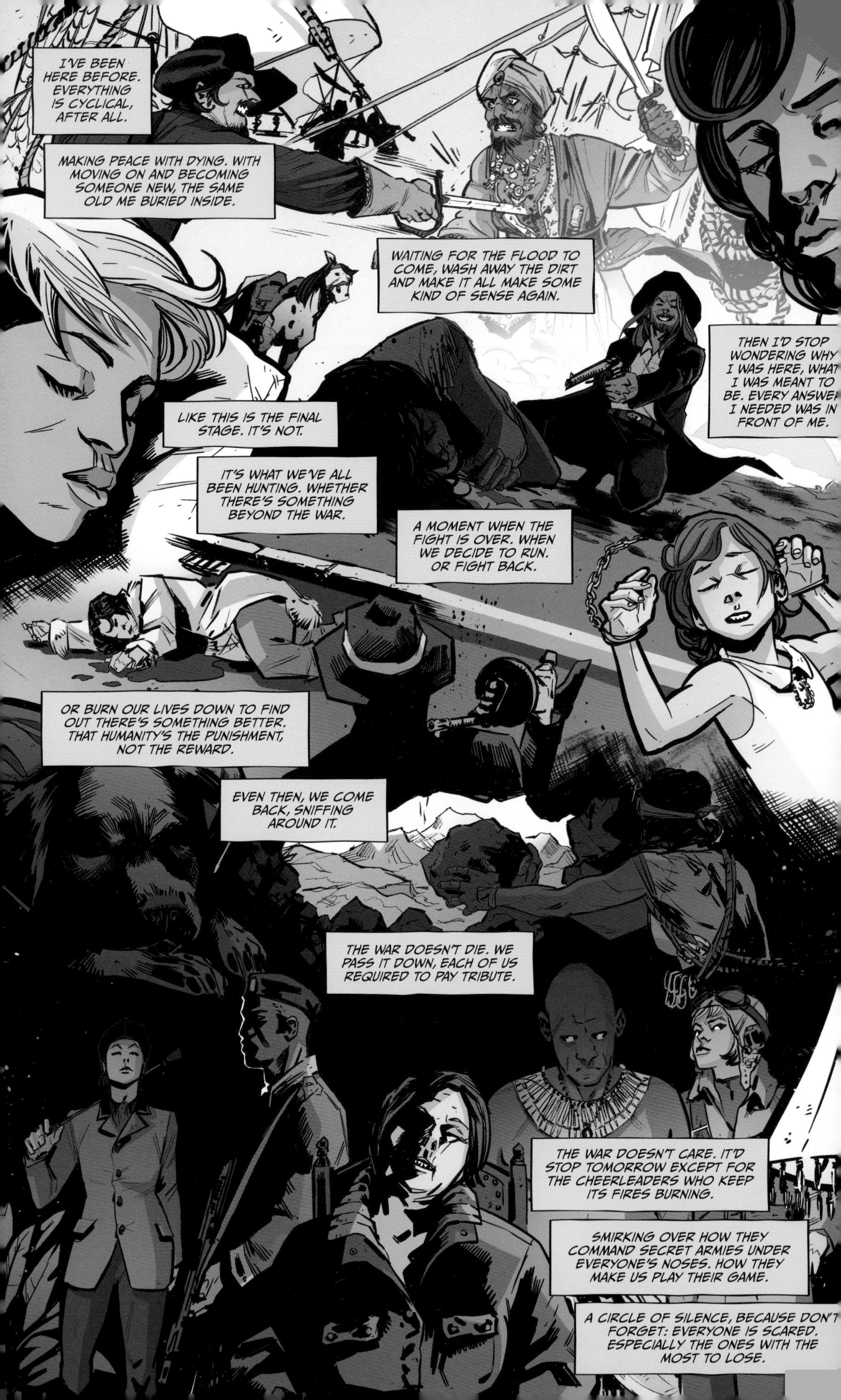
I'VE BEEN HERE BEFORE. EVERYTHING IS CYCLICAL, AFTER ALL.
MAKING PEACE WITH DYING. WITH MOVING ON AND BECOMING SOMEONE NEW, THE SAME OLD ME BURIED INSIDE.
WAITING FOR THE FLOOD TO COME, WASH AWAY THE DIRT AND MAKE IT ALL MAKE SOME KIND OF SENSE AGAIN.
THEN I'D STOP WONDERING WHY I WAS HERE, WHAT I WAS MEANT TO BE. EVERY ANSWER I NEEDED WAS IN FRONT OF ME.
LIKE THIS IS THE FINAL STAGE. IT'S NOT.
IT'S WHAT WE'VE ALL BEEN HUNTING. WHETHER THERE'S SOMETHING BEYOND THE WAR.
A MOMENT WHEN THE FIGHT IS OVER. WHEN WE DECIDE TO RUN. OR FIGHT BACK.
OR BURN OUR LIVES DOWN TO FIND OUT THERE'S SOMETHING BETTER. THAT HUMANITY'S THE PUNISHMENT, NOT THE REWARD.
EVEN THEN, WE COME BACK, SNIFFING AROUND IT.
THE WAR DOESN'T DIE. WE PASS IT DOWN, EACH OF US REQUIRED TO PAY TRIBUTE.
THE WAR DOESN'T CARE. IT'D STOP TOMORROW EXCEPT FOR THE CHEERLEADERS WHO KEEP ITS FIRES BURNING.
SMIRKING OVER HOW THEY COMMAND SECRET ARMIES UNDER EVERYONE'S NOSES. HOW THEY MAKE US PLAY THEIR GAME.
A CIRCLE OF SILENCE, BECAUSE DON'T FORGET: EVERYONE IS SCARED. ESPECIALLY THE ONES WITH THE MOST TO LOSE.

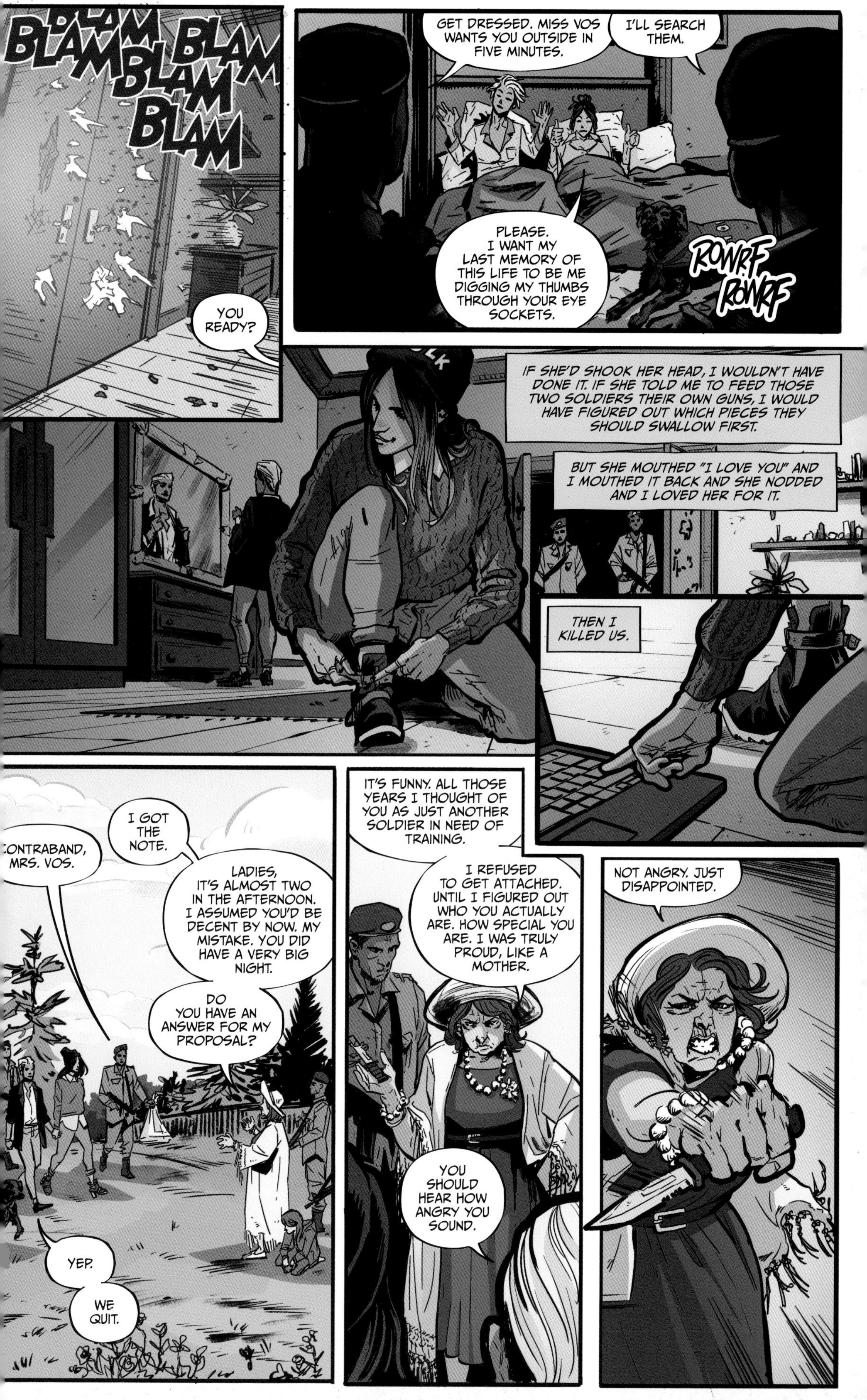
BLAM BLAM BLAM BLAM BLAM BLAM
YOU READY?
GET DRESSED. MISS VOS WANTS YOU OUTSIDE IN FIVE MINUTES.
I'LL SEARCH THEM.
PLEASE. I WANT MY LAST MEMORY OF THIS LIFE TO BE ME DIGGING MY THUMBS THROUGH YOUR EYE SOCKETS.
ROWRF ROWRF
IF SHE'D SHOOK HER HEAD, I WOULDN'T HAVE DONE IT. IF SHE TOLD ME TO FEED THOSE TWO SOLDIERS THEIR OWN GUNS, I WOULD HAVE FIGURED OUT WHICH PIECES THEY SHOULD SWALLOW FIRST.
BUT SHE MOUTHED "I LOVE YOU" AND I MOUTHED IT BACK AND SHE NODDED AND I LOVED HER FOR IT.
THEN I KILLED US.
CONTRABAND, MRS. VOS.
I GOT THE NOTE.
LADIES, IT'S ALMOST TWO IN THE AFTERNOON. I ASSUMED YOU'D BE DECENT BY NOW. MY MISTAKE. YOU DID HAVE A VERY BIG NIGHT.
DO YOU HAVE AN ANSWER FOR MY PROPOSAL?
YEP.
WE QUIT.
IT'S FUNNY. ALL THOSE YEARS I THOUGHT OF YOU AS JUST ANOTHER SOLDIER IN NEED OF TRAINING.
I REFUSED TO GET ATTACHED. UNTIL I FIGURED OUT WHO YOU ACTUALLY ARE. HOW SPECIAL YOU ARE. I WAS TRULY PROUD, LIKE A MOTHER.
YOU SHOULD HEAR HOW ANGRY YOU SOUND.
NOT ANGRY. JUST DISAPPOINTED.

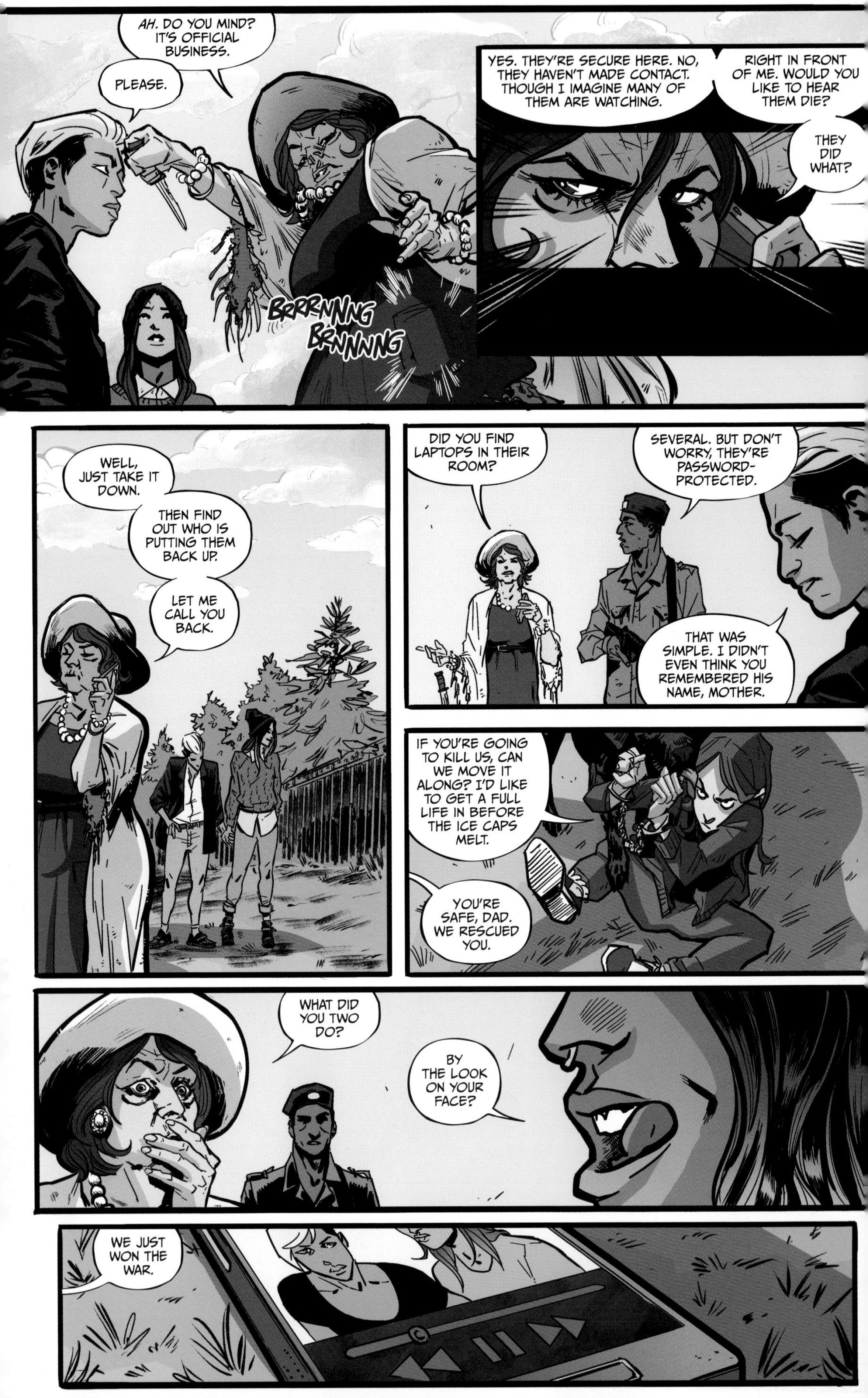
AH. DO YOU MIND? IT'S OFFICIAL BUSINESS.
PLEASE.
BRRRNNNG BRNNNNG
YES. THEY'RE SECURE HERE. NO, THEY HAVEN'T MADE CONTACT. THOUGH I IMAGINE MANY OF THEM ARE WATCHING.
RIGHT IN FRONT OF ME. WOULD YOU LIKE TO HEAR THEM DIE?
THEY DID WHAT?
WELL, JUST TAKE IT DOWN.
THEN FIND OUT WHO IS PUTTING THEM BACK UP.
LET ME CALL YOU BACK.
DID YOU FIND LAPTOPS IN THEIR ROOM?
SEVERAL. BUT DON'T WORRY, THEY'RE PASSWORD-PROTECTED.
THAT WAS SIMPLE. I DIDN'T EVEN THINK YOU REMEMBERED HIS NAME, MOTHER.
IF YOU'RE GOING TO KILL US, CAN WE MOVE IT ALONG? I'D LIKE TO GET A FULL LIFE IN BEFORE THE ICE CAPS MELT.
YOU'RE SAFE, DAD. WE RESCUED YOU.
WHAT DID YOU TWO DO?
BY THE LOOK ON YOUR FACE?
WE JUST WON THE WAR.

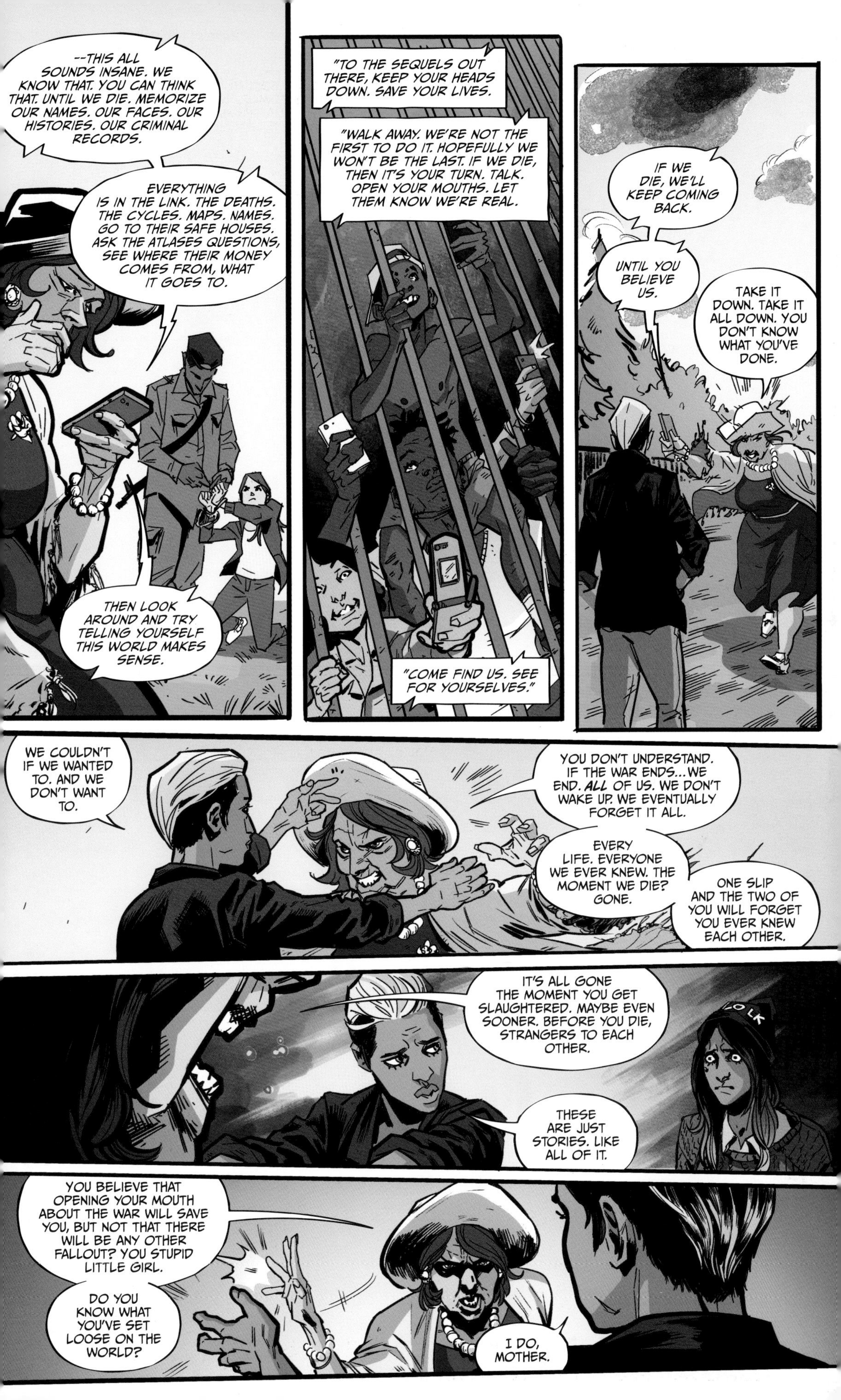

--THIS ALL SOUNDS INSANE. WE KNOW THAT. YOU CAN THINK THAT. UNTIL WE DIE. MEMORIZE OUR NAMES. OUR FACES. OUR HISTORIES. OUR CRIMINAL RECORDS.
EVERYTHING IS IN THE LINK. THE DEATHS. THE CYCLES. MAPS. NAMES. GO TO THEIR SAFE HOUSES. ASK THE ATLASES QUESTIONS, SEE WHERE THEIR MONEY COMES FROM, WHAT IT GOES TO.
THEN LOOK AROUND AND TRY TELLING YOURSELF THIS WORLD MAKES SENSE.
"TO THE SEQUELS OUT THERE, KEEP YOUR HEADS DOWN. SAVE YOUR LIVES.
"WALK AWAY. WE'RE NOT THE FIRST TO DO IT. HOPEFULLY WE WON'T BE THE LAST. IF WE DIE, THEN IT'S YOUR TURN. TALK. OPEN YOUR MOUTHS. LET THEM KNOW WE'RE REAL.
"COME FIND US. SEE FOR YOURSELVES."
IF WE DIE, WE'LL KEEP COMING BACK.
UNTIL YOU BELIEVE US.
TAKE IT DOWN. TAKE IT ALL DOWN. YOU DON'T KNOW WHAT YOU'VE DONE.
WE COULDN'T IF WE WANTED TO. AND WE DON'T WANT TO.
YOU DON'T UNDERSTAND. IF THE WAR ENDS...WE END. ALL OF US. WE DON'T WAKE UP. WE EVENTUALLY FORGET IT ALL.
EVERY LIFE. EVERYONE WE EVER KNEW. THE MOMENT WE DIE? GONE.
ONE SLIP AND THE TWO OF YOU WILL FORGET YOU EVER KNEW EACH OTHER.
IT'S ALL GONE THE MOMENT YOU GET SLAUGHTERED. MAYBE EVEN SOONER. BEFORE YOU DIE, STRANGERS TO EACH OTHER.
THESE ARE JUST STORIES. LIKE ALL OF IT.
YOU BELIEVE THAT OPENING YOUR MOUTH ABOUT THE WAR WILL SAVE YOU, BUT NOT THAT THERE WILL BE ANY OTHER FALLOUT? YOU STUPID LITTLE GIRL.
DO YOU KNOW WHAT YOU'VE SET LOOSE ON THE WORLD?
I DO, MOTHER.

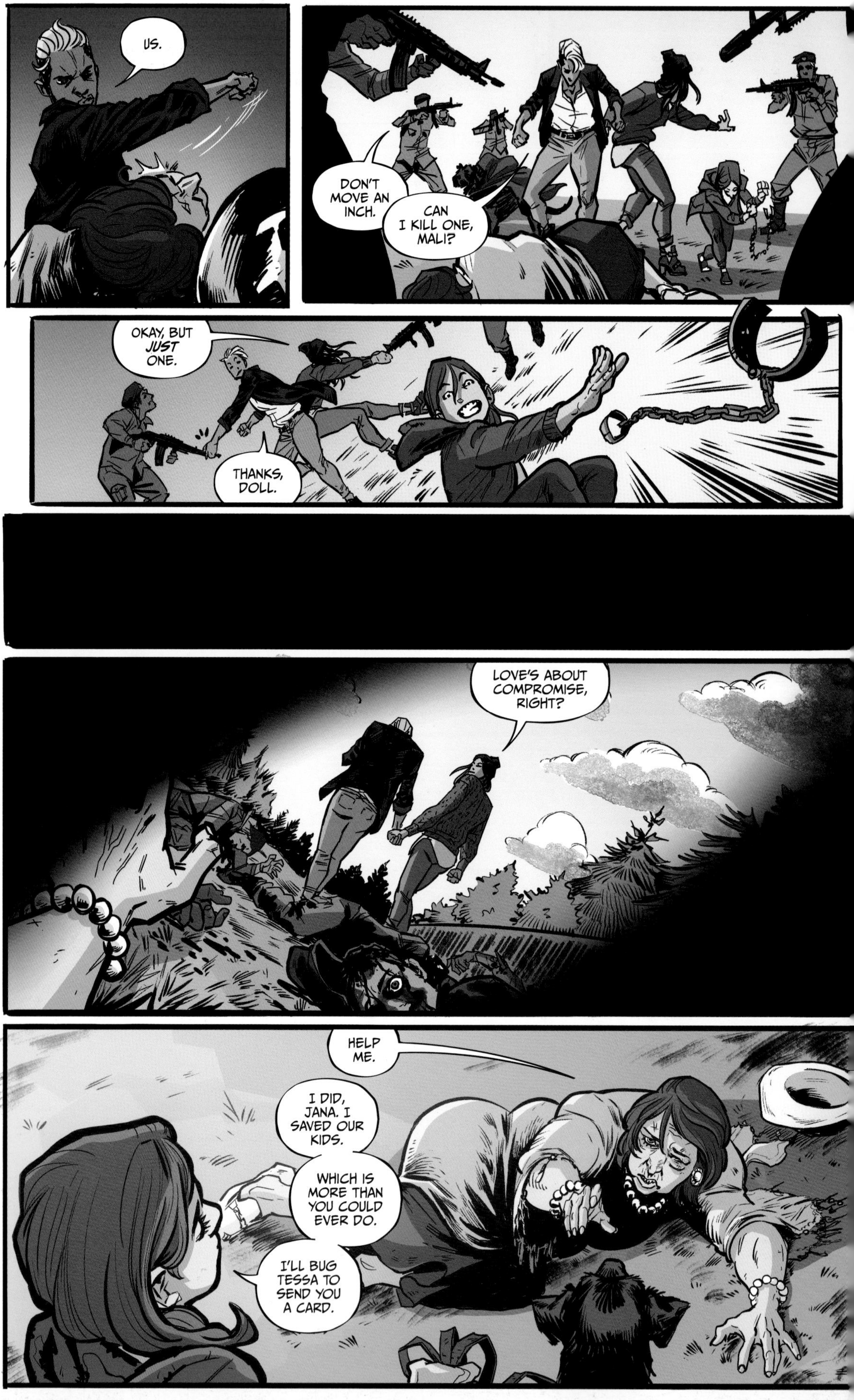
US.
DON'T MOVE AN INCH.
CAN I KILL ONE, MALI?
OKAY, BUT *JUST* ONE.
THANKS, DOLL.
LOVE'S ABOUT COMPROMISE, RIGHT?
HELP ME.
I DID, JANA. I SAVED OUR KIDS.
WHICH IS MORE THAN YOU COULD EVER DO.
I'LL BUG TESSA TO SEND YOU A CARD.

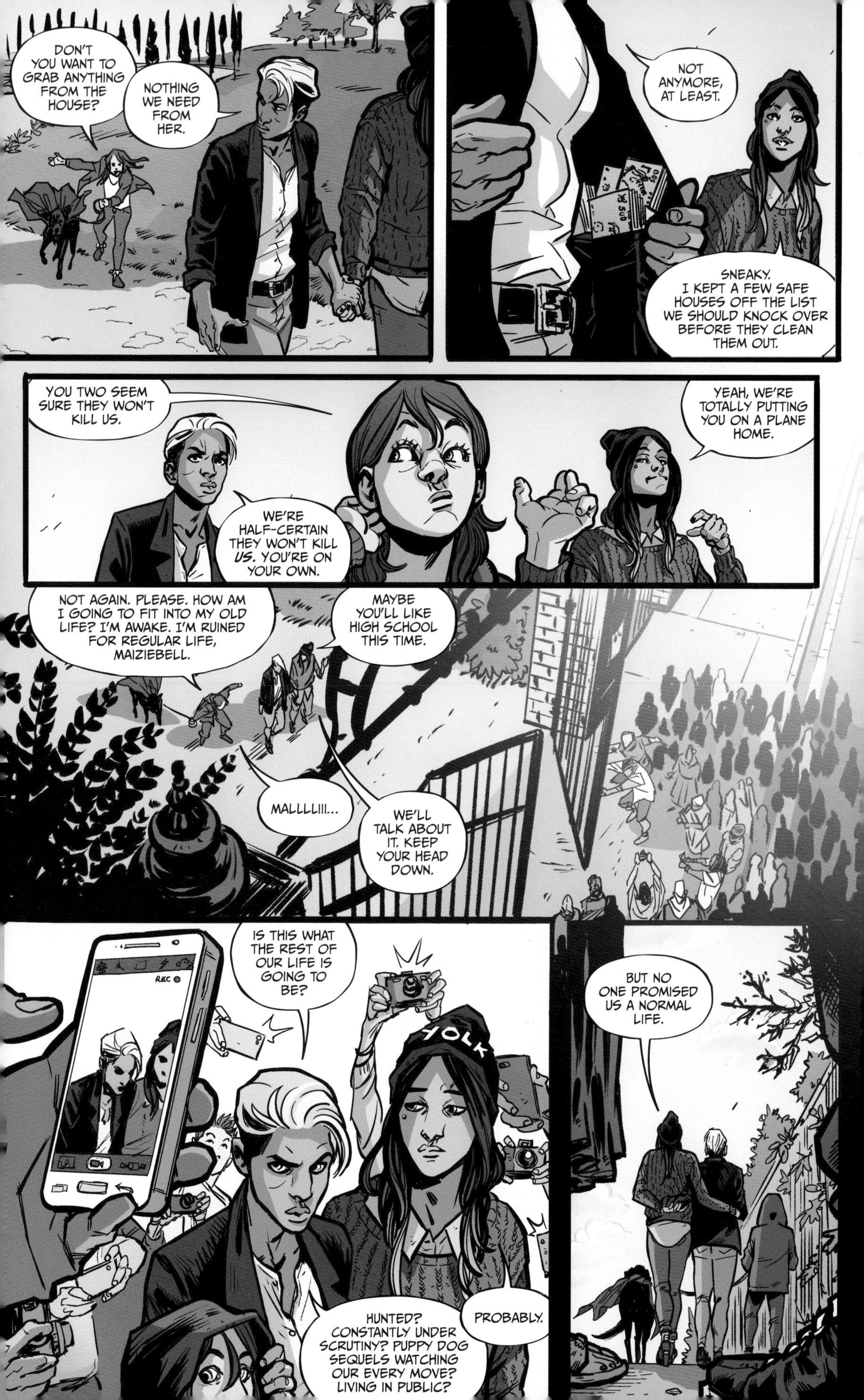
DON'T YOU WANT TO GRAB ANYTHING FROM THE HOUSE?
NOTHING WE NEED FROM HER.
NOT ANYMORE, AT LEAST.
SNEAKY. I KEPT A FEW SAFE HOUSES OFF THE LIST WE SHOULD KNOCK OVER BEFORE THEY CLEAN THEM OUT.
YOU TWO SEEM SURE THEY WON'T KILL US.
YEAH, WE'RE TOTALLY PUTTING YOU ON A PLANE HOME.
WE'RE HALF-CERTAIN THEY WON'T KILL *US*. YOU'RE ON YOUR OWN.
NOT AGAIN. PLEASE. HOW AM I GOING TO FIT INTO MY OLD LIFE? I'M AWAKE. I'M RUINED FOR REGULAR LIFE, MAIZIEBELL.
MAYBE YOU'LL LIKE HIGH SCHOOL THIS TIME.
MALLLLIII...
WE'LL TALK ABOUT IT. KEEP YOUR HEAD DOWN.
REC
IS THIS WHAT THE REST OF OUR LIFE IS GOING TO BE?
YOLK
HUNTED? CONSTANTLY UNDER SCRUTINY? PUPPY DOG SEQUELS WATCHING OUR EVERY MOVE? LIVING IN PUBLIC?
PROBABLY.
BUT NO ONE PROMISED US A NORMAL LIFE.

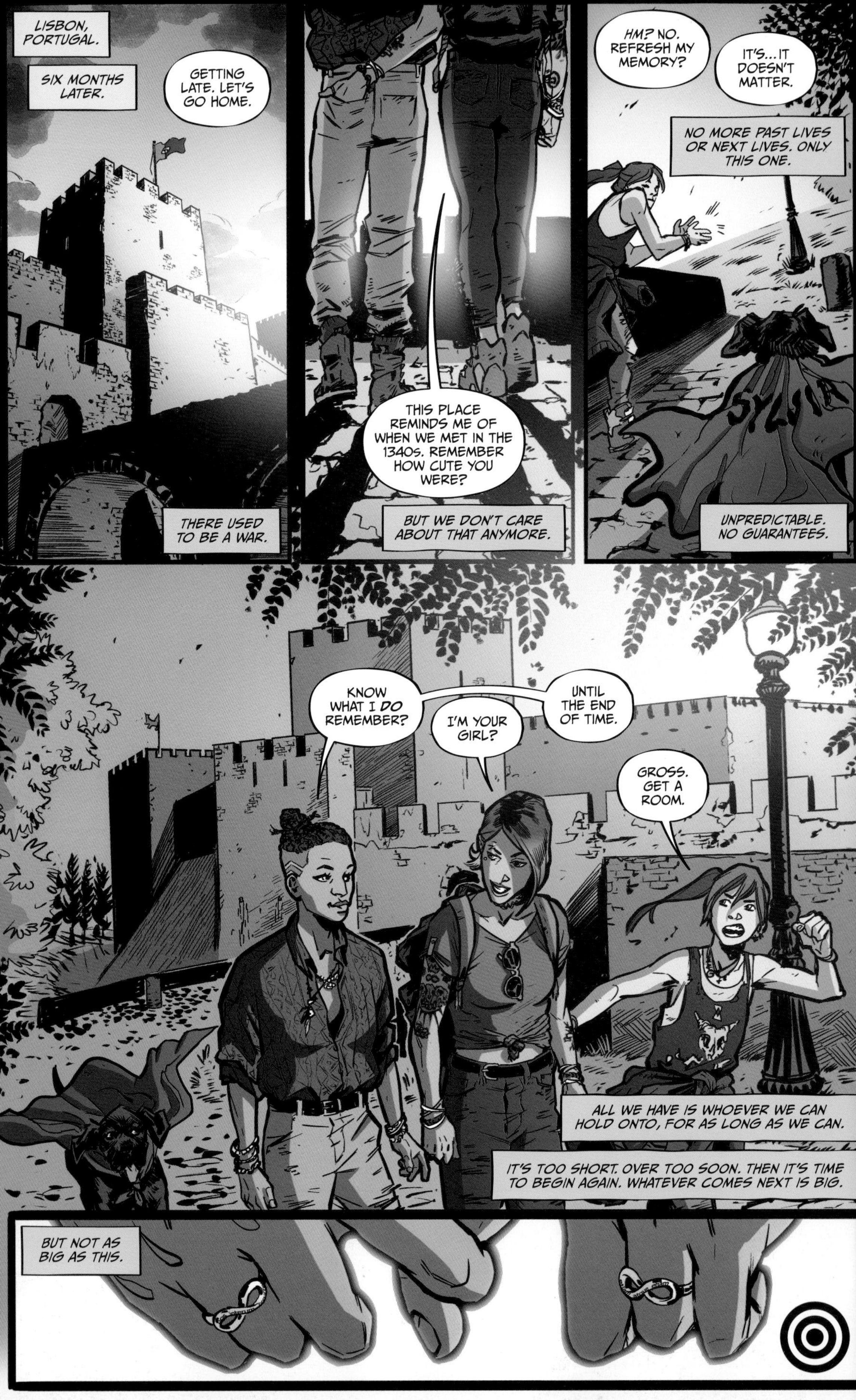
LISBON, PORTUGAL.
SIX MONTHS LATER.
GETTING LATE. LET'S GO HOME.
THERE USED TO BE A WAR.
THIS PLACE REMINDS ME OF WHEN WE MET IN THE 1340S. REMEMBER HOW CUTE YOU WERE?
BUT WE DON'T CARE ABOUT THAT ANYMORE.
HM? NO. REFRESH MY MEMORY?
IT'S... IT DOESN'T MATTER.
NO MORE PAST LIVES OR NEXT LIVES. ONLY THIS ONE.
UNPREDICTABLE. NO GUARANTEES.
KNOW WHAT I DO REMEMBER?
I'M YOUR GIRL?
UNTIL THE END OF TIME.
GROSS. GET A ROOM.
ALL WE HAVE IS WHOEVER WE CAN HOLD ONTO, FOR AS LONG AS WE CAN.
IT'S TOO SHORT. OVER TOO SOON. THEN IT'S TIME TO BEGIN AGAIN. WHATEVER COMES NEXT IS BIG.
BUT NOT AS BIG AS THIS.

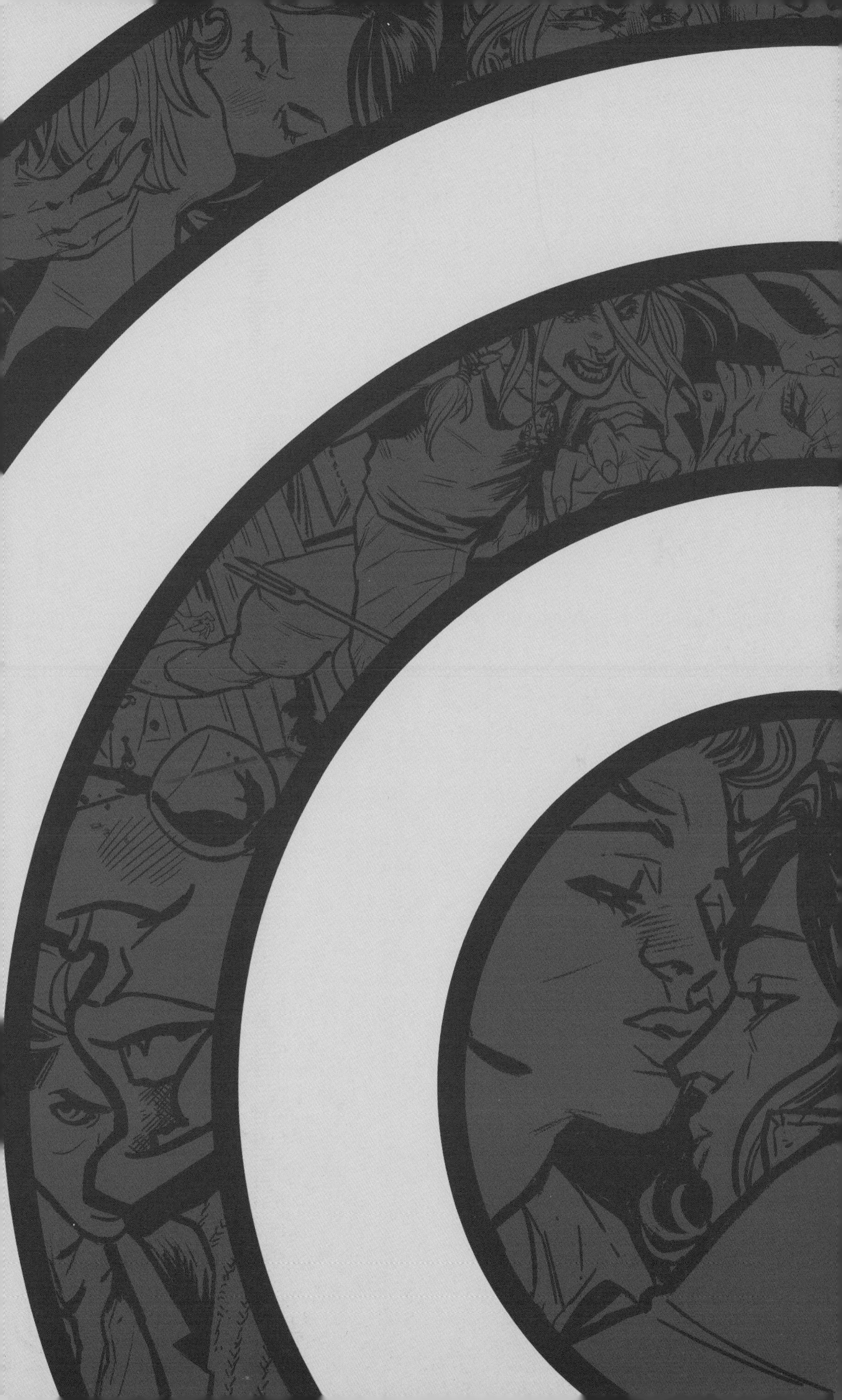

COVER

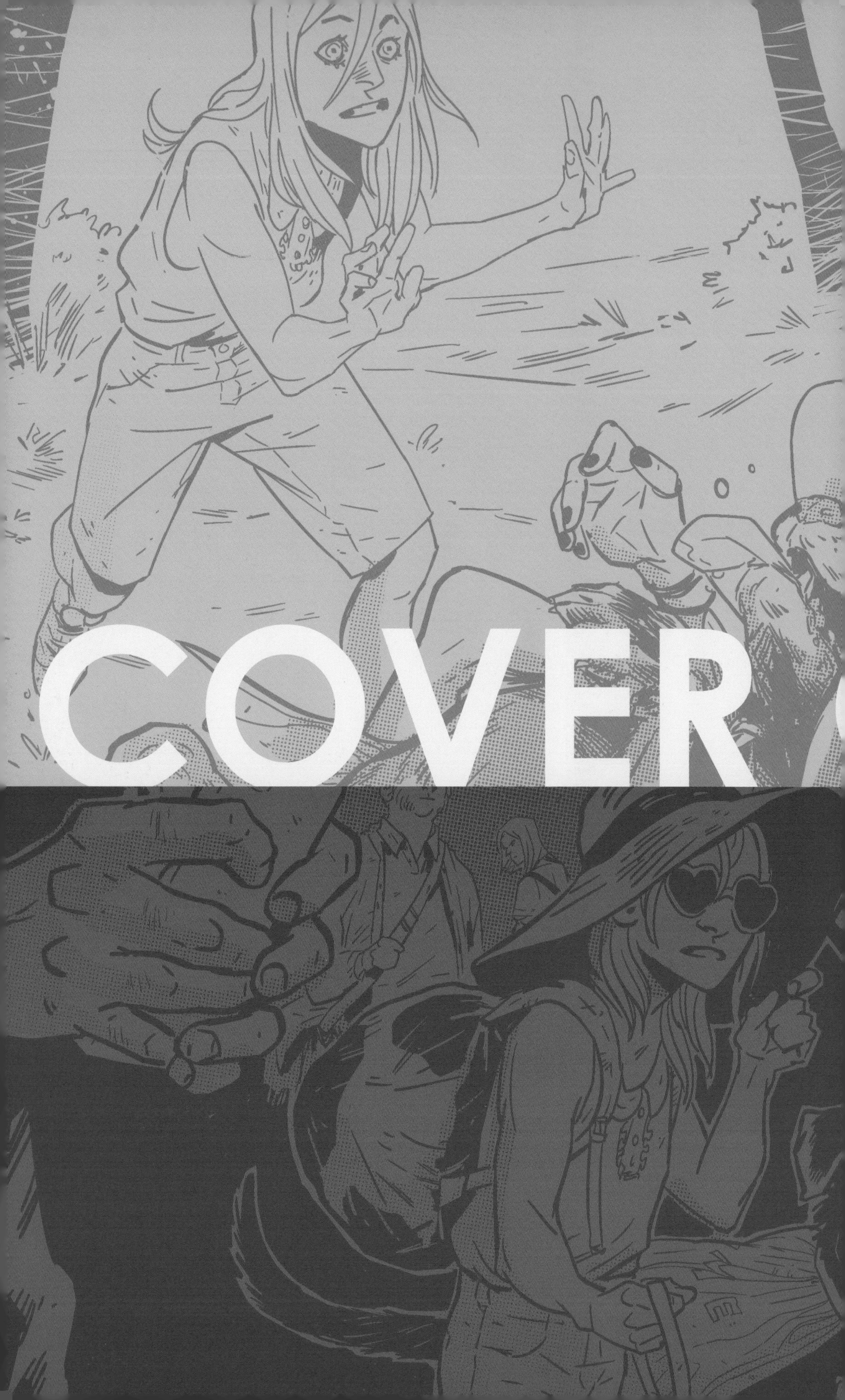

GALLERY

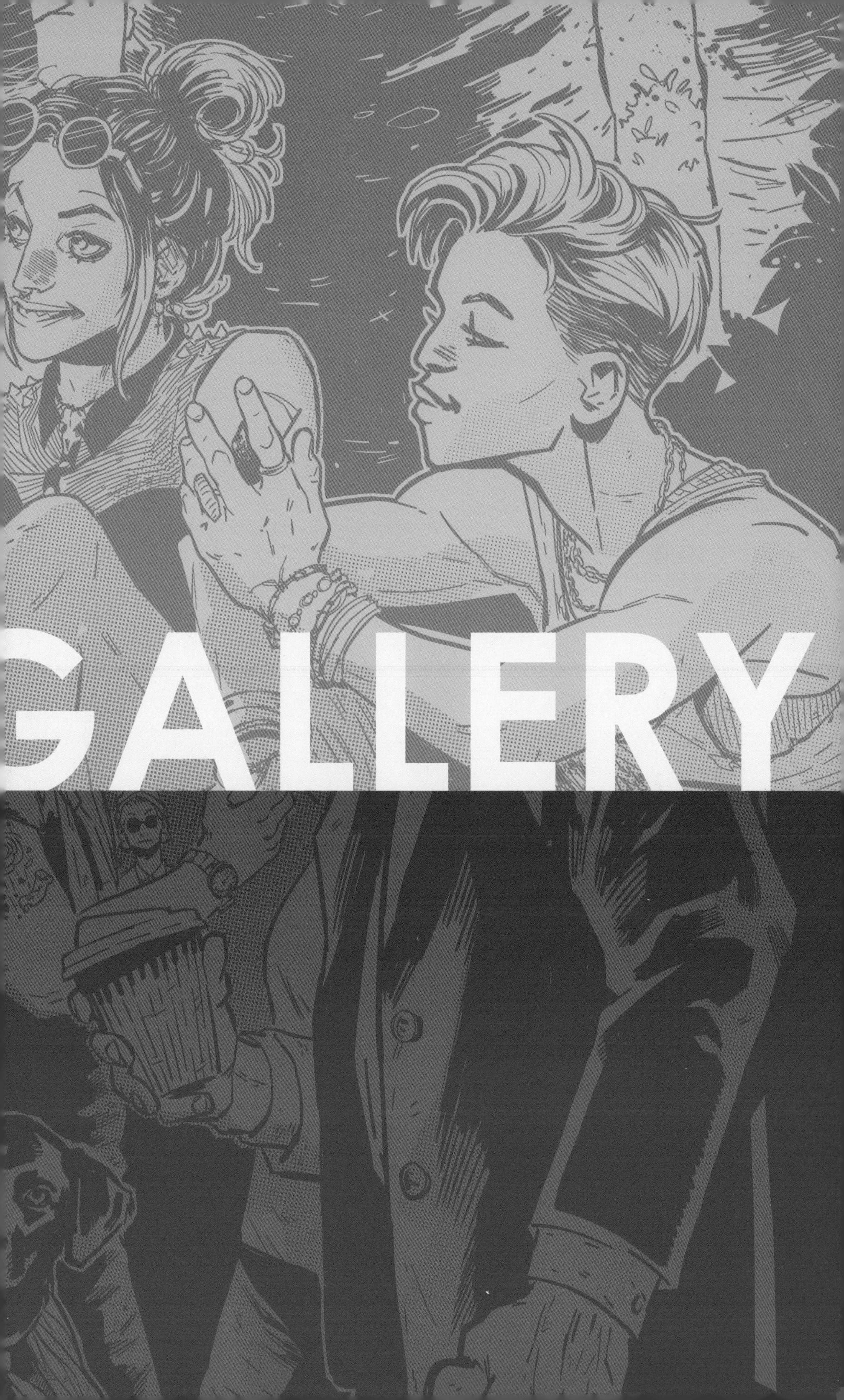

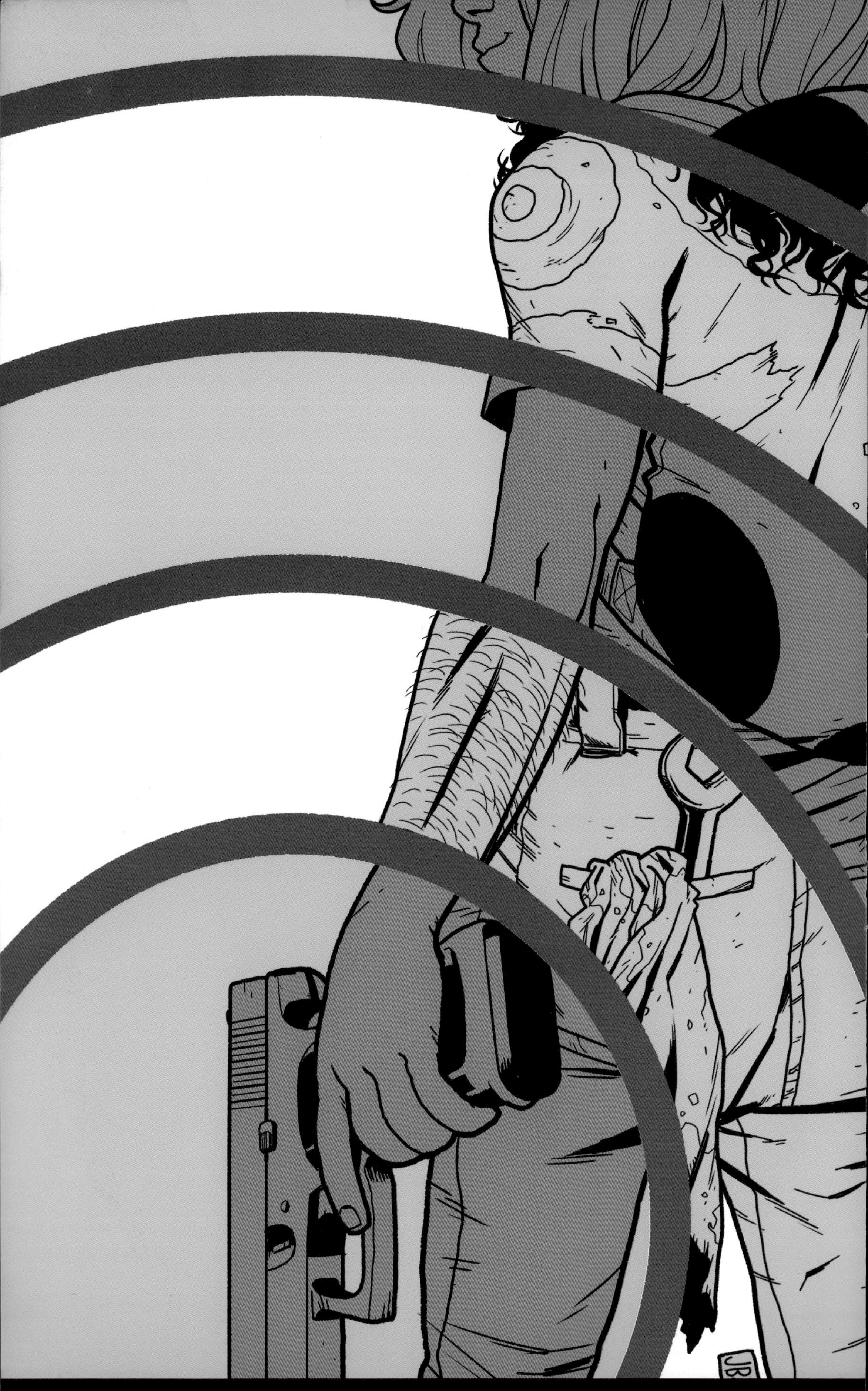

Issue Five Cover **Jonathan Brandon Sawyer**

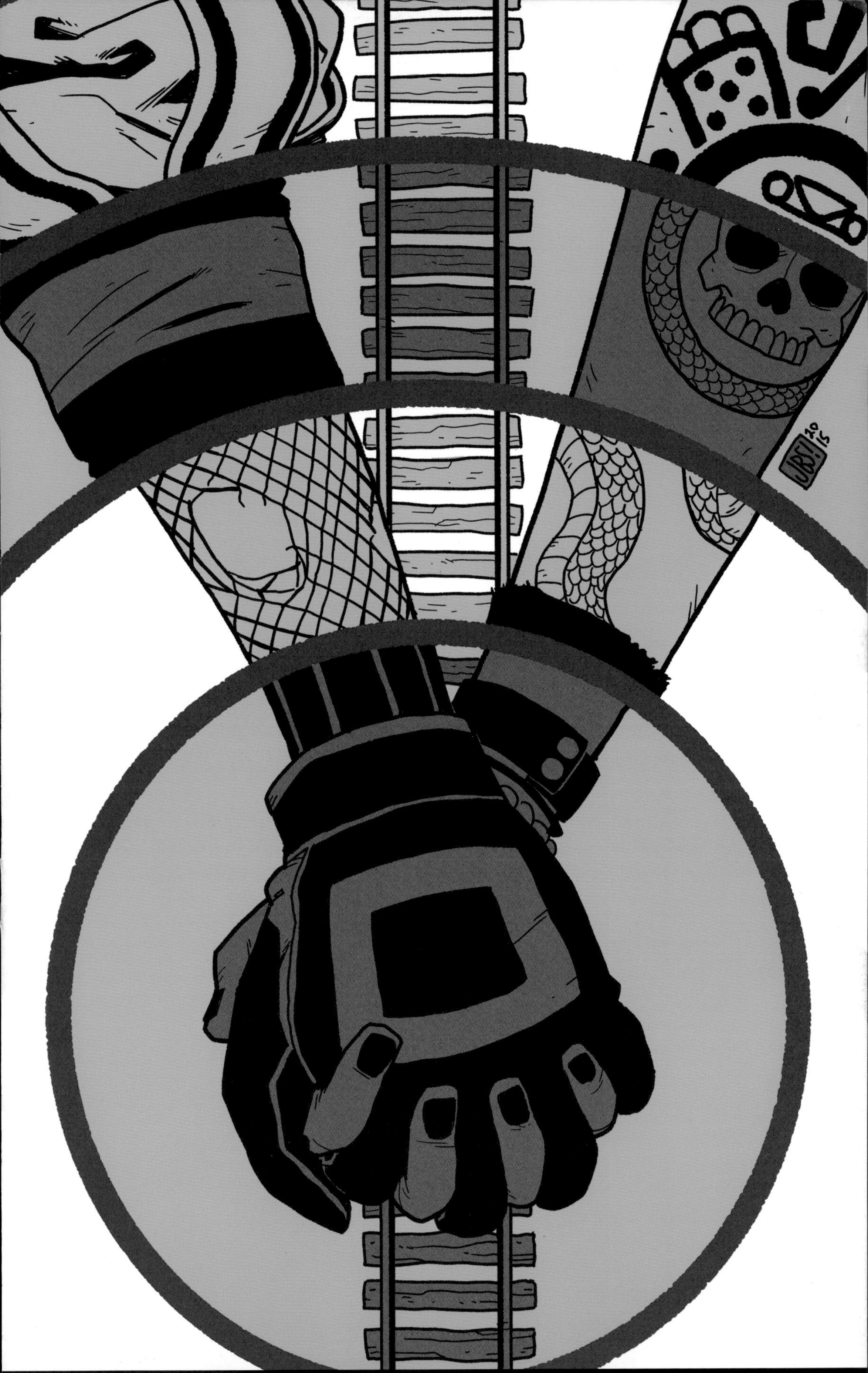

Issue Six Cover **Jonathan Brandon Sawyer**

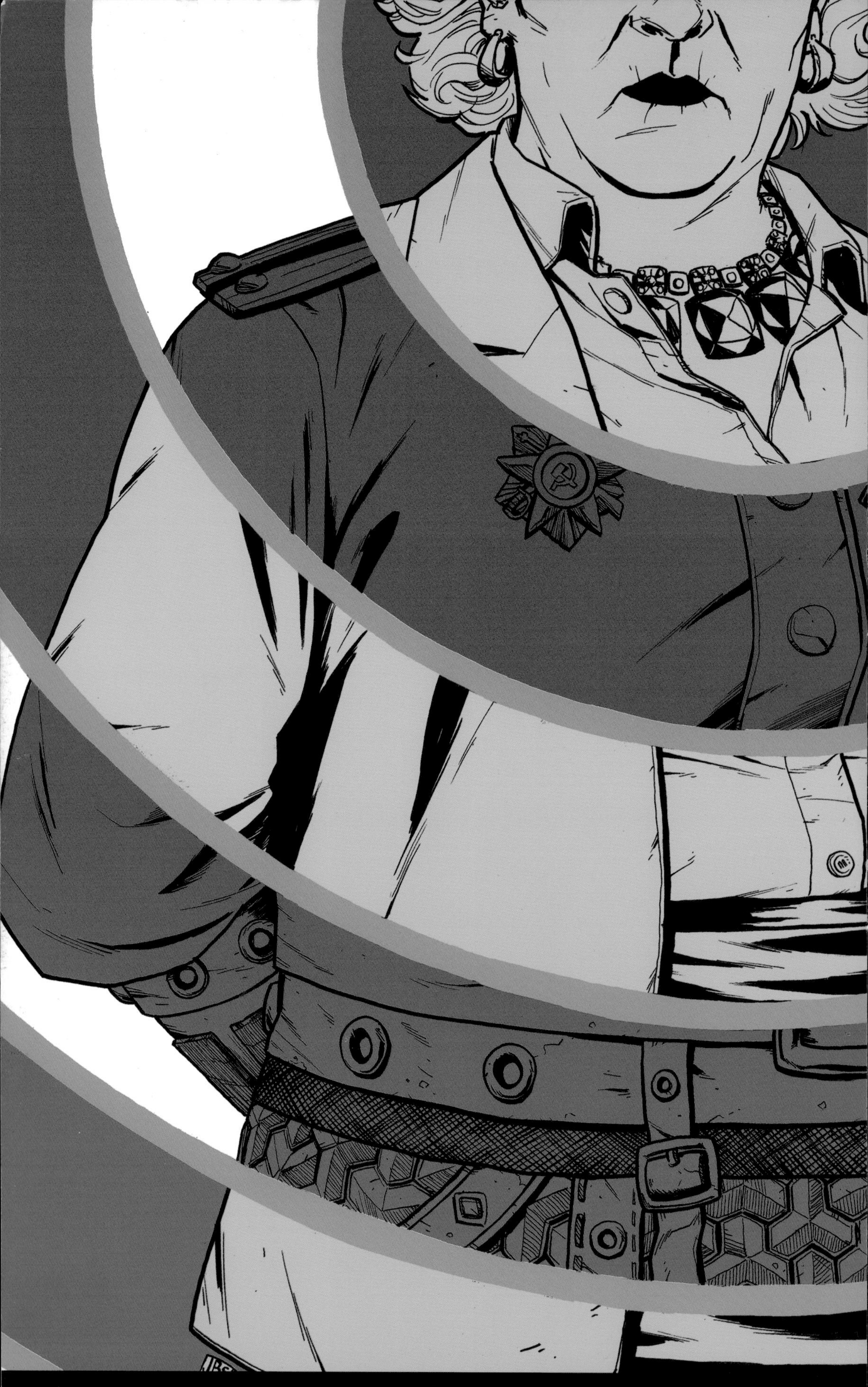

Issue Seven Cover **Jonathan Brandon Sawyer**

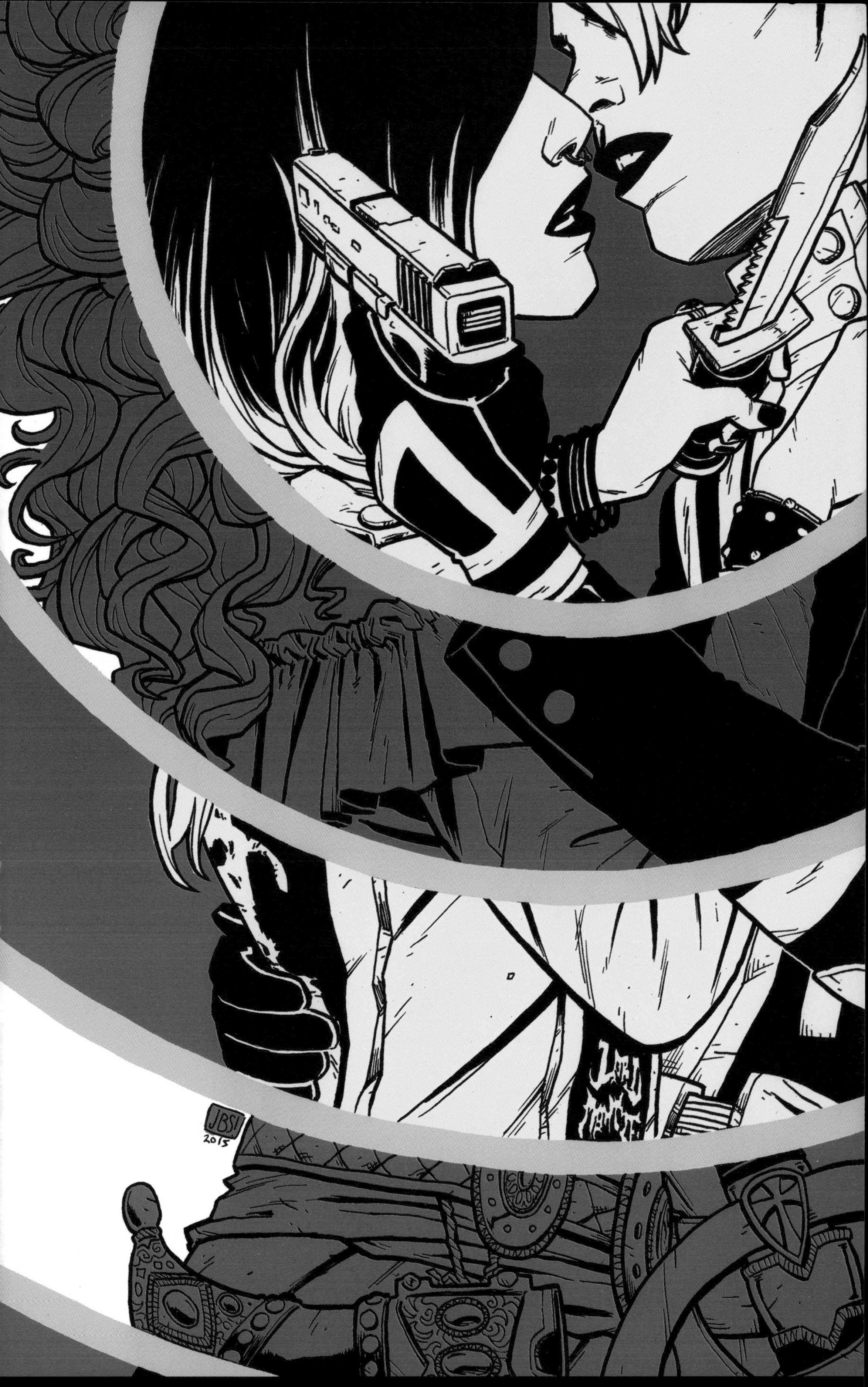

Issue Eight Cover **Jonathan Brandon Sawyer**

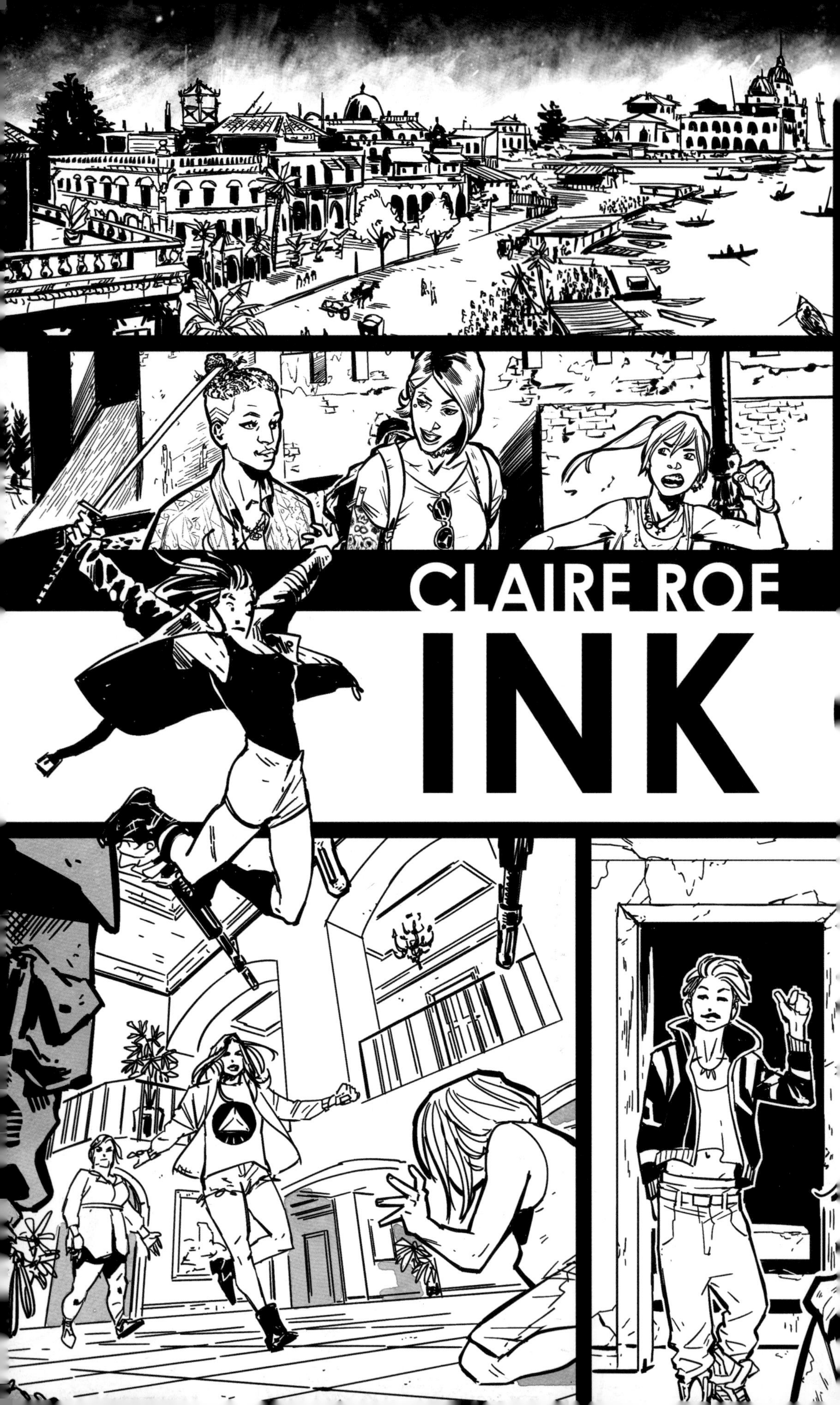
CLAIRE ROE
INK